Rethinking Class

Rethinking Class

Culture, Identities and Lifestyles

Edited by

Fiona Devine

Mike Savage

John Scott

and

Rosemary Crompton

First published 2005 by
PALGRAVE MACMILLAN
Houndmills, Basingstoke, Hampshire RG21 6XS and
175 Fifth Avenue, New York, N.Y. 10010
Companies and representatives throughout the world

PALGRAVE MACMILLAN is the global academic imprint of the Palgrave Macmillan division of St. Martin's Press, LLC and of Palgrave Macmillan Ltd. Macmillan® is a registered trademark in the United States, United Kingdom and other countries. Palgrave is a registered trademark in the European Union and other countries.

ISBN 0–333–96894–8 hardback
ISBN 0–333–96895–6 paperback

This book is printed on paper suitable for recycling and made from fully managed and sustained forest sources.

A catalogue record for this book is available from the British Library.

Library of Congress Cataloging-in-Publication Data
Rethinking class : culture, identities and lifestyles / edited by
    Fiona Devine ... [et al.].
      p.   cm.
    Includes bibliographical references and index.
    ISBN 0–333–96894–8 (cloth) — ISBN 0–333–96895–6(pbk.)
    1. Social classes.   2. Social stratification.   3. Culture.
    4. Social classes—Case studies.   5. Social stratification—Case
    studies.   I. Devine, Fiona, 1962–

    HT609.R44 2004
    305.5—dc22   2004054819

10   9   8   7   6   5   4   3   2   1
14   13   12   11   10   09   08   07   06   05

Printed in China

Contents

List of Figures and Tables

Figures

Tables

Notes on Contributors

Floya Anthias is Professor of Sociology at Oxford Brookes University, UK. She has published extensively on social divisions, racism, ethnicity, migration and gender as well as Cypriots in Britain. Her latest books are *Gender and Migration in Southern Europe: Women on the Move* (co-edited, 2000) and *Rethinking Antiracisms: From Theory to Practice* (co-edited, 2002). She is currently completing a book on *The Social Division of Identity: Identities, Inequalities, Intersectionalities* 2005 and researching into the life chances and social position of the children and families of ethnic entrepreneurs.

Gaynor Bagnall is Lecturer in the School of Education, Community and Social Science at Liverpool John Moores University. She has published papers on the cultural aspects of museum visiting and has research interests in lifestyles, consumer culture and identity.

Talja Blokland is Fellow of the Royal Netherlands Academy of Arts and Sciences at the Amsterdam School for Social Science Research, and author of *Urban Bonds* (2003). Her research interests include historical sociology and memory, urban studies, social inequality and ethnic and racial studies. Her current research focuses on the effects of spatial diversity of neighbourhoods on residents' social networks and access to resources, based on empirical work in New Haven, CT, USA and Rotterdam, the Netherlands.

Rosemary Crompton is Professor of Sociology at City University, London. She has published widely on the areas of class, stratification and employment. Her current ESRC-funded research is exploring the topic of the integration of employment and family life across a number of European countries.

Fiona Devine is Professor and Head of Sociology in the School of Social Sciences at the University of Manchester. Her books include *Class Practices: How Parents Help Their Children Get Good Jobs* (2004), *Social Class in America and Britain* (1997) and *Affluent Workers Revisited* (1992). She is the co-editor, with Mary Waters, of *Social Inequalities in Comparative Perspective* (2004). She is currently undertaking ESRC-funded research on participation and democracy in Britain.

Brian Longhurst is Professor of Sociology at the University of Salford where he is Head of the School of English, Politics, Sociology and Contemporary History. His research interests are in middle-class lifestyles and popular culture and recent publications include *Audiences* (with Nick Abercrombie 1998) and he is also co-author of *Introducing Cultural Studies* (1999).

Tim Phillips is Senior Lecturer in Sociology at the University of Tasmania, Australia. He has empirical research interests in the areas of culture, identity and deviance. He has had articles in these fields published in *The British Journal of Criminology*, *The British Journal of Sociology*, *Sociology* and *The Sociological Review*. He is currently undertaking a national survey of experiences of 'everyday incivilities' in Australia. This study has been funded by the Australian Research Council (ARC) Discovery Project Scheme between 2002 and 2004.

Mike Savage is Professor of Sociology at the University of Manchester where he works on the study of social stratification, urban sociology and the study of lifestyles. Recent publications include *Class Analysis and Social Transformation* (2000).

John Scott is Professor of Sociology at the University of Essex and has previously taught at the University of Leicester and Strathclyde University. His main work has been on social stratification, sociological theory and research methods. His main books include *Power* (2001), *Social Structure* (with Jose Lopez 2001), *Who Rules Britain* (1991), *Poverty and Wealth* (1994), *Sociological Theory* (1995), *A Matter of Record* (1990) and *Social Network Analysis* (2000). With James Fulcher, he is the author of the textbook, *Sociology* (Second Edition, 2003).

Beverley Skeggs is Professor of Sociology at Goldsmiths College, London. She has written books on media, feminist methodology and class. She is the editor of *Transformations: Thinking Through Feminism* series. She has just published two books, one on *Class, Self and Culture* (2003) and one, on the culmination of an ESRC project on *Sexuality and the Politics of Violence and Safety* (with Paul Tyrer, Karen Corteen and Leslie J. Moran 2003).

Michael Vester is Professor at the Institute of Political Science at the University of Hannover. He is an expert in the study of social structures, social movements and mentalities and has published widely on the German class structure and social relationships. His books developing the milieu approach include *Soziale Milieus in Ostdeutschland* (with M. Hofman and I. Zierke 1994).

Mark Western is Associate Professor in Sociology, School of Social Science, and Co-Director, the University of Queensland Social Research Centre, both at the University of Queensland. His recent publications include *Reconfigurations of Class and Gender* (co-edited with Janeen Baxter 2001) and 'Postmaterialism and Economic Voting in Australia, 1990–1998' (with Bruce Tranter, *Australian Journal of Political Science*, 2001). He is currently working on projects relating to the effects of marriage on life outcomes for women and men; the nature of postmaterial values change in contemporary societies; and the continued significance, or otherwise, of class for social inequality, identity formation and politics.

1
The Cultural Turn, Sociology and Class Analysis

Fiona Devine and Mike Savage

It is widely recognised that the discipline of sociology, especially in the UK, has been profoundly affected by the 'cultural turn' in recent years (e.g. Chaney 1994; Abbott 2001). Not only has the study of culture become a significant area of sociological research, but key debates now explore the cultural dimensions of a variety of economic, social and political processes (e.g. Archer 1988; Melucci 1996; Bennett 1998; Du Gay and Pryke 2002). This shift has several facets. These include an interest in anti-foundational social theory, such as that associated with post-structuralism and post-modernism, and an interest in the possibility that the cultural dimensions of economic, social and political life are becoming more pronounced. In addition, there is an interest in reworking sociology's political relevance by making it relevant to political concerns with 'recognition'. The cultural turn has necessitated a settling of accounts with the traditional sociological canon, in terms of its theoretical foundations and its substantive areas of research expertise. In this settling of accounts, the relevance of stratification is a key terrain of dispute. In the UK, as in other nations, it can be argued that the sociology of stratification was pivotal to the discipline as a whole in the 1960s and 1970s, but it is precisely this pre-eminence that has been challenged by the cultural turn. Criticisms have been made that much stratification research ultimately prioritised employment as the key axis of inequality (see the discussion in Crompton 1998), leading to the marginalisation of other axes of inequality such as gender, race, ethnicity and age, and that it relied on discredited, 'enlightenment' theoretical foundations (Bauman 1982; Lash and Urry 1994; Lockwood 1988).

Until recently, the dominant British response from stratification researchers has been to ignore or denigrate the cultural turn and to retreat from a broader engagement with these new developments. In

1

the US, there has been a similar (though less marked) trend, linked to a tendency to rely on statistical and methodological sophistication rather than theoretical engagement (see the discussion in Sorensen 2000). Either way, the result has been to reduce the centrality of stratification research for the discipline of sociology as a whole. However, it is noteworthy that in recent years the cultural turn is itself being reappraised, with some writers exhibiting unease at its implications. Turner and Rojek (2001), for example, are critical of what they see as a 'decorative sociology', which they see as a 'sociology that is obsessed with the immediacy of commercial and popular cultures, has no sense of historical depth, does not engage in comparative research, and has little political relevance' (Turner and Rojek 2001: vii).

It is also noteworthy that increasing numbers of stratification researchers are abandoning their defensiveness and becoming more interested in relating their work to broader theoretical debates. In the UK the work of Bradley (1996, 1999), Crompton (1998), Charlesworth (2000), Devine (1992a, 1998) and Savage (2000), is indicative of a recent interest in thinking through the relationship between culture and stratification. It is also striking that writers with interests in cultural studies have also become more interested in relating their concerns to stratification (for instance Skeggs 1997; Reay 1998; Bennett *et al.* 1999; Lawler 2000a). In the US, there is also evidence of a new opening up of stratification studies as writers such as Sorensen (2000) and Tilly (1999) have developed new theoretical frameworks.

Most of the chapters in this book were first presented at a seminar held at the University of Manchester in 1999, which was funded by the ESRC as part of a seminar series on 'Rethinking Stratification Research' (for another collection from this series, see Crompton *et al.* 2000). The chapters chosen for this book are designed to further the emergent debate in three main ways. They all engage, albeit in different ways with theoretical concerns with culture, identity, and subjectivity. Secondly, the majority of them seek to develop their theoretical concerns using empirical research of some kind, in the view that theoretical debates are best made if empirically embedded. Thirdly, they have tried to broaden out coverage of relevant issues away from the UK alone, either by drawing on research outside the UK, or by drawing on theoretical currents from outside the heartlands of British stratification research. It can readily be seen that the work of Pierre Bourdieu is especially important here, and he serves as a key reference point in a number of papers.

In our introduction, we seek to place these contributions in broader context by providing an account of how the recent engagement between cultural studies and the sociology of stratification relates to older debates in the discipline. Our main concern is to show that there is nothing inherently reductive about stratification research, and indeed much of history of stratification has involved a strong concern with culture. Rather than seeing the issue of culture as being a new one, we concur with Abbott (2001) that it has always been one of the core concerns in the discipline. Abbott notes the general shift away from talk of structure to that of culture in much social scientific understanding. He is not perturbed by the recent shift in focus, in part, because he is not proposing a different set of foundations for sociology. Rather, his observations about the cultural turn arise from his interest in the evolution and development of the social sciences in general and sociology in particular. He argues that the fundamental principles of sociology have long been characterised by dichotomies such as that between structure and culture, quantitative and qualitative research and so on (Abbott 2001: 10). Interestingly, he argues that these dichotomies are fractal distinctions that are reproduced in a similar way at each level of the discipline. Thus, the division between sociologists who are interested primarily in structure and those who are interested in culture are to be found in the various sub-fields of sociology such as class analysis, sociology of education, criminology and so on.

This is not to say that Abbott is uncritical of such developments. He does not think that sociology or other social sciences are progressive in the sense of making new discoveries about society. Rather, knowledge changes as the different protagonists vie for dominance although when they achieve victory, they find they must take up the problems of the old order. Sociologists, in this respect, are good as 'reinventing the wheel' using new terminology for old concepts and making out that new knowledge is far superior to old ways of seeing things over time. Nevertheless, Abbott is not contemptuous of this process since the re-mapping of core concepts allows sociologists to know the same things in different ways and to reach that knowledge by different routes. Such changes in knowledge, which 'arise through the reshuffling of these affiliations between the fractal distinctions within the context of individual fractal cycles' (Abbott 2001: 32), contributes to a comprehensive understanding of social life in terms of breadth and depth. From this viewpoint, Abbott remains cheerful about the discipline.

Our theoretical aim in this chapter is to show how Abbott's view that disputes over core dichotomies that are a feature of the social sciences as a whole are also present in sub-fields of the different disciplines, and we consider how future stratification research can best progress in the light of this. Our interest therefore focuses on the study of stratification and class as a sub-discipline of sociology. More specifically, we address the growing interest in the cultural dimensions of class – especially around issues of habitus and identity – and think about how this relates to older bodies of research on class-consciousness and images of society. This allows us to judge whether newer debates about culture and class really resolve older problems in understanding class-consciousness or whether they simply re-label and re-iterate them. We will show that prior to a recent revival in the cultural dimensions of class, there was a steady elimination of interest in the cultural in class analysis. This field of study was gradually eroded because research on class cultures invariably found them to be incoherent and fragmentary in character in highly complex ways. This argument, outlined in the first section, is developed with reference to debates on class-consciousness and images of society in the 1960s and 1970s.

In the second section, we consider the more recent ways of thinking about cultural issues in class analysis. Adopting a similar spirit to Abbott (see also Crompton *et al*. 2000), we are of the view that the recasting of the sub-discipline should not simply be dismissed as 'old wine in new bottles' since the exploration of habitus and identity – inspired by the work of Bourdieu – represent new and exciting ways of exploring the cultural dimensions of class. At the same time, we acknowledge that incorporating the cultural into class analysis is not without its problems and, indeed, throws up new as well as old issues to be addressed. In the third section, we outline the contributions to this book while, in the fourth section, we return to Abbott's account of the evolution and development of the social sciences. From our review of the study of culture in class analysis, we embrace his optimistic view of how knowledge changes and advances in the sub-discipline and sociology more generally.

Consciousness and imagery

In what might be seen as 'the golden years' of stratification research, from the 1940s to the 1970s, issues of culture were central to the study of class. The cultural meanings of class – issues of subjectivity, awareness of, perceptions about, feelings towards class and so on – were discussed within the context of debates about class-consciousness and class imagery.[1] Of course, these discussions were limited, above all by their silence with respect to issues of gender and ethnicity. Furthermore discussion about class-consciousness was itself confined to working-class consciousness

(Savage 2000, see Chapter 7). focusing on whether the working class would play a historic role, identified by Marx, in moving from a 'class in itself' to being a 'class for itself' ready to overthrow capitalism. For this reason, studies were organised around a 'class formation problematic' that examined the ways that people might become aware of their structural class position. The extent to which the articulation of class-consciousness was an inevitable feature of capitalist development or contingent upon historically specific circumstances became a chief debating point between Marxist and non-Marxist sociologists (Scott 1996: 228), and paved the way for a series of empirical studies that commanded considerable attention. These studies tended to adopt what has been labeled an 'S–C–A' approach (Pahl 1989), where researchers saw consciousness as the intermediary between structure and action. An example is the classic sociological study 'Coal is Our Life', a study of a mining community in Featherstone, Yorkshire by Dennis *et al.* (1956). This showed how brutal working conditions in the mines generated a strong sense of occupational solidarity amongst men, whilst close-knit family and community ties sustained a powerful community solidarism. The miners' distinctive way of life, therefore, was the source of cultural values that emphasised communal concerns over individual pre-occupations, and these values in turn informed perceptions about class, upholding a strong sense of 'them and us'. Finally, such solidaristic feelings were the bedrock of an unswerving loyalty to working-class organisations like the trade unions and the Labour Party.[2]

In this study we see the concern to establish an association between class position and class-consciousness, and projects such as this formed the staple of British stratification research at this time (see also Frankenberg 1966). The main issue of disagreement concerned the extent to which there was a necessary association between structure and action, and how this might lead to political action. Most British research emphasised that the nature of the association was complex: even the uncritical allegiance to the trade unions and the Labour Party found by Dennis *et al.* (1956) fell a long way short of Marx's conception of revolutionary class-consciousness. Still, the working class could be seen as a potentially radical force for change. Commentators, however, soon heralded the demise of a culturally distinct working class (Abrams *et al.* 1960; Zwieg 1961). Affluence in the late 1950s and 1960s, it was argued, undermined the unique way of life and the values and beliefs associated with it among the working class. The demise of occupational and community solidarity in turn undermined the solidarism that underpinned working-class views of class and politics. A new working class of privatised workers and their families saw themselves as middle class and distanced them-selves from the trade unions and the Labour Party. Goldthorpe *et al.* in the *Affluent Worker* series (1968a,b, 1969), based on research in Luton, quickly refuted what became known as the 'embourgeoisement thesis'. Affluence was enjoyed but at the price of long hours of overtime doing dull, repetitive work. Lifestyles were privatised rather than communal but they were not middle class in form. Finally, views about class and politics were instrumental but an allegiance to the trade unions and the Labour Party, albeit a critical one, remained strong. The Luton team, therefore, stressed continuities in working-class structural conditions and cultural practices while also acknowledging economic and cultural change by identifying a 'new working class' that was normatively converging with the lower middle class. A distinct working-class culture was dissolving.

The Luton team's research was important in generating a fresh wave of thinking about class-consciousness. At one level, it was a portrayal of an essentially conservative working class preoccupied with monetary concerns, which implied that it was not a revolutionary force for change. This conclusion did not go down well in the late 1960s when theories of embourgeoisement appeared misplaced in view of an out-break of worker insurgency, especially in France and Italy in 1968, but also in the same Vauxhall car plant in Luton where Goldthorpe *et al.* had undertaken some of their research. Blackburn (1967), for examples, interpreted a strike at Vauxhalls as an explosion of revolutionary class-consciousness. That sociologists could come to such different conclusions about the nature of class-consciousness was addressed by Mann (1970, 1973) in his secondary analysis of attitudes in Britain and the United States and his review of implications of events in France and Italy in 1968. He famously argued that class-consciousness should be clearly distinguished into four elements: namely, class identity, class opposition, class totality and conceptions of an alternative society. He stressed that finding a combination of all four elements was a rare occurrence indeed (Mann 1973: 13). Mann argued there was little evidence of a normative acceptance among the working class of their subordinate position. There were no indications of a consistent commitment to any general societal values. Rather, working-class compliance rests on a pragmatic acceptance of their position. Fatalism and ambivalence are the psychological defence mechanisms by which workers adapt to their life situations (Mann 1973: 29). In sum, Mann emphatically concluded that the class position of workers did not generate a clear and coherent class-consciousness (see also Parkin 1972).

Similar conclusions were reached in a debate about class imagery. Lockwood (1959) had argued that clerical workers had different market and work situations to manual workers. Consequently, they held different cultural values and beliefs that meant they were less class-conscious than blue-collar workers (Lockwood 1959). Building on these ideas about the impact of people's immediate social context and personal experiences on how they visualise the class structure of the society in which they live, he identified three types of worker with different 'work and community relations' that generate different images of society.[3] First, he described a traditional proletarian worker whose solidaristic work and family relations sustained a power model of society. Second, he identified a traditional deferential worker, working in rural settings or small firms, who perceived social inequality in terms of a status hierarchy. Third, he outlined a new privatised worker, whose home and family-centred lifestyle sustained a pecuniary view of the class structure (Lockwood 1975: 17). It was this new working class, of course, who were regarded as prototypical by the *Affluent Worker* team. The conceptual clarity by which Lockwood clearly and succinctly specified the links between people's everyday experiences and their cultural beliefs and practices was hugely influenced in the sub-discipline spawning a number of research projects on the traditional proletarian, traditional worker and deferential worker.

No sooner had Lockwood's model been developed, than it quickly collapsed under the weight of counter empirical evidence. This was well captured by the contributions to Bulmer's (1975a,b) edited collection around Lockwood's seminal article. Neither of his ideal types of traditional proletarian or deferential worker stood up to close empirical scrutiny. Moore (1975), for example, found limited evidence of an antagonistic proletarian worker from his study of Durham miners noting, instead, the impact of religion – specifically Methodism – in shaping class imagery. Bell and Newby's (1975) study of farm workers found that deferential attitudes were often situationally specific and ambivalence was more the order of the day. All in all, it seemed as if people's work and community relations did not generate clear and coherent images of society. Class imagery was often incoherent, contradictory, fragmentary, ambiguous and uncertain. The prevailing view was that there was no tidy relationship between class structure and position and cultural beliefs and practices (Bulmer 1975a,b). Culture could not simply be made reducible to structure for it appeared that cultural meanings were much more indeterminate than he had allowed. These views were reinforced by the feminist critique of 'malestream' stratification research that pointed to the distinctive gendered elements of class-consciousness (see Hunt 1980 and more generally Crompton and Mann 1986).

By the late 1970s, therefore, the debates on class-consciousness and class imagery had reached similar conclusions about the need for a more complex understanding of the relationship between class and culture. However, it was unclear how sociologists should proceed in thinking about understanding the relationship between the two in terms of acknowledging links between class position and cultural meanings without reducing cultural values and beliefs to structure. No alternative accounts of the social structuring of cultural beliefs and practices while also recognising a certain degree of indeterminacy in them was proffered. Lockwood (1988), for example, was highly critical of the economic determinism that underpinned Marxist theories of action but did not acknowledge the same problems that confronted non-Marxist studies of class as well.[4] Little was said about overcoming the problem. Increasingly, sociologists of class came to talk of there being an impasse in the sub-discipline (Newby 1982; Marshall 1988) since novel ways of overcoming the problematic dualisms of objective and subjective class, structure and culture and so on were not forthcoming. Frequent reference was made to how such dualisms were false anyway and that, for example, class and culture are mutually constitutive of each other but it was unclear how this observation should shape a new research agenda. Consequently, issues of culture disappeared from view in the field of class analysis as the sub-discipline turned its attention, almost exclusively, to issues of class structure in the 1980s. In terms of Abbott's argument about the centrality of the division between culture and structure as a fractal divide, sociologists of stratification largely staged a retreat from the 'cultural' pole of inquiry and focused their energies on a better appreciation of the 'structural'.

The beginning of the decade saw the publication of research on class structure and social mobility and class and education in Britain by the Nuffield School (Goldthorpe 1980; Halsey *et al.* 1980). Goldthorpe's nationally representative survey of social mobility enjoyed the most attention although his substantive findings on patterns and trends in social mobility caused less controversy than how he and his colleagues conducted the research. Thus, there was considerable debate about his class schema and the different class categories he defined prior to conducting the research. The limitations of these class groupings, drawn from proxy data on the occupational and employment status of men, in relation to understanding the position of women and social class was also widely discussed. The employment aggregate approach, therefore, generated numerous technical discussions about how to define the class structure (Savage *et al.* 1992; Crompton 1998). Consequently, issues of class structure dominated the last major national study of class undertaken by Marshall *et al.* (1988) at Essex. They compared and contrasted three alternative conceptions of the class structure: the Registrar General's (RG) prestige and skill-related class categories, Erik Olin Wright's Marxist-inspired class schema (1985) and Goldthorpe's occupational class schema. Unsurprisingly, their adjudication between the different schemas came out in favour of Goldthorpe's class categories. Goldthorpe's (revised) schema has stood the test of time and its underlying foundations have been used to update official RG categories (Rose 1997). Be that as it may, the debate was rather narrow in its substantive concerns and inspired few in the sub-discipline. It is probably safe to say that this controversy has now run its course.

Issues of class identity and class-consciousness were not neglected altogether. Marshall *et al.* (1988: 149) found a high level of class identity in Britain that, they argued, was far more salient than other identities.[5] Class identification, however, did not sustain class activism for a desire for equality was tempered by a fatalistic evaluation of the ability of the trade unions and the Labour Party to deliver on redistribution. It was this critical evaluation of working-class organisations that the Essex team stressed in their account of the lack of class action in Britain. The argument was confirmed in their wider consideration of class-consciousness where they confirmed earlier studies by Mann, Parkin and so on. Like them, they argued that few people have unambiguous views of class and, more often than not, they lack a coherent package of beliefs and values about class (Marshall *et al.* 1988: 188). This led Marshall *et al.* (1988: 193, 194) to conclude that class-consciousness should not be considered as the property of individuals so less attention should be devoted to examining 'the developing subjectivity of groups of class members' and more time be directed to collective organisations and their 'class practices'. However, whilst again highlighting the problems of a traditional class formation approach, it was not clear how this stress on collective organisations and class practices could be operationalised, especially in a period when the labour movement was on the retreat. Somewhat disappointingly, therefore, the Essex team's research on class identity and class-consciousness did not move the debate on the relationship between class and culture beyond the impasse in class analysis in the 1970s. Their call for a reconceptualisation of class-consciousness from individuals to groups has been made many times before – see Scase (1977) and Gallie (1983) – although, in fairness to them, the call has not been taken up by fellow sociologists in the field.[6]

The Essex team's findings on class identity and class-consciousness generated controversy that in many ways mirrored that triggered off by Goldthorpe and Lockwood's work in the 1960s. Marshall *et al.* were criticised for overstating the strength of class identity and the weakness of other identities in Britain (Saunders 1989, 1990b; Emmison and Western 1990). Critics stressed the importance of contextualising the salience of identities and Devine's (1992a,b) in-depth study of affluent workers in Luton, for example, noted that working-class identification was weaker in abstract discussions about class and more strongly articulated in conversations about politics. Marshall and Rose (1990) eventually conceded this point when they acknowledged the strength of class identity in relation to political beliefs and practices specifically. In relation to class-consciousness, Evans (1992) criticised the Essex team for overstating the social structuring of beliefs and values noting that very few of them can be linked back to particular class locations and this is true even of attitudes towards issues of class and inequality. Arguably, the implication of this argument is that the relationship between class and culture is even looser than has been imagined and cultural beliefs and practices are even more indeterminate than has been previously envisaged. There were some innovative twists to their argument, for instance in coining the phrase 'class identity', but it is worth noting here that the concept of identity was used in a commonsensical way in terms of thinking about who people identify with rather than in the way in which the concept is more widely used today. Overall, this body of work was a long way from offering the radical re-conceptualisation of class and culture that would have been necessary to overcome deep-rooted problems in class analysis.

Habitus and identity

We have seen how the traditional sociological interest in class-consciousness ultimately had two major problems. First, the empirical problem unraveled by Mann (1973), Bulmer (1975a,b) and Marshall *et al.* (1988) was that there was no coherent class-consciousness amongst the population. One Marxist response to this issue was to see this as the result of the commodity fetishism inherent to capitalism, which led to the systematic 'hiding' of the real nature of class relations in capitalism. However, this approach then begged the question as to how class-consciousness might ever develop. The teleological view which held that class-consciousness might emerge as the contradictions of capitalism became ever more apparent seemed ever less convincing as capitalism found ways of reconstructing itself. Another view, originating in Marx and Lenin's ideas, emphasised the role of political leadership in breaking from the restricted trade union consciousness of the workers and inculcating revolutionary class-consciousness. As we have seen above, there are echoes of this approach in Marshall *et al.*'s (1988) account, but it ultimately leads to a simplistic account which over-privileges the role of institutions in general and political parties in particular in generating ideas.

Weberian approaches superficially seemed better placed to deal with this issue, but ultimately their reliance on the subject–object dualism meant they faced similar concerns. Lockwood's (1992) account still provides the most powerful criticism of this approach. Insofar as class-consciousness can be related to class position, this relies on an instrumentalism that sees ideas and values as linked to the interests of particular structurally defined groups. This entails a reductionism that is unable to satisfactorily account for the complexity of values and ideas in evidence. Insofar as values and norms are recognised as powerful in their own terms, this involves breaking from a tradition that links them to structural foundations. You cannot have your cake and eat it. As we saw above, Goldthorpe's response that has been followed by a number of other stratification researchers (e.g. Breen and Rotman 1995) was to make the best of the necessary reductionism identified by Lockwood and adapt a version of rational choice theory (see Goldthorpe 1996, 2000). The merits and de-merits of this intellectual move have been subject to some considerable discussion (see Devine 1998; Savage 2000) and we do not plan to discuss them again here. What needs to be pointed out is that the advocacy of rational choice theory is very much a minority concern within the discipline as a whole, and the dominant approach has been to adopt the view that taking culture seriously involves breaking from stratification research, at least as conventionally conceived (e.g. Lash and Urry 1994; Pakulski and Waters 1996; Urry 2000). Is it possible to develop a genuine reconciliation between these choices and show that ideas from the cultural turn genuinely allow stratification researchers tools to allow them to understand class cultures in ways that do not fall back on the kinds of problems identified above?

This leads to the second main problem of conventional stratification approaches which is that, theoretically, they failed to resolve deep-rooted problems linked to their reliance on a subject–object dualism, and its associated binaries (such as base/superstructure, or economic/social class).

By conceiving class-consciousness as some kind of reflection (even if distorted) on class position, it relied on a conceptual dualism between structure and agency that proved problematic. These conventional approaches relied on a theory which was effectively been criticised by proponents of the cultural turn who claimed that language (and hence understanding) does not develop as a means of 'naming' referents, but rather develops through signifying processes that depend on the relational contrasts between signifiers which allow the 'signified' to be evoked (famously, Saussure 1959, see Giddens 1984 for discussion).

One of the starting points of recent work has been to show how once class-consciousness is not seen as the 'reflex' of class position, it can be studied in a variety of more innovative ways. Thus Charlesworth explores in his study of working-class identities in Rotherham that once one recognises that working-class culture is 'not enshrined in self conscious cultural representation' a variety of interpretive and hermeneutic methods can be deployed. Both Skeggs (1997) and Reay (1998) use the reluctance of working-class women to define themselves in class terms as the linchpin of their analysis. Because approaches to language and culture from within the cultural turn emphasise the constructed nature of identities, and in particular their 'relational' qualities, older problems can be sidestepped. Identities are not labels of your position, but 'claims for recognition' (see also Honneth 1995) which are both contested and fraught. It is therefore highly indicative that there has been a reorientation from studies of 'class-consciousness' to 'identity'. This can be traced to the work of Devine (1992a: 7) who reports her concern to show how interviews with respondents might indicate how their aspirations are related to their 'collective working class identity', but the term 'identity' is now legion in current work (see, for example, Scott 1996: 243; Charlesworth 2000; Savage *et al.* 2001). The paper by Phillips and Western is an indication of how this interest in identities can be developed.

As is evident from various contributions in this book, there are multiple influences at work in this shift to identity. Nonetheless, although in some respects disparate, a number of common threads run through recent research. Firstly, there is a wide reliance on in-depth interviews and ethnographies rather than survey analysis, which allows a much fuller account of the nuances of class identifications. Related to this is a concern to place awareness in context of people's everyday lives, rather than to relate it to abstract expectations of what class awareness should be, or even might be, like. This relates to a third similarity, which is a common awareness that the complexities and ambivalences of class awareness should be analysed in their own terms, rather than as a difficulty to be explained away whether this be through recourse to a dominant ideology, organizational forms, or whatever. This has led to an interest in thinking through how the ambivalences and complexities of popular identities and forms of awareness can be understood.

In addressing this issue, a central point of reference is the work of Pierre Bourdieu. All the writers mentioned above (with the partial exception of Devine and Bradley) take his work as their main theoretical source, and Bourdieuvian perspectives now command the stage. For some writers (Alexander 1994) Bourdieu's framework is similar to conventional sociological approaches, and it can appear reductive because it appears to link values, taste and perception (as deployed in Bourdieu's concept of habitus) to class interests. Such a perception is only possible if Bourdieu is read partially, with particular attention given to his accounts of economic, cultural and social capital (e.g. Bourdieu 1999a). Here, it appears that Bourdieu sees economic position, cultural taste and social networks as a resource that people can instrumentally deploy for self advancement. However, these concepts need to be put in a broader context, where they are inter-related to the ideas of habitus and field. Briefly (see further Jenkins 1992; Longhurst and Savage 1996; Swartz 1997), Bourdieu (1977b) develops a 'sociology of practice' which identifies inequalities as the result of an interplay between embodied practices and institutional processes which together generate far-reaching inequalities of various kinds.

Bourdieu explores this broad issue through his conceptual trinity of field, capital and habitus. The concept of field has some of the same property as structure in the conventional sociology of stratification. Fields 'present themselves' as 'structured spaces of positions (or posts) whose properties depend on their position within these spaces and which can be analysed independently of the characteristics of their occupants' (Bourdieu 1993: 72). However Bourdieu sees fields as relatively fluid (compared to some notions of structure, for instance), in that they only delineate stakes and interests between competing groups. The actual outcomes of the struggles depend on the actions of individuals, and may lead to a transformation or modification of the field itself: there is therefore no question whether fields can automatically reproduce themselves. 'In order for a field to function, there have to be stakes and people prepared to play the game, endowed with the habitus that implies knowledge and recognition of the immanent laws of the field, the stakes and so on' (Bourdieu 1993: 72). Fields only operate when there are skilful people, interested in the stakes that field can offer, who are prepared and able to make it work. People have to be competent to operate in these fields (see Bourdieu 1993: 158–167 for the example of political competence, for example). People's competence to participate in fields is critically related to their habitus, and their socially and historically acquired dispositions. Capitals can only be mobilised in particular fields and by people with appropriate habitus.

This formulation points towards a different kind of approach to culture and subjectivity than in older forms of class analysis:

(1) Traditional approaches within stratification see awareness as linked to self-recognition of one's position in the system, an ability to name your social location. Marxists and Weberians alike have considered the kinds of conditions that may allow individuals to correctly (or incorrectly) identify their own position in society. Bourdieu's approach, however, is consistent with a structuralist or post-structuralist theory of language which means that identification, for Bourdieu, is not based on recognising oneself as a belonging to a given position, but as differentiating oneself from others in a field, through comprehending and playing the game with its various stakes and players. This allows awareness to be seen not as a reflection of one's position, but related to tactical and strategic 'moves' within a field. This involves a more fluid and contextual approach to exploring how identities are mobilised and deployed. There is no question of there being a relationship between a 'base' and 'superstructure' or between 'economic' class and 'social' class; these terms are simply meaningless within a Bourdieuvian perspective.

(2) In the conventional SCA model structures of inequality are seen to reproduce themselves unless (subordinate) agents become aware of their position and act consciously to challenge it. For Bourdieu, by contrast, inequalities depend on the incorporation of agents into fields. Becoming conscious of one's position in a field actually can make the stakes of that field more compelling and powerful so actually rein-forcing the legitimacy of the field itself. Thus, identification of one's own position reduces the ability to challenge the stakes of the field. Claims to recognition are claims by subordinate groups to be taken as agents within a field, and can have the paradoxical effect of validating the rules of the game as a whole. Identity, whether of class, gender, ethnicity, sexuality or other axis, is hence not to be seen in celebratory way: as an indication of 'becoming'. Rather, it is seen as a relational claim to other players in the field. This, incidentally, offers an approach to the issue of recognition politics rather different to that developed

by Fraser (1995) during the course of her debate with Butler (1998, see the discussion in Adkins 2002).

(3) Classical stratification theory relies on a macro-social theory which specifies the relationship between the structures of inequality. This can take the form either of a theory such as Marxism which asserts the pre-dominance of one overarching social structure (the mode of production), or more pluralistic forms such as that offered by Weber which specifies a number of different dimensions of inequality (notably class, status and command, e.g. Scott 1996). Bourdieu, however, sees a multiplicity of fields, with no clear, pre-determined relationship between them, with the result that his account is more fluid and attentive to change and the power of agency. Insofar as fields are inter-related, this depends on the activities of dominant classes who are able to traverse different fields more easily than those whose stakes are confined to fewer fields.

(4) Bourdieu's work offers a distinctive paradox of reflexivity. As people move between fields they become aware of the different kinds of stakes that exist in diverse fields, and hence can become more reflexive about the kinds of practices they can pursue, their respective ethics, strategies and tactics. As McNay (1999) and Adkins (2002) explore with respect to gender, reflexivity arises through mobility between fields. However, the ability to move between fields is itself variable and dependent on par-ticular kinds of habitus that support mobile personality characteristics, personal flexibility and so on. It is those with stakes in many fields, namely male members of dominant social classes, who thereby find it easier to develop various kinds of reflexivity.

This schematic account suggests the potential of Bourdieu's approach to offer a distinctive new approach to issues of class, culture and identity that focus on the complex interplay between habitus, reflexivity and identity. We have seen that traditional stratification theory attempted to model forms of distinct class-consciousness and ultimately failed to provide a convincing account of the complex and fractured nature of class-consciousness. For Bourdieu, however, this is not a problem. One should expect to find ambivalent, contradictory and complex values, identities and forms of awareness. The issue is then to show how these ambivalences are explicable according to the interplay of fields, habitus and capitals. An interesting example of this is Skeggs's (1997) argument that the 'mis-recognition' of class by young working-class women can be taken as evidence of the power of cultural and economic capital to shape their lives. The fact that people may not see themselves as members of classes does not mean that class is unimportant: indeed, it can be taken as evidence precisely of its overarching power. There is no reason why one cannot simply work with the complex and ambivalent values, awareness and evident identities. Above all, this means seeing values in the context of lived practices, and taking discursive forms of awareness, especially articulate identities, as linked to strategic and tactical moves within a field.

Research inspired by Bourdieu suggests a way of repositioning stratification research with a much richer concept of culture. However, as several of the chapters in this book examine, there continue to be issues and problems, and we are some way from a fully elaborated new paradigm for cultural class analysis. We raise three problems here, which reverberate in various parts of this book.

First, there continue to be concerns as to whether Bourdieu's approach to culture is reductive in some ways. Perhaps the most significant point here is the extent to which Bourdieu's emphasis on cultural capital leads him indirectly to denigrate the vitality, fluidity and complexity of various kinds of popular culture. His account of field and habitus can be construed as implying a form of neo-structuralist analysis in which people are ultimately compelled to conform to wider forces (e.g. May 2001; Boyne 2002). In some respects his arguments can be seen to validate largely discredited ideas that one can read popular culture as a form of false consciousness. For instance, Skeggs's (1997) arguments are open to criticism because the ideas of dis-identification and mis-recognition implies a 'correct' recognition or form of identification, and hence have residues of older stratification theory, with its associated notions of a dominant ideology thesis. Perhaps, here there are things still to be learnt from older studies which were more attentive to the positive virtues of working-class cultural forms. This theme is taken up in some chapters.

Secondly, and relatedly, the relationship between discursive and more practical forms of awareness remains unclear. By emphasising the power of everyday practice, and the ways that people become actively involved in various fields through 'playing the game', it is unclear in Bourdieu's thought where critical and discursive consciousness arises from. How do people's actual elaborate identities relate to the complexities of their everyday lives, and how is it possible for these identities to take on more critical forms? It is not clear that whether Bourdieu himself addresses these issues clearly. In parts of his work he seems to evoke a naïve scientism where only (properly sensitised) sociologists are able to fully understand social relationships. There is also a tendency in his writing to dismiss identities as itself the product of middle-class habitus, and argue that the ability to feel competent in articulating an identity is itself the result of privilege (Wacquant, personal communication). This issue is further taken up by Anthias in Chapter 2.

Thirdly, and again relatedly, Bourdieu's work can be seen as continuing to work with assumptions about the existence of 'society' that are open to challenge in an increasingly fluid and complex social world. Bourdieu assumes the existence of national societies in his work, and is not spatially sensitive in reflecting on the way that flows and mobilities may lead to social processes that cross boundaries (see Urry 2000). It is not at this stage clear whether this issue can be remedied by working with Bourdieu's concepts, or whether it is a fundamental limitation of his approach as a whole. Savage *et al.*, in this book, attempt to use Bourdieu's work to develop a more spatially sensitive account of social process, whereas Vester largely adopts Bourdieu's own practice of conducting research within given national boundaries.

Finally, we have to attend to methodological uncertainties. Bourdieu's own research practice has been subject to criticism, for instance in its naïve use of personal testimonies in *The Weight of the World* (1999b). Whilst there is now considerable theoretical discussion of Bourdieu's work, there is less methodological discussion. Do we re-work national sample survey methods? Do we use detailed ethnographies, and if so, how, in globalising and fluid conditions? What is the status of correspondence analysis, Bourdieu's own preferred method but which continues to be largely ignored, in much social science research practice? To put these issues another way, whilst we now have a clear sense of the limitations of the 'employment aggregate approach', it is unclear how to develop an alternative. Hopefully the chapters in this book, which use a variety of methods, will allow readers to develop their own thoughts on this fundamental issue.

The contributions

The contributions in this book all share, in varied ways, the concern to re-open the issue of class culture – in terms of habitus and identities. We should make it clear that despite the arguments made in this chapter there is no 'party line' that the contributors have been expected to follow. Rather, we have left them all to raise issues as they see fit. There are both similarities and differences in the ways in which the issues are discussed as some draw heavily on Bourdieu while others do not. Moreover, Crompton and Scott take up the issues raised by Devine and Savage in their conclusion.

In Chapter 2, Anthias develops a theoretical overview of the non-class factors in social differentiation and inequality, and, in particular, divisions of gender and race/ethnicity. She identifies three models of stratification and how they have dealt with gender and race. She rejects the 'reductionist' model, which is associated with attempts to reduce them to class relations. Interestingly, she is also critical of the 'identity' model, which is associated with trends in post-modernist theory. In place of these, she allies herself with a modified variant of what she calls the 'intersectionality' model. According to this model, it should be acknowledged that people occupy multiple and overlapping social positions. They can both reinforce and undermine individual and collective identities. Anthias argues that recognising this 'translocational positionality' of social inequality must not focus on the purely descriptive. Rather, the model should highlight the processes through which such multiple positions are reproduced. In arguing this point, she very much stresses that such 'translocational positionalities' are fluid and often contradictory and these facets have to be embraced in the study of social stratification and system integration.

Skeggs develops a culturalist reading of class, in which she charts a powerful yet also hidden process towards cultural re-branding, in which it becomes difficult for those lacking middle-class resources to claim entitlement to cultural presence. Drawing on Bourdieu's concept of symbolic violence, and linking it to other elements of recent cultural theory, she uses a series of perceptive case studies of cultural change to skillfully point to the way in which class cultures are tied up with the making of the self. Even where cultural forms do not appear to be superficially about class, she shows how issues of class and entitlement are implicitly bound together. She emphasises the need to recognise the significance of cultural class struggles.

Michael Vester's chapter explores how Bourdieu's framework can be applied to examine class relations in Germany. Like many of the chapters in this book, his main concern is to show how a Bourdieuvian perspective allows different ways of understanding class to the occupationally derived accounts of Goldthorpe and Wright. Vester shows how it is possible to delineate a number of common milieu in Germany which are relatively stable over time, but which also have changed in form, largely as a result of the growing amount of cultural and economic capital. A particularly important element of Vester's argument is his examination of the skilled manual worker habitus, where he is able to demonstrate the existence of positive cultures of autonomy.

Although Savage *et al.*'s chapter is very different in subject from Vester's, there are some striking overlaps. Savage *et al.* report the results of a local study in the Manchester conurbation where they show how a practical habitus related to the deployment of manual skills is embedded in place. Like Vester, Savage *et al.* argue that this culture of skilled manual work is distinctive and cannot be seen simply as stigmatised or marginalised. Savage *et al.* also show, however, the lack of clear fit between people's practical habitus and their sense of class identity, but they reveal how a sense of exclusion and marginality are related to respondents' sense of nostalgia, which means that they continue to remain distinct from middle-class groups.

Blokland's chapter also uses a local study to consider issues of class identity. She is especially interested in nostalgia. Like Savage *et al.*, Blokland is concerned with how to understand the ways in which nostalgia is used to construct senses of class and identity. She shows that the elaboration of a nostalgic sense of a homogeneous class community is related to the breakdown of communal boundaries and, in particular, is related to the significance of immigration. In this way she is able to show how more discursive identities develop in the gaps left as everyday practices fragment.

Chapters 7 and 8 consider issues of identity although they return to the national arena. Devine, for example, considers class identities in America. She has not adopted Bourdieu to shape her theoretical concerns and empirical research that has left her out of step with current fashion. Nevertheless, she acknowledges that the application of Bourdieu's ideas in the work of Savage *et al.* (1992) and Skeggs (1997) has raised interesting ideas about old problems around ambivalence, mis-recognition and dis-association from (working-) class labels. Drawing on her comparative work in the US and the UK, however, she describes her surprise at finding how her American interviewees happily and frequently used the language of class to describe themselves and their life histories in contrast to the British informants. Moreover, while the British middle class were invariably silent about their class background, the Americans defined themselves as middle class without discomfort or unease. Contrary to the public view, therefore, people's everyday lives in America, in their families and communities, in schools and in jobs, generate and sustain class sentiments. Moreover, it seems they can be more readily expressed in America than in Britain because they are not so bound up with status distinctions and notions of superiority and inferiority that have a long historical legacy in Britain.

Phillips and Western address identity formation in Australia. They demonstrate the way in which the issue of social identity has become central to the discipline of sociology in a very succinct review of diverse literatures. They note, correctly, however, that empirical research on social identity has not kept abreast of theoretical ideas about modernity and post-modernity although the measurement and the distribution of social identities need to be established empirically to critically evaluate such theories of social change and social identity. They fill this gap by way of quantitative research addressing changes and continuities in patterns and trends in social identification among Australians from the mid-1980s to the mid-1990s. Contrary to the postmodern emphasis on flux, they found considerable consistency and commonality in identities; especially territorial identities such as an identification with Australia, and positional identities such as class. They call for more research, among other things on identities and place/space and, of course, the content and meaning of identities in different contexts.

Crompton and Scott return to the issue of the cultural turn in class analysis in Chapter 9. They are less critical than Devine and Savage of the structure–consciousness–action model that predominated in the mid-twentieth century, highlighting the many strengths of the empirical work on class undertaken at this time. Consequently, they are also less enamored with the work of Bourdieu and the extent to which his approach to class culture replaces or improves upon the older research tradition. Their chapter rightly discusses the shifting positions about methods of social research in the study of class over the last fifty years. In its current form, this debate now focuses on the pros and cons of variable-oriented research as opposed to case-oriented studies of class. Returning to theoretical disputes, they suggest that the popularity of Bourdieu's work has lead to culture being taken 'too seriously' to the extent that the economic and material aspects of structured inequality have been lost. They compare different approaches to the way in which the concept of culture has been incorporated into the study of class distinguishing between a 'dual systems approach' and a 'unitary approach'. They argue that while a unitary approach to issues of the economic and culture has become increasingly dominant, claims that cultural factors are now more important than economic factors in shaping class inequalities require some element of dual systems thinking. Thus, Bourdieu's work, for example, does not overcome the dichotomy of the economic and the cultural that has dominated class analysis and, indeed, sociology more generally. As yet, there is 'no best way' to address these issues and they reassert 'their pluralist stance' to research on class and stratification.

Conclusion

In this opening discussion to this introduction, we drew on Abbott's account of the evolution and development of social sciences and how knowledge changes and advances. We saw how he rejected the idea that the social sciences are inevitably making progress. Instead, disciplines constantly reinvent fundamental concepts as part of debates around common oppositions in theory and method. Opposing perspectives on fundamental concepts are also reproduced as 'fractal distinctions' in sub-disciplines. We applied Abbott's thought provoking ideas by focusing specifically on the concept of culture in sociology and in the sub-disciplines of 'class analysis' in particular. Against the backdrop of debates about their being a 'cultural turn' in sociology, we charted how interest in class cultures has waxed and waned in class analysis since the 1940s. Up to the late 1970s, the study of class cultures – notably working-class culture – was central to the sub-discipline. Class cultures were considered in terms of class-consciousness and class imagery within a structure–consciousness–action theoretical perspective. When empirical evidence uncovered ambivalent attitudes towards class and a reluctance to position oneself in relation to class, however, the S–C–A model became a straightjacket that stifled research on ambivalence. Stuck in this impasse, sociologists of class abandoned the study of culture for class structure that came to dominate the sub-discipline in the 1980s and early 1990s.

Interest in class cultures has now returned to the centre stage of the sub-discipline however. While not inevitable, research on class structures seemed to generate a series of technical debates rather than fire discussion on substantive issues and interest in issues of structure quickly waned as the limitations of this research agenda became obvious. At the same time, Bourdieu's work generated a renewed enthusiasm for the study of class cultures in terms of habitus and identity. Most importantly, the S–C–A model no longer dictated the parameters of research – or at least, the consciousness–action coupling was not longer taken for granted – opening up the possibilities of exploring issue of class ambivalence, dis-association from class and so forth in their own terms. This new found freedom has opened up the research agenda for those working from Bourdieu's perspective as well as those who do not feel compelled to see the world from his theoretical perspective. In other words, those working in the field of class analysis have found themselves returning to issues of culture and to seek to break out of the impasse, both theoretical and methodological, that so perplexed sociologists in the late 1970s. As Abbott cleverly suggests, old problems have a habit of returning and there are familiar limitations to Bourdieu's ideas too. As we noted in this chapter, the extent to which Bourdieu's approach to culture is reductive to the economic continues to be an issue of concern.

Be that as it may, the re-emergence of interest in the concept of culture in class analysis is, in our view, to be welcomed. It has led to a renewal of the sub-discipline both in terms of theoretical ideas and empirical research. We concur with Abbott's view that this re-mapping of the core concept of culture should not be dismissed by older generations of sociologists of class. Rather, it indicates the way in which new generations of sociologists know fundamental principals of sociology and its sub-disciplines. Like Abbott, we remain optimistic about the development of sociology and class analysis. The contributions to this edited collection amply demonstrate our reasons to be cheerful.

Notes

1. In this discussion, we confine ourselves to previous research on class cultures in class analysis. For a consideration of class cultures in social and labour history and cultural studies, see Savage (2000).
2. Of course, as Scott (1996: 288) reminds us, this portrayal of a homogeneous working class can be situated historically alongside the advent of more organised forms of capitalism from the 1880s through to the 1950s. Both Scott (1996) and, more recently, Roberts (2001) acknowledge that working-class communal solidarity was stronger in more isolated, single industry villages and towns than in other localities. Such local variations are, of course, often missed in stereotypical portrayals of the traditional working class.
3. It is interesting to revisit Lockwood's (1966) paper and note how his opening discussion comments on how previous research portrayed the working class as either proletarian (i.e. radical) or deferential (i.e. conservative). This open statement is very similar to Mann's (1973) initial discussion of debates about working-class consciousness.
4. What Pahl (1989) subsequently called the Structure–Culture–Action model of class was as determinist as Marxist theories of class. Pahl (1993) directed his critique against Goldthorpe's social mobility research and his views about the 'promising future' of class analysis.
5. Such high levels of class subjectivity were used in justification of the continued significance of class analysis. Scott (1996) and Savage (2000) have subsequently argued that the relevance of class analysis cannot be justified on the basis of its frequent use in everyday language.

6. This call for research was also made in the closing pages of the *Affluent Worker* study. We agree that the role of organisations such as trade unions and parties are crucial in understanding 'links in the chain' as Lockwood might say although in the current context, we would prefer to emphasise the need for more research on action (or practices) that may or may not be organised by such institutions.

2
Social Stratification and Social Inequality: Models of Intersectionality and Identity

Floya Anthias

We live in a world torn apart by inequality, conflict and injustice. Not only is there a global division in the very capacity to sustain life in different parts of the world, in what Hall (Hall *et al*. 1992) has called 'the West and the rest', with more than half the world living in poverty and disease, but there are conflicts manifested in war and other forms of violence, with people being pitted against each other in the name of nationalism, religion or territorial claims. This is only one arm of the divided world we live in. Within societies and nations, within so-called 'communities', there are divisions and conflicts around class, around ethnicity and racialisation, and around gender as well as other social categories and social positions. Moreover, old people, single mothers, those living on benefits, the long-term unemployed, the sick, the disabled are terms we use to describe both the boundaries we place between different categories of people (although as we shall see these are not mutually exclusive), categories embodied in state practices and regulations, and unequal economic and social positions around income, housing, employment opportunities, education, skills and social rights as well as forms of social honour and rank. In this quagmire of inequality what means do we have for their understanding?

There are a number of terms in the sociological vocabulary that attach themselves to the understanding and explication of inequality. If 'social inequality' is the broad frame by which sociology identifies its object of reference, then social stratification is the most used para-conceptual means for identifying the issues at stake. Essentially social stratification conceptualises inequality as a process of layering or classifying according to a hierarchical principle. In this way social stratification points our attention to vertical rather than horizontal differences. However, social stratification theory is currently in crisis. There is a long tradition of treating class as coterminous with social stratification or at least as structuring those social relations that produce and reproduce the structures of material inequality. Recognising that the concept of class has failed to deliver the understanding of broader forms of social inequality that are not derived from labour markets, the problematic of social inequality has tended to be colonised more recently by a cultural studies framework. This is not so much concerned with resource distribution and allocation but rather with inferiorisation at the cultural or ascriptive level, as well as the level of identity and access to cultural or symbolic resources. Concerns with racism and sexism are incorporated within this problematic (for example, through a notion of spoilt identities) although concurrently recognising the implication of labour markets and social welfare practices in this process.

In addition, given the recognition of the multiform nature of inequalities, there is an increasing attempt to incorporate gender and ethnic difference into the understanding and analysis of social stratification. In this chapter, I will examine a number of ways in which non-class forms of differentiation have been dealt with in relation to inequality. There are three major models for this that can be summarised as: the reductionist model, the intersectionality model and the identity model. This chapter will deal primarily with the intersectionality model and the identity model since the reductionist model has already been heavily discredited. I will then propose that questions of stratification could be reframed through the lens of a reformulated notion of social location and positionality, proposing the notion of translocational positionality. Such an approach marries the idea of narrations of location and positionality with processes of boundary making and hierarchisation in the social sphere and recognises the fluid contextual and dialogical/contradictory processes involved.

Terminological issues in the study of inequality

Given the crisis in social stratification theory, a number of alternative concepts have been used to 'bridge the gap' so to speak. One of the most important of these is the notion of *status*. This has been proposed as a way of thinking about non-class forms of social hierarchy/stratification and as 'relating to the overall structuring of inequality along a range of dimensions' (Crompton 1998: 127). In some current analyses, status has been used to refer to a wide range of social relations including citizenship rights (Lockwood 1996). Certainly citizenship rights constitute a place for formulating a range of conditions about resource access and allocation but the juridical and other categories implicated are themselves highly gendered and racialised in quite specific ways. I would argue that the concept of 'status' is not able to attend to the complex range of social relations involved here.

Dividing people into permanent class and status groupings simply does not work or have any heuristic value because the people in class groups are concurrently crosscut by gender and ethnicity. Moreover, treating gender and ethnicity as 'groupings' and then allocating them to the 'status' category fails to attend to their specific characteristics and their differences, both from each other as well as other types of status groupings such as occupational or consumption-based groups. Class, ethnic and gender attributions and competencies are centrally important in the market place, both as resources that individuals bring to it, but also in terms of the allocation of value to the places in the market (e.g. see the discussion of skill in the works of Phillips and Taylor 1980 and Cockburn 1991).

Other alternative notions to social stratification are those of social exclusion, which has had a great deal of currency, and social polarisation which is tied more closely to a Marxist analysis on the one hand and an underclass thesis (Murray 1990) on the other. Social exclusion as a way into exploring social inequality has some merit in as much as it recognises the importance of boundary formation. To be excluded is to be prevented from entering a social boundary of entitlement, whether it is of wealth, access to jobs, housing or citizenship (and many other social 'goods'). To be included, however, may not eliminate inequality as one might be included on unequal terms, as are migrants who lack citizenship but are included in the labour market say on short-term contracts, or women. Therefore, inclusion in one social sphere, such as the labour market can go hand in hand with exclusion from another social sphere, such as the political process vis-à-vis citizenship. In this way, the notion of exclusion, whilst being broader to some extent than traditional notions of stratification, cannot adequately substitute the latter's concern with hierarchy and therefore inequality.

The concept of social polarisation, whether of the Marxist or the 'underclass' variant, also has merits but constructs a binary model of inequality with those outside a specifically denoted boundary being heralded as polarised from a norm or normal society, as well as implying the expression of antagonism or systematic opposition.

One way in which the multiplicity of sites of inequality is depicted is through the notion of social divisions. The study of social divisions has also been prompted by the demise of class identities and mobilisations as well as the increasing fragmentation of identities in the modern/global world. Within this problematic the first issue at stake is the parameters of social divisions, which I will briefly discuss here before looking at the three models of reductionism, intersectionality and identity.

What is a social division?

Although the term 'social division' is much used, it has been both seriously under-theorised and used in a variety of very different ways. In some texts (e.g. Payne 2000), a social division is any social difference linked to differential treatment. From this point of view, a social division becomes a shorthand descriptive term for differences and inequalities of gender, age, health, ethnicity and so on. In yet other versions a social division refers to any conflictual group, as found in the idea of class divisions. A social division is however more than a taxonomy or a descriptor on the one hand and does not necessarily require the expression of conflict, on the other. It is more useful to treat social divisions as those dimensions of social life relating to boundary formation, which classify human populations according to ontological claims and attributions of difference, involving differential treatment on this basis, including systematic social processes of inferiorisation, hierarchisation and unequal resource allocation.

The term 'social division' has very little analytical value if it is used merely as a descriptor of all forms of social inequality or social difference. It is also problematic to view social divisions as social groups with certain fixed characteristics that can be identified analytically by using the common-sense assumptions of actors, or by using juridical categories of the state and social practice (although both of these aspects are part of the process). This is because population groupings are fluid and contextual/located features of social life rather than given and fixed. Furthermore, population groupings are never empirically given. Rather they are constituted through the hailing process of collective imaginings and embodied practices, as well as the social regulations and other taxonomic devices in the social sphere in a time/space framework. The latter denotes the central importance of treating social divisions as emergent features of social relations, that is in terms of their locational, spatial and chronographic contexts and in terms of a concern with both their practices and their outcomes. This is why it is not possible to specify, outside concrete social formations, the types and character of social divisions. However, the matrix of gender, ethnicity and class generally provides the core of analysis of social divisions in society. Acknowledging the importance and indeed centrality of gender, ethnicity and class should not imply that other social divisions do not or cannot exist. In addition, it becomes important to treat the social divisions themselves as both analytically distinct but essentially constitutive in relation to each other and broader social processes and this is where the discussion of intersectionality, later on in this chapter, is important.

Boundaries and hierarchies

Arguably, the question of social divisions can be encapsulated by the notion of boundaries on the one hand and hierarchies on the other. The issue of the boundaries for defining particular class groupings has been a long-standing concern in class theory, with its problematic of homogeneity of positioning within class groupings. On what dimensions do people have to share (or have similar) functions, conditions, life chances or solidarities to be placed in one social class rather than another? A concern in contemporary class theory has been particularly with defining the boundary between the petit bourgeoisie and the working class as well as bourgeoisie (e.g. see Poulantzas 1973; Carchedi 1977; Wright 1985; Scase 1992).

The issue of boundaries, however, raises questions about *who* does the classifying, *what uses* this is put to, and what are its *effects*. Within any particular population there are boundaries around different *diakritika*. For example, the *diakritika* used for placing individuals into gender groups are different to those used to place them into ethnic and class groups. Individuals, therefore, will not always be placed together using different *diakritika*. Putting the two terms of unities and divisions together helps us to see that within any unity there are also divisions, and within any divisions or boundary points, there are unities. The constructed rather than essential or fixed nature of the boundaries becomes clear. Different markers may be used to define the boundaries. This is raised for example by the debate on the category Black and the shift from seeing it as incorporating both Asians and Afro-Caribbeans, to seeing it as describing only Afro-Caribbeans (e.g. Modood 1988; Brah 1991; Anthias and Yuval Davis 1992; Anthias 1998b). Alternatively, it may be used as a form of self-identification and not dependent necessarily on ascriptive criteria, or may be used as a political identity. A group may be defined, at different times, in terms of culture, place of origin, or religion; for example, Jews may be seen as a cultural group, as a diaspora with a reclaimed homeland (Israel) or as a religious community. These are labels, as well as claims, that are produced socially and enter into the realm of assertion, contestation and negotiation over resource allocation, social positioning and political identity. Recognising the shifting and contextual nature of the boundaries that fix the unities is important without this meaning that they are treated as *ad hoc* or uninvestigable.

This discussion does not imply that class, gender and race are equivalent types of relation for there are distinct features to each, both as boundaries and hierarchies. Class classification starts off from the allocation of individuals, sorting their competencies on the basis of criteria of marketability of skills, competencies, property and knowledges. Membership of individuals in ethnic and race groups is also determined by the possession of criteria of entry, but using other markers, such as colour of skin or language. Individuals are attributed levels of competencies on that basis; in other words competencies are endowed a posteriori on the basis of already meeting other criteria of entry. In the case of class there is no natural reproduction posited, although individuals may be seen to inherit characteristics from their parents, which means that they may be regarded as fated to be members of a particular class. But movement in or out is seen as a product of individual capacities. In the case of race/ethnicity and gender, there can be no movement in and out in terms of capacity. The capacity is written into the very classification. However, we should note that Cohen (1988) has argued for the racialisation of class, as has Miles (1993). In real labour markets the two systems are intertwined: in the first case *what* is regarded as a marketable skill may be dependent on *who* possesses the skill (e.g. the market value of a medical degree may go down if the people who have them are endowed with intrinsically lower social worth are regarded as not so deserving: feminisation and ethnicisation of occupations may lead to this syndrome).

The construction of *collective attributions and the production of unitary categories* is a particularly salient aspect of ethnic and gender divisions and construct those inside (and often outside) in unitary terms. Constructions of sexual or 'racial' difference in terms of a biological or somatic difference come to signify or postulate necessary social effects, to produce gendered or racialised depictions and dispositions. Moreover, collective attributions often become internalised. For example, racist attributions produce negative self-concepts, that is endowing positive value to Whiteness (Fanon 1986) and negative value to Blackness. Collective attributions are also about We-ness and are involved in political or social mobilisation to pursue collective projects. We-ness is always undercut by Other-ness within the group; as in women's position and that of subordinate classes within ethnic groups or ethnicities within gender and class groups. Such a notion of We-ness is particularly important in the construction of ethnic and national boundaries.

What characterises social divisions at the level of *hierarchical positions/difference* (a pecking order of places, symbolically and materially) is inferiorisation and unequal resource allocation (concrete access to economic, political, symbolic and cultural resources). *Hierarchical difference (or hierarchisation)* relates to the ways in which ethnic divisions (along with those of gender and class) construct *places* or *positions* in the social order of things. The hierarchisation is a complex one because it is not just a matter of a hierarchy of places (and specification of which types of individuals may or may not fill them) within any one category. For example, in the category of 'race', there exist class and gender differences that interplay with those of race to produce complex forms of hierarchy.

Unequal resource allocation indicates not only economic resources but also the allocation of power, authority and legitimacy in relation to political, cultural and representational levels as well as the validation of different kinds of social and symbolic capital (Bourdieu 1990b). For example, dominant ethnic, 'race' and gender categories within the modern state have determinate powers in terms of cultural production and reproduction (even though not all individuals attributed in this way will have these powers).

The shifting and located ways in which individuals interpellate and are interpellated means that the social divisions should be seen as forms of signification around particular areas of social life rather than merely being treated as given population groupings. These forms of signification function to produce claims at particular spaces, locations and contexts in a time frame for individuals but these are not exclusive or fixed. However, where the forms of signification are totally prescriptive around attributes, which appear as visible signifiers of difference and as stigmata of the body or the person (like colour, physiognomy, deportment, genitalia or secondary sexual or gender characteristics), then groupings are produced of a more 'fixed' and entrenched nature. However, even here individuals can and do hail themselves and are hailed in different ways (if this were not the case we would all be social 'dupes' or resistance and challenges like homosexuality or transcultural and transethnic relations would not be possible) and the significance given to the visible attributes will shift and change over time with regard to specific social processes of a material and symbolic kind.

The reductionist model: explaining ethnicity and class

The attempt to incorporate gender and ethnic divisions into the analysis of social stratification has typically taken the form of reducing them to some form of class division. For illustrative problems I will focus on ethnicity and class here. Ethnicity and class, when twinned together, have led to problems of reductionism, where ethnicity becomes a disguise of class or its symbolic manifestation. Marxist approaches may treat it as false consciousness, where the real divisions of class take on symbolic forms. Ethnicity may also be seen as being a way that classes organise (not as a disguise but as a vehicle), in order to struggle over economic resources, as in the work of writers such as Hechter (1987). This is less reductionist, but again ethnicity is treated as a dependent phenomenon, whereas class is treated as about 'real' resource claims.

Alternatively, twinning ethnicity and class may focus on the correlations between the actors who occupy particular ethnic positions, and those in particular class positions. This is to focus on how actors within each coincide on scales relating to social position. As an example, black groups who suffer racial disadvantage are then seen to occupy a particular class position, or class fraction (Phizacklea and Miles 1980). Another facet of this is to treat one as an *effect* of the other, in terms of the influence of the valuation (and prejudice/racism/discrimination) that accrues to particular ethnic positions, and how this is manifested in terms of class effects or outcomes. Or it can be done in terms of the mutually reinforcing disadvantages of ethnicity and class (Myrdal 1969).

These positions are problematic. One underlying difficulty is that whilst the delineation of connections, correlations and so on between ethnicity and class are useful, as long as there is a clear operationalisation of the terms in substantive analyses, it is much more difficult to specify the mechanisms at work. Moreover, the attempts to find correlations assume each one is homogeneously constituted, has a unitary role and is mutually exclusive; for example, that all class members belong to a particular ethnic group.

Many of the difficulties of these forms of analysis relate to the ways in which class is seen to be a division marked by material difference, and inequality of positioning around material resources, whether conceived in the area of production or distribution, determined by relations of exploitation or by relations of the market. Ethnicity, on the other hand, is treated as relating to being positioned in terms of culture, or in the symbolic and identificational realm, with particular behavioural or action elements flowing from this. The lasting effect of these traditions of exploring social inequality, through the primacy of the economic realm, heralded by the Marxist framework and revised within the Weberian tradition and the aftermath, have seriously skewered academic conceptions of inequalities and social stratification. They have been impediments to thinking about inequalities in a more holistic and multidimensional way, and are premised on the ontological and epistemological primacy of economic/material needs and their social organisation in human life.

The distinction between the 'material', on the one hand, and the 'cultural/symbolic', on the other, underpins the distinction made between class and other social divisions. My view is that whilst it is useful to hold on to these distinctions at the analytical level, however fraught and difficult their delineation might be, they cannot be used to posit a particular configuration of relations as the exclusive domain of particular kinds of groupings of people. This is because material and cultural/symbolic elements are to be found across all the social categories. Categories therefore may be distinguished not through the polarity of the material and the cultural/symbolic realms, but rather in terms of the specific *forms* these take. In addition, it is necessary to disassociate the economic and the material from one another. Materiality is here defined in terms of the production and allocation of socially valued resources of different types. Once 'the material' is formulated around the idea of resource allocation and hierarchical placement, with regard to different types of socially valued resources which can be cultural as well as strictly economic (although economic resources may possess cultural value and cultural resources may possess economic value), this allows ethnicity and gender a definitive role in a theory of social stratification.

The intersectionality model

The matrix of gender, ethnicity and class now occupies a central place in academic and political life as suggested earlier. Since the early 1980s this triad has been the subject of a great deal of social debate and commentary. Triple oppression, interconnections, interplay, multiple oppressions, fractured identities, overlapping systems and simultaneous oppressions, all come to mind. The ways in which these forms of social organisation and identification intersect in specific sites to produce forms of social asymmetry is undoubtedly the most central development in the social theorisation of inequality and a central facet of the social system in the last twenty years. However, it is useful to pause and ask the extent to which the matrix of gender, race and class continues to be useful and the extent to which the idea of intersectionality can yield the types of analysis, which can cover new forms of inequality in the global world.

Intersectionality may be seen in two ways: one is to look at it from the point of view of the intersections in people's lives in terms of the different positions they hold in relation to gender, race and class and other social categories. To show, for example, that black working class women are particularly disadvantaged may be fairly easy by looking at concrete data that exist in terms of such a category of persons. What is at issue however is the manner in which this occurs. The second way of looking at intersections is not so much a question of finding out what inequalities exist and for whom, but to understand the processes involved. This latter is a far more difficult task.

Since about the 1980s particularly, feminists have tried to answer this question, what are the links between gender, 'race' and class? One way in which they have been connected in some of the literature (for a review see Anthias and Davis 1992) was to argue that one of them was most determining. This found its currency in debates on 'race' and class and gender and class, where the tendency was to reduce gender and 'race' to class (see the reductionist model discussed earlier). Gender and 'race' were treated as epiphenomena, as super-structural elements built upon a real foundation, which was to do with class relations.

Another way that the divisions were linked was in terms of ideas about a triple burden faced by ethnic minority women. Here class, gender and 'race' inequalities were treated as separate but as being experienced simultaneously. This position can be criticised as being too mechanistic. Nira Davis and I (Anthias and Davis 1983, 1992), amongst others, have criticized additive models of the oppression of gender, race and class.

Much recent analysis has posited the idea of interconnecting divisions: that each division involves an intersection with the others (e.g. Collins 1990; Anthias and Davis 1992; Crenshaw 1994; Brah 1996; Anthias 1998b). In this way classes are always gendered and racialised and gender is always classed and racialised and so on. Although this appears a more fruitful way ahead for the analysis of the connections between the social divisions, the question of intersections raises fundamental problems relating to the concrete and analytical relations between social divisions. Some caution therefore is needed when intersectionality is discussed. There is a need also to disentangle the notions of social position (concrete position vis-à-vis a range of social resources such as economic, cultural and political) and social positioning (how we articulate, understand and interact with these positions, e.g. contesting, challenging, defining).

An underlying difficulty is that whilst the delineation of connections, correlations and so on between ethnicity/race or gender and class are useful, as long as there is a clear operationalisation of the terms in substantive analyses, it is much more difficult to specify the mechanisms at work. Moreover, the attempts to find correlations assumes each one is homogeneously constituted, has a unitary role and is mutually exclusive; for example, that all class members belong to a particular ethnic group or gender group. The depiction of Black people as an underclass (Castles and Kosack 1973) or as a class fraction (Phizacklea and Miles 1980), for example, underemphasises the heterogeneity given by the distinct employment characteristics of different 'racialised' groups (e.g. Asians, Afro-Caribbeans and other colonial migrants in Britain). It also takes no account of gender differentiation. The concern to show the class bases of 'race' leads to glossing over the differences and divisions within racialised groups.

One danger with the notion of intersections is therefore found in constructing people as belonging to fixed and permanent groups (e.g. ethnic, gender and class groups) which then all enter, in a pluralist fashion, into their determination. This undermines the focus on social processes, practices and outcomes as they impact on social categories, social structures and individuals. The issue is whether it is useful to maintain talking about categories at all in the first place. The second issue is whether each category can be overlaid on to the others and what that means. If the notion of intersections, in this sense, is inadequate what other terms might be more useful for signalling the constitutive nature of discursive and practical arrangements organised around the existence of social ontologies and how do the social ontologies themselves depend on each other in constituting themselves as analytically discrete and socially active?

This is further complicated by the fact that, despite the danger of seeing people as belonging to fixed groups, groups exist at the imaginary or ideational level as well as at the juridical and legal level. Therefore, the membership of people in groups is important in two ways. One is in terms of attributions of membership and the consequences that flow from these attributions. For example, being labelled as a member of a spoilt or racialised group is related to both one's position in the world and how one sees oneself and in terms of ideas of belonging and otherness. In terms of the second this may have an important role in terms of determining forms of social engagement and participation and in the construction of claims about belonging that may be vehicles for a range of political, cultural and economic resource struggles.

However, it is not just a question of looking at the concrete experiences and positions of subjects in terms of a multiplicity of identities; for example, black working-class women or white middle-class men. Such accounts cannot pay attention to the range of social processes which cannot be encapsulated by the sex/gender, race/ethnicity and class, that is the multiple situational elements that produce social outcomes. The metaphor of intersection may not be an apt one either as it signals roads that meet. On the other hand, the intersection can be a place where the different roads occupy a singular space through coming together.

One view of intersectionality (e.g. around human rights) is that categories of discrimination overlap and individuals suffer exclusions on the basis of race and gender, or any other combination (Crenshaw 1994). One can see the usefulness of this approach. For example, the understanding of the sexual trafficking of young Albanian women in Greece for example cannot be seen as either a gender problem (about the position of women) or a racist problem (about the position of Albanians in Greek society). One aspect of this is the production of data, which cross references the divisions within formulated groups. However, the very act of already presupposing the groups *per se* as useful classificatory instruments, as opposed to groups who are positioned in a particular relation to the state (e.g. focusing on Albanians rather than working class or poor migrants who are located in Greek society in a particular way) has the danger of placing too much emphasis on the origin of the migrant and not enough on a shared terrain of disadvantage across rather than merely within country of origin-based lines (or those of religion, etc.). Being sensitive to the differences in the position of men and women from different social classes and different religions, countries of origin or linguistic and cultural communities is important. However, how to implement strategies of inclusion, which do not concurrently exclude or are ethnocentric, is more problematic. Reaching agreement, within the terms of multiculturalist policies for example, on universally applicable norms of what should be done around thorny areas of practice and culture (such as polygamy) is also far from simple.

In existing legislation, different aspects of human rights or equality mechanisms are treated separately and different aspects of human identity such as sex discrimination, race equality and disability rights are addressed by separate laws and organisations. Some of us have been arguing for the need to integrate them and cross reference them but this need not be interpreted as entailing the abolition of political intervention on specific sites of oppression also, as long as action and politics is coordinated. Mechanisms are needed for the pulling together of these. A coordinating group, which additionally focuses on their integration and intersection, is needed rather than the abolition of sex or race discrimination agendas. The Beijing Platform for action, adopted by 95 countries in 1995 recognises the 'multiple barriers' to girls and women's empowerment and advancement through 'race, age, language, ethnicity, culture, religion, or disability or because they are indigenous people'. The UN Committee of Racial Discrimination is taking on board the need for intersectional analysis.

The argument has been that forms of inequality and subordination are distinctive yet interlocking. However, in the argument that they are distinctive it is important to note what this might mean: here we enter the terrain of what is shared and what is different in the social divisions both in terms of analytical tools for examining social relations, as classificatory principles, attributions and claims and in terms of practical processes. In the attempt to say that each individual has a unique position in terms of the triad of gender, race and class (e.g. Collins 1993: 28) and that each person is simultaneously oppressor and oppressed (ibid.) the danger is the steady disappearance of systematic forms of subordination and oppression. There is also the assumption of race, gender and class position being unproblematically ascertainable leaving out the understandings of subjects themselves who are not divided into fragments in the way some of these arguments might suggest or necessarily think of themselves in such terms. Issues emerge about the power of definitions and who makes them here. The question of the political nature of claims and attributions at the intersectional level is also raised. Identities of legitimation and identities of resistance are useful ways of thinking about this (Gimenez 2001). Contradictory locations where dominant and subordinate ones intersect (Wright 1985) make it a useful arena. The concrete depiction of intersections is very different to finding explanations for these. The sources of the inequalities experienced by people at the intersection might not be a product of the intersection at all but may be manifested in that space, for example, something happens at the junction which is not necessarily a product of the different roads that lead to it. Nor can the notion explain the reproduction of discrimination/subordination. In other words it is power relations within social processes and practices that need to be considered for this. Such power relations can be treated as both emergent and institutionalised. There is a danger of race, class and gender becoming taken for granted categories for social analysis.

Despite the difficulty of the notion of intersections, it may be possible to see ethnicity, gender and class, first, as crosscutting and mutually *reinforcing* systems of domination and subordination, particularly in terms of processes and relations of hierarchisation, unequal resource allocation and inferiorisation. Secondly, ethnicity, gender and class may construct multiple, uneven and *contradictory* social patterns of domination and subordination; human subjects may be positioned differentially within these social divisions. For example, white working-class men may be seen to be in a relation of dominance over racialised groups, and over women, but may themselves be in a relation of subordination in class terms. This leads to highly contradictory processes in terms of positionality and identity. The exploration of *reinforcing aspects of the divisions, and their contradictory articulations*, opens up fundamental political questions also. In other words the discussion of connecting social divisions is not purely theoretical. It has a direct relevance in terms of how inequalities, identities and political strategies are conceptualised and assessed.

Given the above, social divisions are *emergent and subject to historical contingencies, variable, irreducible and changeable* but not *ad hoc* or uninvestigable. They *intersect within specific and local contexts and in relation to agency (as social action rather than will)*. Agency is not only at the level of the person but also at the collective level, involving solidary and collective allegiances and struggles.

This discussion of intersectionality indicates the need to be cautious in using the term as an unproblematic means of auditing and correcting social disadvantage and raises the following issues:

- A simple model of descriptive intersectionalities is not enough and has the danger of making us taken for granted what it means when we use the terms ethnic, race, gender and class and their interlocking.
- The notion of contradictory locations that I have written about (Anthias 1998a, 2001) can help us but it is not just a descriptive term. We need to theorise the processes that give rise to them and these are not just the roads that lead to our junction.

Identity model

Having discussed the intersectionality approach, I will now turn to the identity model. Theorists have tried to correct the objectivist and often socially mechanistic models of class and to insert ethnicity and gender as forms of inequality into frameworks of analysis in terms of a model of identity and its importance in the structuration of inequality (e.g. see Hall 1990). The concerns of identity within class discourses have been more about the link between consciousness and political practice or class mobilisation. More recently the demise or refusal of class identity has been highlighted (Pakulski and Waters 1996). As forms of social differentiation are marked by commitments of the actors to certain forms of positioning vis-à-vis gender, ethnicity and class, then issues of social location cannot be separated in any fundamental way from issues of the taking up of positions or identities for the purpose of negotiating social relations, as well as projects of political importance for social actors. It is this implication of expanding the concern of social stratification that I will look at as it has brought into focus issues of identity, which have been subordinate in discussions on class. However, the way people perceive their social location, and the taking up of particular political positions, is not only indeterminate (see the classic conception of this in the work of Hall 1978) but issues of identity are slippery means for finding alternative political voices as well as analytical inroads.

Issues of identity in the debates on social class have usually been thought of using the idea of consciousness. A distinction that has traditionally been made is that between 'a class in itself' and 'a class for itself'. The analogous concept of false consciousness has been used to explain the point at which a class is in itself but not for itself. This false consciousness can be thought of either in terms of a misapprehension of class identity (i.e. a falsehood) or in terms of an absence altogether of class identity. In the first case, the class exists as more than a classificatory system vis-à-vis production (or distribution) of resources in as much as it exists as a totality of misunderstood social identity. In the second case, that is when false consciousness depicts an absence of class identity, then a class is merely a classification in terms of function of a population who are waiting to discover their identity. The parameters of class debates have been about the links between the objective social location of a 'class', that is a group of people functionally connected, and the forms of identity and consciousness in terms particularly of mobilisation.

Let us examine how this occurs in the case of ethnic and gender debates. The entry point to consciousness differs in the case of ethnicity and in the case of 'race' and gender. In the case of ethnicity the entry point to identity is usually articulated through the idea of culture. Here it is the lifestyle, the values, the stuff of everyday life in its entirety, but particularly in terms of a *modus vivendi* that is associated with identity. However, the assumption is that the commonalities of culture establish a form of identity in the expression of statements such as 'I am' or 'I belong'. So for example it is predicated on the idea that a set of cultural practices or beliefs will automatically become translated into forms of consciousness and identity or collective belonging, in the process of the enactment of cultural idioms. Hence, in the case of those who are identified as having more ambiguous or synthetic cultural attributes, the issue of identity becomes problematic. This is found in ideas of hybridity, identity crisis or being 'between two cultures'. However, the notion of culture is highly contestable (see Anthias 2001) and the conflation of culture with identity highly problematic as an overarching principle.

In the case of race and gender (in different ways), consciousness and identity are not tied so much to the internalisation or performativity of cultural idioms (as in ethnicity), but rather to the inescapable logic of physiognomy or bodily characteristics (but see the work of Butler 1993 for example). Here it is performed because of the stigmata of the body, as imprinted or performed vis-à-vis a reaction/response to the social attributions and positions bestowed on individuals through social recognition/misrecognition.

I believe that the concept of 'identity' has over-run its limits (Brubaker and Cooper 2000; Anthias 2002). First, the concept has been expanded so much that it has lost its specificity, so it can embrace everything, for example, when shifting or multiple notions are used to correct the essentialising of earlier concepts. Secondly, the concept always takes us back to the theoretical baggage about communal identity as generic and fundamental in social processes. Whilst acknowledging that people's notions of belonging are important social facts, we cannot presuppose that they are always necessary or determining elements in collective placement or action.

There is no doubt that social divisions are not only features of social structure but are implicated in claims and attributions of identity, social practices and social action. Indeed one of the major characteristics of social divisions is that they construct forms of belonging and otherness. However, it is important to frame this within the context of the emergent and differentially salient nature of identity claims and attributions, and not to assume that identity is the quest that drives categories and hierarchies relating to social classification.

'Where do I belong' is a recurrent thought, however, for most of us. Asking this question is usually prompted by a feeling that there are a range of spaces, places, locales and identities that we feel we do not and cannot belong to. Such quests involve a range of different kinds of questions relating to how we are positioned, how we are perceived, our identifications, our self-understandings and our visions of the future. Not only do these relate to our own belonging but also to the ways in which the collective spaces and places of 'others' are understood and thought about. Some of the ways in which I think about my belonging involves fragments of memories (and forgetting), of feeling and of evocations of loss. Crossing borders, real and imaginary is part of this process. These are multiform and the borders may be fluid or rigid. These borders and boundaries are shifting and changing, some are more a product of external constraints, like political, legal or national rules relating to membership, others are inscribed in the body which presents the stigmata of absence or deformity via gender or disability, or inscribed through the body in the effects of body style in class relations, or very importantly through colour, physiognomy or the bodily and personal style/gait associated with ethnic difference.

Collective imaginings constitute points of reference for the formation of uncertainties about belonging. This is not just an existential question but one relating to ideas of what we share with others, and where we feel comfortable. In a sense though, the places we feel at least we do not belong to (this in itself is a form of certainty) are as important as those we feel with certainty that we do. Part of the construction of belonging within a boundary involves knowing that you do not belong to another from which it is constructed as a binary. From this point of view belongingness is always framed within difference and alterity. But we do not need to accept analytically that the binary of self and other or sameness and alterity have a sociological equivalence or indeed that the processes are as dyadic as they may appear. Moreover, not all these boundaries of belonging and non-belonging have equal effects: some are more violent and damaging than others: some construct our very ability to survive in the world: oppression constructed by the colonialist power and the violence of ethnic cleansing, racism and sexism are all examples of this.

Being sceptical of the heuristic or analytic value of treating social divisions as forms of 'identity' is not equivalent to saying that the issues addressed are not important. Indeed, quite the opposite. This includes both the way individuals have personal and political investments in their 'identity', found in Giddens notion of self identity in high modernity (1991a) and Beck's notion of the 'risk society' (1992), and identification with particular cultures, lifestyles or work, 'racial' or sexual identities (Bradley 1996). Such encoding of the self implicates a sense of human value and worth and may counter the construction of otherness, ascribed or internalised. Within globalised relations, there is a decline of interest in what might be called social determination via institutional arrangements or structures, and the growth of interest in 'travelling' cultural and symbolic expressions (which could be seen as the colonisation of the social by the cultural). Moreover, there is an increasing economic value given to cultural forms (Crook *et al.* 1992; Lash and Urry 1994). There has also been a growth of social movements and campaigns that forge under the banner of a politics of recognition or what might be called a politics of displacement (Phillips 1998). Such processes have gone hand in hand with an increasing focus by the polity on multiculturalisms and the growth of different forms of exclusion, inferiorisation or differential incorporation (Wievorka 1998).

Being cautious of using notions of identity in the area of social inequality also does not mean that 'identity' is no longer treated as socially meaningful, since individuals and groups (not only may, but often do) use the term to signify a range of processes, ideas and experiences relating to themselves and others. However, it is possible to problematise the epistemological and ontological status of identity and critique the forms of politics based upon these whilst still treating identity as a *socially* meaningful concept. Such a position is able to pay attention to spatial and contextual dimensions, treating the issues involved in terms of processes rather than possessive properties of individuals (as in 'who are you' being replaced by 'what and how have you'. Moreover, such an approach points out attention to the intricacies of the links between different forms of position structured in the interstices of social divisions and their intersections, for example, ethnicity, gender and class location.

Displacing the identity problematic: narratives of location

Issues of collective identity, whilst related to those of self-identity (in the sense that the self is embedded in collective idioms and draws defining characteristics from them) contain important differences also. Whilst an essential step to the production of self is the boundary of the self from the other (in the first instance the recognition of the bodily and psychic separation from the mother), in the case of collective identity it involves the step of recognising many others that can stand as 'selves' (e.g. in the family, in the ethnic group, in the gender category, etc.) and similarly those that are constructed as collective 'others'.

In current literature, static and essentialised views of difference and identity have been challenged systematically by a range of approaches, particularly via the growth of postmodernist and poststructuralist social theory, drawing on and developing the important work of Saussure (1959), Freud (1949), Lacan (1977), Derrida (1981) and Foucault (1972). In such approaches notions of the fragmentation of identity come to the fore, along with a critique of unitary notions of identity, treating the latter as emergent and contingent, whilst putting in its place the notion of multiple and fragmented identities (e.g. see Shotter and Gergen 1989; Hall 1990; Brah 1996). There has also been an important debate about the failures of 'identity politics' as modes of pursuing inclusion and incorporation into society and achieving full social rights (e.g. Butler 1993; Phillips 1998).

Narratives of location and positionality might be useful concepts for reframing issues of identity. A narrative is an account that tells a story and a narrative of location, as it is used here, is an account that tells a story about how we place ourselves in terms of social categories, such as those of gender, ethnicity and class at a specific point in time and space. The narrative is both a story about who and what we identify with (i.e. a story about identification) and it is also a story about our practices and the practices of others, including wider social practices and how we experience them. These stories however, do not necessarily have a beginning, plot or ending; they are composed of fragments whose place in the whole text is emergent and at times contradictory. Nor does the sequence or chronological citing of information necessarily mirror the 'life' trajectory or have any particular significance (Stanley 1993). From this point of view, any account that is given about a person's place in the order of things (in the broader sense) constitutes a story about 'location'. Such stories will also be articulated in terms of notions of identity making claims to 'who I am', which groupings 'I identify with' and which groups 'I participate within'. These stories at one level draw on, and therefore are derived from, collective stories told around us (which often *do* have a component of a narrative that unfolds genealogically), that is from discourses, representations and normative systems as well as stories told within our families and by a range of significant others. At the same time, these stories are ways in which we try to order and organise our experiences in terms of certain conventional norms or rules. These relate to the type of narration that is deemed appropriate in a particular context and in relation to a particular audience, imagined or real. Therefore these stories have both a conventional and strong intersubjective component.

Narratives of location are also narratives of dislocation and alterity. This is particularly relevant to the study of what has been termed ethnicity in migration, involving as it does dislocation and relocation at multiple levels – structural, cultural and personal. The migrant is also placed in terms of a range of other attributions and claims of difference and identity, constructing group belonging, such as those of gender, class, age and so on. In the formation of positionality, gender and class may be seen as important as ethnicity.

I suggest that narratives of location are structured more in terms of a denial, that is through a rejection of what one is not rather than a clear and unambiguous formulation of what one is. This is not only a question of identity and its narration being relational (see Anthias 1998a), but also being defined in terms of the refusal of certain attributions (e.g. see the work of Skeggs 1997). Such narrations involve imaginaries of collectivities and how borders are constructed. Imaginaries of borders can entail territories/geographies/spatialities of belonging, cultural ingredients, somatic aspects, as contra to the group one is not part of, as the structuring through the negative. Stories are told in terms of bipolar: positive and negative, partly framed through the relation *to whom and for what* and in the case of research, the interview process. This must be separated from the stories we have of our inner world/ identity that is not the concern of the chapter, although clearly impacts upon it. The narrative constitutes a means for understanding the ways in which the narrator at a *specific point in time and space is able to make sense and articulate their placement in the social order of things. This however, also means the recognition of the narrative as an action, as a performance.*

The focus on narratives of location avoids assumptions about subjective processes on the one hand and culturalist or materialist forms of determinism on the other. Moreover, it acknowledges that identification is an enactment that does not entail fixity or permanence, as well as the role of the local and the contextual in the processes involved. Narratives may then be seen as forms of social action, that is as actively participating in the very construction of subject positionalities.

In this part of the chapter, I have argued that the insertion of identity into debates on social inequality fails to deliver an understanding of the contradictory, located and positional aspects of constructions of belonging and otherness and overemphasises the role of such constructions in the structuration of inequality since gender and ethnic lived experience is not synonymous with belonging and otherness notions alone. It is through the narration and enactment of location and position that such spaces become meaningful for social actors. The narrational aspects of location/dislocation are important for sociological understanding and political contestation and can be seen as both outcomes and as effective social processes. These narrations of individuals are the stories that they tell and retell about their collective placement, about their place in the social order of things.

Concluding remarks: implications for the study of social inequality

Forms of social inequality are complex and cannot be accounted for through some single mechanism or principle (such as found in arguments of class, gender or race inequality). Social divisions and 'identities' attribute and claim social location and entail the construction of boundaries of difference and sameness along particular dimensions (or codes/markers). Here the term 'identities' is used to demarcate boundaries of differentiation and classification. Such collective identities are framed within one another. They constitute ways of thinking about others and ourselves in terms of the social order of things and are therefore never innocent of stratification, entailing hierarchy and distinction characterised by different forms of particularism and partiality. The binary, naturalised and collectivised forms of these (Anthias 1998a), for example male/female, Black/White, inclusion/exclusion, self/other, are central parameters which enter into individual narrations of location.

With the recognition of the importance of meaning and context, such categories can no longer be thought of as unities and divisions in any clear sense. In the area of ethnicity and migration, for example, there has been an interest in what has been called transethnic, transnational and hybrid identities (Hall 1990; Gilroy 1993; Brah 1996; Anthias 1998b). In terms of social relations that are hierarchical, it is not purely a question of a hierarchy of individuals within a category. For example in the category of race, where the distinction between say White and Black is constructed, the White is dominant over the Black. The White is able to reproduce advantages and privileges and reproduce the evaluative components of Whiteness. However, within this construct, there exist class differences and gender differences also which interplay with those of race to produce hierarchical outcomes for individuals. These may lead to complex forms of hierarchy across a range of different dimensions. If the constructs are read as 'grids' their salience will not only vary in different contexts but the interplay of the different grids needs to be always considered in any analysis of social outcomes or effects (Anthias 1998a).

Positionality is a term that references the interplay between *position* within each of the divisions (such as ethnicity/nation, class and gender) and its representation, and *positioning*, the intersubjectively and experientially constituted placing that the individual makes in specific contexts. The focus on contradictory social processes relating to what we might now think of as hybrid social class positions is found in earlier accounts such as those in the work of E.O. Wright (1985) for example and the debates around Carchedi (1977) and Poulantzas (1973) on the lower middle classes. 'Contradictory locations' is also a way of connecting together class, ethnicity and gender for social actors since they may occupy different places in each of these vis-à-vis the stratification principle. There are, however, particularly *contradictory* locations (positions and positionings), which construct translocational positionalities. *Translocational* positionalities are those where there is an uneven placement in different collective imaginings or social divisions, as in example occupying a higher position in one (such as being white), but a lower in the other such as being female or black. Translocational positionalities are particularly open to new forms of imaginings which are not necessarily more progressive or transgressive but which open up possibilities of thinking and being, stressing the fluid and contradictory as well as making transparent the 'imaginary' sphere of collective belonging. Contradictory and in between positions constitute important points of departure for understanding the dynamics of social stratification, on the one hand, and social integration on the other.

3
The Re-Branding of Class: Propertising Culture

Beverley Skeggs

This chapter draws on debates from France, Australia, the US and the UK that work on issues of class, feminism and gender, sexuality and race. It assumes a knowledge of Bourdieu's use of capitals – economic, social, symbolic and cultural as they accrue in bodies over periods of time in different social spaces (see Bourdieu 1987, 1989; Skeggs 1997). Drawing on the historical processes of moral attribution, atavistic positioning and using the working class as constitutive limit, it demonstrates how these processes are being re-worked in the contemporary,[1] through the sites of popular culture and political rhetoric, thereby providing systems of interpretation for how we come to know and understand class. The emphasis is therefore on the symbolic production of class.

My central concern is how bodies, people and groups *attain value* through different systems of symbolic exchange, which enable and limit how they can move through social space. Part of this process involves how discourse sets limits on the *evaluation* of particular bodies and practices. Discourse is part of the process by which social positioning is known. An integral part of this process is the attribution of moral value to particular bodies; what (Foucault 1979) would identify as the 'dense transference point for power'. So the emphasis here is on the transference, *the process by which value is transported into bodies and the mechanisms by which it is retained, accumulated, lost or appropriated.* In order to understand these evaluation processes we need to know the different forms of exchange from which they emerge. It is argued that culture has become a central site for the exchange of value and the ability to convert, or not, cultural practices are seen to be central to contemporary class formation.

As a challenge to the classical political economy of Adam Smith and Ricardo, Marx argued that we have to move away from paying attention to generalised exchange and to focus our attention instead on production.[2] Here I am calling for a reversal of this analysis, arguing that we need to focus on the different forms of exchange that make up the symbolic economy (of which the monetary system is just one element). The reason I argue for this reversal is because of two economic processes, which have promoted the *de-materialisation* of commercial production and therefore the predominance of symbolic exchange in post-industrialisation (the shift from manufacturing to services). Waters (1995) identifies these as: hypercommodification and the industrialisation of culture. Both imply the production of more mobile and easily tradable products; hence globalisation will increase the extent that world production is devoted to these non-matter commodities (the de-materialisation he identifies), precisely because they are so mobile. Culture can be converted into a highly mobile commodity and is used effectively as the sign/symbolic economy of transnational advertising (e.g. the use of racial signifiers to generate a 'multi-cultural appeal' for Bennetton; see Back and Quaade 1993; Franklin *et al.* 2000; Lury 1996). But in order to do this, new markets need to be identified and opened. It is the search for these new markets that makes explicit the value that is attributed to particular bodies and groups. So this is not about a shift from economics *to* culture, but how culture is being deployed as an economic resource in the contemporary and how this shapes our understandings of class.

The contemporary unrelenting capitalist desire for new markets is a different search than that historically produced through imperialism (see Hardt and Negri 2000). This is because it is located in the logic of late capitalism which, as Deleuze and Guattari (1977) suggest, was premised on – unlike all previous social systems – a continual overcoming of its limitations, contradictions, or 'lines of flight', that which escapes its regimes. With diversification, capital increasingly comes to operate directly *on* its lines of flight. That is, it seeks less to maintain fixed moulds – which are not always so quick to capture that which escapes – but operates through increasingly flexible and varying modulations of social activity (see Thoburn 2001). There is therefore little beyond its commodification. It is also what (Zizek 1997) reveals to be perfectly attuned to the identity politics of multi-culturalism, offering capitalism new possibilities on a global scale. It is a way of capital capturing what was previously beyond commodification; not resorting just to the exploitation of labour, but making culture *central to* exploitation and surplus value production.

The search for new markets and new experiences exists within and beyond national frames. The contradictions between the capitalist desire for global markets and the ways in which people are able to have personhood within the nation exist simultaneously and often mark fracture lines in capital – state relations (e.g. pink pound search for new markets and punitive legislation such as Section 28 in the UK). But this also marks different ways in which political claims can be made and who can make them (e.g. through the territorialisation of commercial space – a symbolic economy, or through citizenship and discourses of rights and responsibilities). So whilst we have the demands of global capitalism looking to open out new markets, via culture, we also have state defined sovereignty – often explicated through political rhetoric – which is still significant for deciding who can belong and what it means to belong to a particular nation. So I want to explore how both these frames – markets and national belonging – set limits on who can be seen to exist with or without value, and how this process makes class difference.

For example, Hage (1998) provides an excellent analysis of what it means to be Australian. He analyses how different groups and bodies (for capitals are embodied: see Bourdieu 1986, 1987) acquire the 'right' type and amount of cultural capital to be seen as having worth, or more importantly as being seen as not pathological and problematic to the safety and security of nation formation. To understand how certain bodies can or cannot belong, he argues, we need to identify the processes by which certain representations become attributed with moral value, thus being defined as good/bad, having worth/being worthless, so that boundaries can be drawn and value attributed.

Branding is one way to think about this process; it illuminates different forms of exchange-value, different transference points of power and different values. Branding is about how value becomes re-attributed and flows from subject to object, object to subject, or does not flow at all. But it is also, importantly, about how experience, feelings and affect become central to the evaluation process. It is about how value is produced from cultural experience, affect and feelings. Franklin *et al.* (2000) identify branding as a process in which the subject is linked to the object in novel ways, making available for appropriation *aspects of the experience of product use*, as if they were properties of the brand. This chapter charts how class is defined currently as a cultural property (something that is owned by the person as an attitude or attribute) and then how this is read back into practices, so that people learn not only what they are worth, symbolically (socially and economically), but also how their cultural practices come to have (or not) a worth and value for others. The significance of this analysis is that it enables an exploration of what makes the culture of some groups propertisable for others. It is the ability to appropriate *aspects of the experience of product use* (aspects of working-class culture), as if they were properties of the brand (the new middle-class self) that leads to the re-branding and hence re-propertising of class via culture and affect.

To understand this process fully we need also to understand the changing formations of the middle-class self (aesthetic, prosthetic, omnivorous, reflexive, enterprising, the subject with value, etc.) but that is another paper (see also Savage *et al.* 1992; Strathern 1992; and Lury 1998 for explications).

This chapter is divided into three sections. The first provides some examples of how the symbolic formations of class relations are being presently constituted in popular culture. It charts the attribution of moral value and shows how this is also worked through gender and race. What is significant is how historical legacies become recombined and refigured through the present. The attribution of moral worthlessness has a very long history in the representation of the working-class, but it is being reworked in new ways. Hence, *re-presentations are constitutive not just reproductive* (Coward and Ellis 1977), producing new forms of value, potential for exchange and national belonging. Representations are not dispositions, however, so how they manifest in practice is central to understanding how value it lived. How they are contested by those who are positioned by them is therefore a site of class struggle. The second section asks how academic understandings are responding to these changes and the third examines the consequences of these changes for contemporary politics. This is part of a more general concern to understand how value is attributed to bodies and how subjectivity is framed through value-attribution.

Rhetoric and re-presentations

This is a massive area but some of the ways in which moral value is attached to and identified with the working class include: as excess, as waste, as entertainment, as authenticating, lacking in taste, as un-modern, backward, as escapist, as dangerous, unruly and without shame and always spatialised. These moral attributions are attached to bodies in different compositions and volumes. Moreover, evaluation and position-ing are completely apparent to those whose bodies are meant to carry the value. That is, the working class know how they are being evaluated and read as my previous research showed (Skeggs 1997). I am now going to outline some of the processes. The first example shows how class is being increasingly defined as a moral-cultural property of the person, related to their attitudes and practices (not named and known directly as class). The second shows how class becomes a defining feature of the nation that is fixed to particular groups of people and specific bodies in a way that makes them constitutive outsiders, the third of how these social positions of class are intimately entwined with gender but also represent a fixed space; the fourth shows how this positioning is 'euphemistically transferred' (Bromley 2000) or spoken through debates on taste and the final example shows how race and class entwine and become a resource deployed by entitled others. My interest is in how that which is a valuable cultural practice for some groups becomes devalued when attached to others. I'm interested in how culture can be propertisable (reference to all the legal debates over property and propriety Davies 1994; Moran and Skeggs 2001b). Each performs a different way of attributing, extracting or denying value.

Exemplar One: This is taken from popular culture and reproduces a long tradition by showing how cultural practices come to define class through the attribution of morality to particular cultural practices. So in the *Daily Mirror* Survey (09.02.1997, with a readership of 2.5 m) (Table 3.1) readers are asked to classify themselves by completing a questionnaire. This of course is ironic in the same way that *Loaded* magazine operates irony. It enables distance to be drawn whilst simultaneously maintaining the distance. So out of a list of 20 questions about cultural practice only 3 relate directly to economic issues (owning/renting a house, employed/ unemployed, pension plan). All the other questions are about cultural practices and attitudes such as 'I own a large dog!', 'I have sex too much', 'I regularly eat out in restaurants', 'I go to Tuscany for my holidays' (agree or disagree to be ticked). Highest scores are achieved by the most middle-class pursuits (holidaying in Tuscany – a venue for which the Blairs are associated). The value that has been attached to each practice can be seen to be based on *morality*: big dogs and excess sex, but also *the right knowledge* (knowing to go to Tuscany, how to appreciate the Theatre and eating out[3]). Morality and the right knowledge here are also dependent upon economic resources as affording to holiday in Tuscany and go to theatre and restaurants relies on having enough money too. In this example the attribution of value and its association to social positioning is made abundantly clear. The significance of this example is in making obvious in popular culture the shift from class as an economic categorisation to one based on cultural practices. Standing alone

Table 3.1 The *Daily Mirror* survey on whether Britain is a classless society

Classless Society

? READ ACROSS FROM LEFT TO RIGHT AND TICK THE STATEMENTS YOU STRONGLY AGREE WITH

I am a vegetarian	☐	I have one pet	☐	I eat meat two or three time a week	☐	I have more than one pet	☐
I exercise two to six times a week	☐	I never smoke cigars	☐	I never exercise	☐	I do not drive a car	☐
I take bottles, papers and cans to be recycled	☐	I drink alcohol only about once a week	☐	I wrote to a newspaper this year about an environmental issue	☐	I smoke cigarettes	☐
I have recently walked in the countryside or along the coast	☐	I exercise two to six times a week	☐	If I won the Lottery I would buy a villa in the sun	☐	I exercise every day	☐
I have a credit card	☐	I have recently walked in the countryside or along the coast	☐	I support the monarchy	☐	I never exercise	☐
I have a £50 cheque guarantee card	☐	I have a cashpoint card	☐	I know someone who has taken crack cocaine	☐	I never finish a book for pleasure	☐
I think the monarchy should be abolished	☐	If I won the Lottery I'd move to a country cottage	☐	I have taken Ecstasy	☐	I support the monarchy	☐
I have taken cocaine	☐	I never read books	☐	I support the idea of a minimum wage	☐	I think it's wrong for couples to live together before marriage	☐

Table 3.1 (Continued)

Classless Society

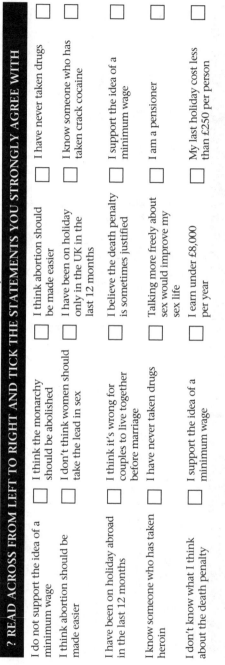

? READ ACROSS FROM LEFT TO RIGHT AND TICK THE STATEMENTS YOU STRONGLY AGREE WITH

I do not support the idea of a minimum wage	☐	I think the monarchy should be abolished	☐	I think abortion should be made easier	☐	I have never taken drugs	☐
I think abortion should be made easier	☐	I don't think women should take the lead in sex	☐	I have been on holiday only in the UK in the last 12 months	☐	I know someone who has taken crack cocaine	☐
I have been on holiday abroad in the last 12 months	☐	I think it's wrong for couples to live together before marriage	☐	I believe the death penalty is sometimes justified	☐	I support the idea of a minimum wage	☐
I know someone who has taken heroin	☐	I have never taken drugs	☐	Talking more freely about sex would improve my sex life	☐	I am a pensioner	☐
I don't know what I think about the death penalty	☐	I support the idea of a minimum wage	☐	I earn under £8,000 per year	☐	My last holiday cost less than £250 per person	☐

Classless Society

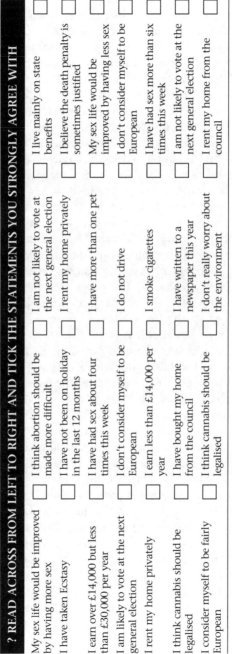

? READ ACROSS FROM LEFT TO RIGHT AND TICK THE STATEMENTS YOU STRONGLY AGREE WITH

My sex life would be improved by having more sex ☐	I think abortion should be made more difficult ☐	I am not likely to vote at the next general election ☐	I live mainly on state benefits ☐
I have taken Ecstasy ☐	I have not been on holiday in the last 12 months ☐	I rent my home privately ☐	I believe the death penalty is sometimes justified ☐
I earn over £14,000 but less than £30,000 per year ☐	I have had sex about four times this week ☐	I have more than one pet ☐	My sex life would be improved by having less sex ☐
I am likely to vote at the next general election ☐	I don't consider myself to be European ☐	I do not drive ☐	I don't consider myself to be European ☐
I rent my home privately ☐	I earn less than £14,000 per year ☐	I smoke cigarettes ☐	I have had sex more than six times this week ☐
I think cannabis should be legalised ☐	I have bought my home from the council ☐	I have written to a newspaper this year ☐	I am not likely to vote at the next general election ☐
I consider myself to be fairly European ☐	I think cannabis should be legalised ☐	I don't really worry about the environment ☐	I rent my home from the council ☐

Source: MORI/Sunday Mirror, 9 February 1997: 23.

this example does not mean much, but when viewed with the cumulative effect across a range of sites listed below (more popular culture, political rhetoric and social policy) we can see a condensation of value signs.

Exemplar Two: The next example also shows how value is *not* attributed to certain bodies and how this is spatialised: some bodies fixed in place whilst some are mobile. Gender here makes a difference. Again drawing from popular culture, this time Hollywood films, Tasker (1998) shows how women's excessive attention to their appearance is used to denote low moral value and to condense lack of value onto certain bodies. This attribution of appearance to conduct has a long history, particularly in distinguishing between the redeemable and unredeemable of Victorian women (Nead 1988). It also has a long history in more general US popular culture whereby 'big hair' or 'big bodies' shorthand white trash (Ortner 1991; Rowe 1995). These are speedy signifiers. Tasker charts a range of transformation narratives in which the visually excessive working-class woman is turned into the subtle and discreet middle-class woman, usually helped into the 'right knowledge' by a powerful man (e.g. *Working Girl, Pretty Woman, Up Close and Personal*). In the British version (*Pygmalion/My Fair Lady*), attention is given to language as well as appearance. In the transformation the audience learn of the change through the gradual loss of excessive style.

Tasker argues that the attraction of these films is the tension and pleasure generated by the risk of the women being exposed, caught out and discovered and then ultimate redemption and escape. This encodes class not only as something that has to be left behind, that which is fixed in order for mobility to proceed, but also as that which has no value. These films also offer middle-class taste and positioning as the mechanism by which being working class can be overcome and eradicated, but also as something which should be aspired to. They reproduce Bourdieu's (1986) definition of cultural capital as high capital. Class here becomes a matter of 'getting it right' by learning middle-class cultural practices and knowledge in order to be able to transcend working-class signifiers. Here the process is to signify appearance (a cultural practice, and a very specific version of working-class femininity) as the short cut to immoral worthlessness, as something that has to be eradicated in order for morality (and hence value) to be established. Again, it is the combination of knowing how and having the resources to escape class that enables worth to be established.[4] This is a very particular way of establishing taste. And as Bourdieu (1986) has shown women's bodies are often used as the carriers of taste cultures. By highlighting movement (or escape) from working-classness, a particular form of fixity is attached to certain cultural practices: those that need to be moved on from for social mobility to proceed. So in this sense the technique of value attribution is produced through the narrative structure, which positions class as that which must be overcome.

In a challenge to the respectability of escaping class the Hollywood film, *Legally Blonde*, sets up this transformation narrative (from West coast excess to East coast tastefulness), but then offsets the transformation by giving credit to the power of feminine knowledge about appearance. This specialist feminine knowledge then challenges the superiority of the legal and the middle-class knowledge.

Exemplar Three: However, the wider discourse of tastelessness continually works to attribute immorality and lack of knowledge to the working class in general. A good example (third) can be seen in the promotion of and resistance to satellite dishes (see Brunsdon 1997 for an extensive account). In the UK a whole traunch of 'alternative' comedy was devoted to making the association tasteless = use of satellite dishes = working-class. Even recently, the same sentiments are being expressed by middle-class cultural intermediaries. In a supposed architectural review of the Lovell Telescope at Jodrell Bank (a 1500-ton, 76.2-meter bowl) in the local Manchester listings magazine, *City Life*, Phil Griffin notes:

> It is particularly touching that so many people in Wythenshawe appreciate it so much, they display little scale models of it on the outside of their houses. (1999: 6)

The spatialisation of class present in the new labour rhetoric of problem council estates is signified through reference to Wythenshawe (the largest council estate in Europe, in Manchester, North West UK). In this statement he manages to insult and insinuate that people from Wythenshawe clearly have no taste. He thus attributes taste to himself because he is the clever, knowing one who can draw ironic distance and make distinctions. It is a subtle move but is one of the ways in which class is frequently played out. Here, lack of knowledge, the subtle association of immorality with watching trash TV (cultural practices) and the spatialisation of class is condensed into one signifier: the satellite dish. So we can see how some cultural attributes become condensed and fixed whilst others are signified as mobile.

This is a general example of how taste can be attributed to some practices by those with access to the distribution and circulation circuits to establish value. Lack of knowledge of how to use and place artefacts appropriately are the central clue in the film *The Talented Mr Ripley*. It is the superior taste of the detective (a narrative device that gets regularly repeated in the BBC TV programme *Inspector Morse*) that enables the villains to be caught.

Whilst all the above examples from popular culture fix class with lack of moral value in particular ways, the following drawn from political rhetoric fixed it even more firmly through association with space and cultural practice.

Exemplar Four: Haylett (2001), in an analysis of new labour political discourse, documents how on 3 June 1997 the British Prime Minister, Tony Blair, chose the Aylesbury estate in South London as the back-drop for an announcement. This announcement was about a mass of people, in mass housing, people and places who were somehow fall-ing out of the nation, losing the material wherewithal and symbolic dignity traditionally associated with their colour and their class, becoming an ugly contradiction: abject and white. She shows how this announcement used the white working-class poor as symbols of a generalised 'backwardness' and specifically a culturally burdensome whiteness. The white working class become represented as the block-age not just to social inclusion, but to the development of a modern nation that can play on a global stage. To consolidate this new labour rhetoric Peter Mandleson (then a man of some significance in the Blair government and now hilariously living in Hartlepool) encapsulates this representation and discourse in his speech to the Fabian Society. This speech used to launch the Social Exclusion Unit sets out what he sees to be the 'problem' confronting government, something which has to be solved in order to re-build the nation, he notes:

> We are people who are used to being represented as problematic. We are the long-term, benefit-claiming, working-class poor, living through another period of cultural contempt. We are losers, no hopers, low life, scroungers. Our culture is yob culture. The import-ance of welfare provisions to our lives has been denigrated and turned against us: we are welfare dependent and our problems won't be solved by giving us higher benefits. We are perverse in our failure to succeed, dragging our feet over social change, wanting the old jobs back, still having babies instead of careers, stuck in outdated class and gender moulds. We are the 'challenge' that stands out above all others, the 'greatest social crisis of our times'. (Mandleson 1997 in Haylett 2000: 6–7)

In defining the 'problem' Mandleson reproduces as 'empirical reality' the threat to the nation. His rhetoric of social inclusion excludes. This can be seen further in the more recent announcement (1 April 2002) by Estelle Morris, then Education Secretary, about 'Yob Parents' (a spin of which Thatcher would be proud). This rhetoric of 'governmental belonging' is a perfect example of Ghassan Hage's argument that the cultural capital of some blocks their possibility of ever belonging to the nation; forever positioned outside of it. This rhetoric is a re-emergence of what Morris (1994) and Levitas (1998) have identified as the discourse of the underclass, a discourse that is used to exclude on the basis of culture and morality. The discourse of evolutionary modernity – in which under stands for backward – is used to illustrate the distance between the forward-thinking middle class at the vanguard of global modernity and the low life no-hopers locked in backward culture. Distance is drawn between the old and the new, the atavistic and the progressive; gaps occur between whiteness and whites, so that white groups sharing the same skin colour are not 'equally white' (Bonnett 1998). This shift takes us back to far earlier conceptualisations, where the white working class were seen to be outside British imperial society, represented as uncivilised, dangerous, a 'race apart' (e.g. Engels 1844/ 1958), or primitive (see Kahn 2001).

But this traditional discourse of degeneration, which has been used over a long period of time to constitute race and class difference (McClintock 1995) is here defined differently: not through biological essentialism but through cultural difference, cultural essentialism or cultural fundamentalism.[5] It is the failure of the culture to enable these people to modernise. The working class are positioned as stuck, with nothing to offer culturally except as an indication of the difference between the civilised and the uncivilised. Their difference is marked through cultural-moral value, through scrounging, being yobs and breeding too much.

Haylett highlights how poor whites reveal a contradiction that threatens to unsettle dominant social systems of class-based and race-based privilege. In particular, it is the symbolic order of the systems of privilege, the way they are visibly marked, that is exposed. First, they show that whiteness does not naturally predispose people to social privilege and success. This is in contrast to (Forde-Jones 1998) who shows how historically the white working class have been pulled into the nation in order to maintain the appearance of 'natural' white privilege. Second, poor whites show that poverty has to maintain an appearance, an order of things, to justify its existence. When large numbers of people are poor *and* white, that symbolic order starts to break down, its legitimacy is called into question. Poor whites, Haylett (2000: 361) argues, thereby come to reveal the symbolically 'worked at', socially produced nature of the order of things.

Inclusion thus becomes cultural: it is inclusion of the culture of the nation, that is the values, aspirations and ways of living as those identified as belonging, respectable, worthy and not spatially and fundamentally different as a result of their culture. But they cannot be included because their culture is of the wrong sort; they do not have the right attitudes and practices, the right knowledge and behaviour. They do not have the cultural capital that could enable them to belong. The rhetoric of inclusion actually excludes by its emphasis on culture. There are no narratives of escape offered here, only pathology and atavism. This is not a matter of taste but of being the wrong people in the wrong place at the wrong time. This is race and class with no value whatsoever.

Yet, Haylett also documents how, in opposition to an atavistic white working class, the white middle class is not racialised at all and is positioned at the vanguard of 'the modern'. The 'modern' thus becomes a moral category referring to liberal, mobile, cosmopolitan, work and consumption-based lifestyles and values, and 'the unmodern' on which this category depends is the white working class 'other', fixed in place and space, emblematically a throwback to other times and places.[6] They are the constitutive limit.[7] It is interesting that many of the 'new' sociological theories of mobility, reflexivity and risk, all promote the modern cosmopolitan whilst denying the existence of class. This is at the same time as post-colonial theorists have recognised how the race figures as the constitutional limit for the category of white.

I now want to shift attention from that which is valued as morally worthless, generated through the wrong cultural practices, which cannot be turned into symbolic value and used for national belonging, to how other aspects of working-class culture are continually reproduced as a resource for others to use. This is where the re-branding analysis fits (reading the experience back into product use).

Exemplar Five: The fifth example, again drawn from contemporary popular culture, but with a long history, Diawara (1998) shows how black (working class) masculinity is a resource, a mobile cultural style that can be used by different characters in film, be they black or white. She shows how in a tradition taken from Blaxploitation films black maleness, coded as cool, can be 'transported through white bodies' (Diawara 1998: 52). This is not a resource that is equally available. Moreover, she shows how Black characters become fixed into playing 'blackness' (Eddie Murphy is probably the most obvious example, even as the donkey in *Shrek*!) whilst white characters who need to achieve 'cool' can move between black and white. Race becomes a resource: fixed and read onto some bodies as a limitation, culturally essentialised, whilst it appears as mobile and trans-textual on others (e.g. John Travolta in *Pulp Fiction*). That is the fixed black character appears to be not acting; they just *are*. Hence they are culturally essentialised and made authentic. This is the most obvious use of re-branding, whereby particular forms of whiteness become re-branded through dispositions initially associated with blackness.[8]

However, this has a long and difficult history and it could be argued that the 'Blues' as a form of music appropriated by white musicians was the site where 'cool' as an attribute was formed. That is it sticks to black bodies in a way that it does not to white bodies is about the repetition of association between dispositions and bodies over a long period of time in which it is not just about the power of those who can influence the dominant cultural symbolic economy, but also about those who have shaped the symbolic through oppositional struggle. So Black power becomes an important intervention in Black representation that served to consolidate earlier representations of Blackness.[9] So using race, class or femininity as a resource only exists for those who are NOT positioned by it.

This use of 'ethnicity' however has different function and the re-branding may not take place. That is it does not alter the dispositions of the one who has the power to appropriate the experience or disposition; it does not stick to the body. The ambivalence of the discursive association of danger and criminality with different categories of race and ethnicity is made apparent in the *Sopranos* (Series One, video 4). In an argument with a Black gangster (who is represented with every heavy-sticking signifier possible) Tony Soprano claims ethnic authenticity 'we were the first niggers in this country'. Yet later after a game of golf with his white middle-class neighbours, he states: 'I never really understood what it was to be used for somebody else's amusement until I played golf with these guys.' Here dispositions are not taken off one body to be re-evaluated when attached to another. Rather, the whole body and culture is used as a source of authentic entertainment.

In fact this process is so well established that the majority of the music industry could be seen to be fuelled by it, as could the tradition of crime movies. It has been described by one journalist as 'one of the most pernicious media trends of the last decade' (Gittins 2002). The movies made by Guy Ritchie (Mr Madonna) – *Lock, Stock and Two Smoking*

Barrels, and *Snatch*, are a perfect example of a cultural intermediary (Featherstone 1991), in which an upper-class British man generates his career and money by using others to reproduce and generate a fascination with low-life danger and criminality. Whilst this appears to be like the traditional colonial use of bodies for labour, for entertainment and for artefact, I would argue that it is in fact different. This is because the experience of product use (i.e. the fun associated in playing with other people's culture, of being a tourist who collects the attributes of others) is now read back onto the marketing of the product itself. Danger as an emotion is read back into the experience of the appropriation of young white working-class men and cool is similarly read back onto the bodies of black working-class men: Rap music, for instance, embodies both of these affects and not surprisingly was used to open up new markets; its biggest market is young white men between the ages of 13–19. Yet, at the same time those who live the lifestyle are increasingly being criminalised, contained and live in poverty (Skeggs 1994). These readings back of experience-use (re-branding) fixes and locks certain attributes onto some bodies whilst others can deploy them as a mobile resource and even make careers out of them, consolidating their cultural capital through the ability to *convert* the cultural capital of others. Re-branding works where aspects of the experience are read into the property itself, so the culture of 'others' become a propertisable resource for those with power to use (Davis 1990).

However, it is only the cultural dispositions that are *user-friendly* that can be used to enhance new middle-class selves. This is one reason why gay male sub-cultural capital may be so plundered. It is only the bits that can be safely incorporated, or commercially useful that are utilised. There is also a temporal aspect to this exchange/appropriation. The use of working-class culture is only temporary. It does not stick to the bodies using it, fixing them in place, physically and metaphorically. And it can be offset in the future by other forms of convertible cultural capital. This is why Bourdieu's analysis of conversion, the possibilities that enable conversion and the use of volume and composition over time are so important.

Payback

However, this is not a straightforward process and a significant class struggle is waged. In the *Soprano* example the white middle-class men display their own stupidity and naivety by their desire to discuss 'the mob' and Mr Madonna becomes a laughing stock through his attempts to do and be the other (through his cultural practices). So re-branding does not always work when there is opposition to it. And it is here where a symbolic battle is waged with morality as one of the main resources. *The Royale Family* and other Caroline Aherne products are devoted to attacks on the pretentiousness and use of working-class culture. There is, as Vicinus (1974) has shown, a long and substantial history to laughing at the middle class. And the ambivalence of the middle classes to identify as such (as shown in the research by Savage *et al.* 2001) may be a result of this cultural struggle. For instance, the immortal lyrics by Pulp for the track *Common People* in which the working-class becomes a *resource* for the entertainment of others, is ridiculed and despised:

> I want to live like common people, I want to do whatever common people do, I want to sleep with common people like you... and the riposte:

> You'll never live like common people, you'll never do what common people do, you'll never fail like common people, you'll never watch your life slide out of view, and dance and drink and screw 'cos there's nothing else to do. (Pulp (written by Cocker/Senior/Mackay/Banks/ Doyle), 'Common People', 1995. Island Records.)[10]

Here the impossibility of being and becoming working-class is made explicit, as is the despisal and resentment of those who know they are being used. However, the ability to fight this symbolic struggle is limited by access to circuits of distribution and circulation.

When the middle-class use working-class culture as a resource, a relationship of *entitlement* is established, which also includes possibilities for resistance. It is not just high cultural capital that relies on the right knowledge; there are also aspects to working-class culture that also need the 'right' accumulated knowledge.

It is how the middle-class resources itself that is crucial to the contemporary re-branding of class. When 'new' debates reference new forms of subjectivity (Rouse 1995; Berlant 2000; Hardt and Negri 2000), they are referencing the new forms of middle-class entitlement. Just as most debates about 'the self' are about a middle-class self. It is the middle-class that is doing the re-branding because they have access to the circuits of symbolic power and distribution, they are the cultural intermediaries. The middle-class are the ones who are positioned as always/already belonging to the nation; they are the ones who need to open up new markets, to find new ways of making profit, or to experience the calculated de-control, so brilliantly expressed by (Featherstone

1991); they want the new experiences without incurring any loss or danger to the social positions that they already inhabit.

So, to summarise so far. In these different processes of representation and discourse class is broken down into cultural elements, some of which are convertible and propertisable and others that have to be firmly fixed as that from which escape is needed. This process is raced and gendered. In this sense class is seen as a cultural resource for some but an abject social positioning for others. For the white working-class in the UK it is something that is becoming directly racialised, positioned as an abject onto which all things bad are projected. Yet, whilst it is fixed by political discourse the user-friendly aspects are becoming propertisable in popular culture, and middle-class cultural intermediaries are making their futures out of them. The progressions and mobility of some relies on the fixing of others. Class is also represented as a fault in the nation, something which represents backwardness, a failure to modernise and a blockage to the inevitability of global trans-national futures. However, it has also become a useful cultural resource and many 'cultural intermediaries' in the media and cultural industries have not been slow to capitalise on this.

What is central to all these processes is the attribution of morality in which certain cultural practices are given value (in the symbolic system) and others are de-valued as immoral. Interestingly it is usually the immoral that becomes the most interesting aspect for appropriation, although working-class women's immorality has never been re-appropriated.

Academic responses

I want to argue that the majority of ways we have of understanding class are no longer adequate to take into account *the constitutive nature of culture and the symbolic economy*. When affect becomes a valued global commodity we need to have ways of understanding what this means for class struggle. Many of our current understandings are not adequate. The two major ways of understanding class were first, Marxist, where emphasis was placed on the labour theory of value (that is the extraction of surplus value from the labour power of the exploited working-class), so emphasis was firmly located in the economic, especially the forces of production and the division of labour. Secondly, the emphasis was placed on occupational stratification, where in the tradition of quantification and 'political arithmetic', counting groups was considered necessary in order to assess their potential for taxation, representation, governance, and so on (see Day 2001). What they both have in common, however, is the centrality of production and economy, even though they were generated by the historical culture of the time; thus they must be *en-cultured* forms of analysis. The term and discourse 'economy', for instance, began as a very specific word to describe the management of a household, it then shifted to the management of national resources and then it became a 'neutral' system, discursively contained, with its own rules and laws. The promotion of a 'discipline' of economics had a lot to do with this, as Bourdieu (1990a) and Fine (2001) show. Moreover, recent attacks on the 'cultural turn' have missed the point. The history of studying culture is as a material force (e.g. Gramsci, Bourdieu; and a significant amount of anthropology), not just a matter of discourse.

To turn attention to culture does not mean to say that capitalisms[11] are not important framing factors. The search for new markets and the ability of capitalism to marketise its own contradictions has enabled the opening out of new markets for which new resources and new consumers need to be produced. It is in this search for new markets that what was once abject, legitimated through biology and science, is now being accessed and re-legitimated in order to produce the 'new' and 'exciting'. Moral boundaries are being redrawn whereby what was once projected onto an 'other' is now being drawn back into the mainstream. Yet, this is not a wholesale incorporation of bodies that were once positioned at a distance. Rather, it is a re-evaluation process, whereby prior immoral abject culture is being used to open up new markets. The expanse of sexuality and violence as mechanisms for selling goods is one obvious example. Another is how the display of sexuality, pathologised when attached to working-class women's bodies, is being re-worked in novel ways when attached to middle-class women's bodies as *Sex and the City* shows most explicitly. Sex is recoded as glamorous when attached to those with enough volume of other forms of cultural capital to offset connotations of pathology and degradation. But this is a piecemeal operation and it is the detachment and separation of the user-friendly bits from the backward bits that creates the re-branding, re-figuring, re-moralising and re-making of class relations. Class struggle becomes not just about the entitlement to the labour of others but the entitlement to their culture, feelings,[12] affect and dispositions. This is a very intimate form of exploitation. The safe and secure boundaries that were seen to be necessary for the formation of the authority claims of the emergent bourgeoisie are now not being drawn so closely, although they are being maintained spatially: Davis (1990) has shown that defensible space is now a positional good that maintains class distinction.

The shift from the politics of redistribution to the politics of recognition has been well documented in the US by Taylor (1994) in relation to multiculturalism, and (Fraser 1995) on feminism and the shift in left politics in general. They suggest that the political landscape has been reshaped by the demands made through identity politics by campaigning groups. The emphasis on identity has led to the eclipse of wider structural issues of class, with focus on race, gender and sexuality instead. Brown (1995) have also illustrated how the shift to identity politics reproduces a particular version of bourgeois individualism, premised on the moral claim of 'injury' which is articulated through Nietzsche's ideas on ressentiment. And my previous work has asked what happens to politics when women who are pathologised symbolically, identifying them as immoral, bad mothers and hypersexual, cannot mobilise an identity category through which to make political claims and who cannot accrue the right sort of capital to acquire 'governmental belonging'.

So what are the consequences of this?

First, the shift into 'recognition/identity' politics re-frames the potential for political understanding and claims-making. If we bring together national belonging, identity politics and the potential for commodification via flexible capitalism, we can see that only some people can acquire the 'right' sort of cultural capital that enables them to belong, to be commodifiable and to generate a relationship of entitlement via access to the commodification of others.

Secondly, the propertising of culture means that economic deprivation is understood again and increasingly through moral evaluation. So being poor becomes represented as a cultural deficiency, as individualised, as a problem of dispositions, of not being able to become the right person (Sayer 2001). This works at the level of subjectivity, at the level of feelings and affectivity.

But what is also interesting is how resentment has also been harnessed by the middle class in their political claims-making. Brown (1995) documents how identity politics generated its moral legitimation through ressentiment – by claiming that the experience of pain and oppression gave them the moral right to establish their claims on a political agenda. The historical analysis of ressentiment has more recently been translated into a more direct contemporary version of resent in political claims-making and a class transfer has taken place. Cameron (McCarthy 2000) details how that the suburban middle class in the US is using the discourse of resentment in an attempt to promote its own moral authority (as shown in the films *Falling Down* with Michael Douglas, or *American Beauty* which visualise this white male middle-class resentment). As Rouse (1995) details, these articulations are from those whose power has been challenged, who have been 'slightly' displaced from the political agenda.[13]

The politics of ressentiment is a mechanism of trying to capture back the moral high ground in order to make political claims and a way of imagining and influencing symbolic relations. McCarthy shows how in the early 1990s *Time* magazine published two articles that documented the rise of suburban middle class. In these articles crime and violence are fetishised, transmuted in the language of the coming invasion of the abstract racial other.[14] In opposition to Fredrick Jameson's argument that postmodernism or the logic of late capitalism sets a new 'emotional ground tone', that is about the waning of affect or the loss of feeling, McCarthy maintains that through the manipulation of difference there is a powerful *concentration of affect and a strategic use of emotions to make a moral re-evaluation*. A critical feature of discourses of resentment is their dependence on processes of simulation, that is the middle-class comes to 'know' its inner-city other through an imposed system of infinitely repeatable substitutions and proxies: census tracts, crime statistics, tabloid newspapers and television programmes. Resentment, therefore, is an emotion distinguished first of all by its concern and involvement with power. McCarthy points out:

> A new moral universe now rides the underbelly of the beast – late capital's global permutations, displacements, relocations and reaccumulations. The effect has meant a material displacement of minority and other dispossessed groups from the landscape of contemporary political and cultural life. That is to say, increasingly the underclass [*sic*] or working-class subject is contemporaneously being placed on the outside of the arena of the public sphere as the middle-class subject-object of history moves into occupy and to appropriate the identity of the oppressed, the racial space of difference. The centre becomes the margin. (2000: 285, my emphasis added)

But we can see how resentment and moral high ground is not just limited to the suburban middle-class or those interested in using identity to make political claims. My prior research showed it being articulated by those groups who have no recourse to identity. The women were seething with resentment at the inequality of how they were represented, and how these representations fed the mis-recognitions made by the middle-class people with whom they came into contact. This resentment was partly produced by being judged by others who were not seen to be worthy to make the judgement. This is strongly echoed in the research of Reay (1998), Lawler (2000b) and Walkerdine and Lucey (1989) which demonstrates how motherhood in particular becomes a site through which moral battles are fought.

Conclusion

We need to be able to reinvigorate class analysis with critical insights on neo-liberal governance and trans-national flexible capitalism. We need an understanding that goes beyond the 'economic', production and occupation which can take into account the consequences of culture, and how this is central to the making of class difference, generating new ways of attributing value, producing new forms of appropriation and exploitation.

We require *a* model which sees class struggle (partially) fought out through the relationship of entitlement to the cultures of others, whereby working-class culture becomes a resource; fixed, fragmented and plundered for elements for others to use and authorise themselves through. This *is* about new relationships being formed in the making of new markets. It is about new connections that are different from the old colonial ones, when it was artefacts or bodies rather than affect or dispositions, that were used to display middle-class distance.[15]

The working-class do not just figure as a culture to be plundered for the opening out of new markets; the progression and progressiveness of the new middle-class self is predicated on holding in place – fixing – that which must signify stagnation and immobility. So the working-class is both fragmented as a resource that functions in a variety of ways to sustain the modernity of factions of the middle class but also fixed in place so that others can be seen to be distant from it. We also need to be aware of the different ways the middle class use working-class culture and experience: some accumulate 'dangerous' and exciting practices and attach them to their bodies in the hope of increasing cultural capital, others just experiment and play; and others use the affect of the working-classes to forge their own political claims and authority. We therefore need to be highly suspicious of the recent theories of mobility as the 'new social condition'. These say more about the social positioning of the theorist and the re-making of the middle class than any universal social condition.

But the working class, both within and outside the circuits of symbolic distribution resist this continual appropriation, exposing and ridiculing the use made of their culture. We thus need to be aware of the fragility and vulnerability of the middle-class self-formation, which has to be continually asserted to be enabled to operate as a form of powerful difference and worthy of moral authority. Entitlements have to be institutionalised, perspectives authorised and property legitimated. These are processes; they can be challenged.

We therefore need an analysis that can understand processes as constitutive across a range of sites such as popular culture, political rhetoric, academic theory, economic discourse and analysis that shows how the rhetoric of social inclusion actually excludes. We need a way of understanding how, what and why bodies accumulate culture and how this can or cannot be valued as a resource (for wealth, for the nation). The class struggle is being waged on a daily basis through culture as a form of symbolic violence, through relationships of entitlement that are legitimised and institutionalised, and it is these processes that set limits on who can and cannot belong, be, and have worth on a national and global stage. These are not just processes of product use, but are painfully felt by those from whom they are extracted. The hidden injuries of class, identified by Sennett and Cobb (1977), are still well and truly intact but now they are being used as a cultural resource by others.

Notes

1. It is a very condensed version of an argument from the book *Class, Self, Culture* (London: Routledge, 2003).
2. Marx always understood the immaterial nature of materialism; hence his theory of commodity fetishism works to make labour invisible.
3. As Erickson (1991, 1996) has shown eating out is a pre-requisite for the display of middle-class cultural omnivorousness and essential to the maintenance of social networks in business practice.
4. See also Lawler (2000b) for an excellent analysis of the difference between escape and escapism when reading bodies.
5. See Strathern (1992) and Stolcke, V. (1995) for the shift from biological essentialism to cultural fundamentalism.
6. This binary representation between old and modern is worked through in contemporary political struggle.
7. Historically, it has been Black and white working-class women's and Black men's sexuality that has operated as the constitutive limit of civilisation, governmental belonging and respectable behaviour. And as Brown (2001) has recently shown how the racialisation of these constitutive limits has been exposed by post-colonial theorists. Yet the class limits have not. In our recent research into Violence and Sexuality it is the excessive noise and sexuality of working-class women, the 'hen parties' that have posed the major threat to the 'comfort' of the gay village. They are the constitutive limit by which the

safety and security is maintained through the imaginary of those who have made an investment or claim on the gay space known as the village (Moran and Skeggs 2001a).

8. In an argument about gender rather than class, but which shows how resources such as identity are mobile for some and fixed for others, Adkins and Lury (1999) show how gender, in this case, femininity and sexuality, can only be performed at work by some groups and women in particular are not able to make this performance because they are already positioned in place. It is already assumed that they *are* gendered. Therefore femininity as a resource only exist for those who are not positioned by it.

9. This is further complicated in the US where a Black middle-class does exist and it cannot be assumed that representations of Blackness have a close association to working-classness. The term 'white trash' highlights the racialisation of the difference. This is not at all similar to the development of Blackness in the UK in which it has always been produced through close discursive association with class. Gilroy (1987), Gilman (1992), Hall *et al.* (1978).

10. The album 'Common People' by Pulp has recently been voted the top 13th CD album in the UK (see www.123cds.co.uk).

11. I use the plural here following Gibson-Graham (1996) who charts the many different types of capitalism that exist simultaneously and in contradiction, making any homogenous representation impossible.

12. The desire for authenticity is a crucial feature in this process.

13. Thanks to Paul Jones who made me think about how resentment was being harnessed and re-branded following a presentation of this paper at Liverpool University, Sociology Dept. on 1 May 2002.

14. He shows how these articles offer a dystopic chronology in two instalments: in the first phase, indigenous criminal elements take over the small town rural suburbs. In the second phase, nameless Third World infidels housed in the UN make a final conquering manoeuvre to rush the whole nation, making their first point of attack a leafy Michigan suburb. In the articles murder and mayhem are everywhere.

15. Thanks to Emma Britain for this point generated from a paper given to the *Sources of Radicalism* seminar series. Manchester, 4 April 2002.

4
Class and Culture in Germany

Michael Vester

In this chapter I will develop a typological map of class cultures in Germany based on research projects organized by a new, dynamic interpretation of the Bourdieu approach to class habitus and social space. My aim is to show how Durkheim's concept of milieu can be used to operationalize Bourdieu's approach so that culturally sensitive approach to class can be operationalized. Following the English culturalists, especially Williams (1963), Thompson (1963) and Hall (Hall and Jefferson 1975) I will develop the necessary hermeneutic methods to allow us to define social classes not as the aggregates of the official employment statistics (see Crompton 1998) but as aggregates of social action, that is as groups united by a common habitus and the respective patterns of practice and taste by which they distinguish themselves from other milieus.

In pursuing this question, I link my presentation of German research with the discussion of two related questions: First, how can Bourdieu's approach be utilized in different national contexts? It is clear that over the past decade a number of important studies have indicated the need to develop approaches attuned to national diversity. Michèle Lamont, in her study *Money, Morals and Manners*, carried out 160 interviews to compare four factions of the French and American upper middle class. Focussing on different types of boundaries drawn by middle-class members, she found that the American middle class were less concerned with cultural boundaries than the French, and that in general Bourdieu underestimates moral boundaries as compared to socio-economic and cultural boundaries.

Savage *et al.* (1992), in *Property, Bureaucracy and Culture*, studied three factions of the middle class, analyzing the life style survey data on public-sector professionals, managers, government bureaucrats and "postmoderns". Much like Lamont and contrary to Bourdieu, they also found a "non-distinctive" group and also stressed the importance of culture as an independent variable concerning class position and habitus. They also differ from Bourdieu's typology of capital assets by paying more attention to the organizational assets in middle-class careers, which they partly relate to the relative weakness of credentialism in British society.

Still another encouragement to widen the scope of the Bourdieu approach was formulated by Rupp (1995, 1997), in *Rethinking Cultural and Economic Capital*. In his study on the educational strategies of workers in the Netherlands, he noted a strong disposition for investments in the children's cultural capital which could be explained not only by vertical mobility striving towards petty bourgeois standards but also by a horizontal movement towards the intellectual pole of social space, towards more personal autonomy and emancipation.

These studies point to the second question, how can the Bourdieu approach be related to issues of social and cultural change? Bourdieu's own work, especially in *Distinction*, mainly concentrates on the static *reproduction* of class. Post-materialism, affluence and modern life styles are explored, but largely viewed from the perspective of how classes change in order to conserve. This interpretation is evidently connected with Bourdieu's concentration on the upper classes and their petty bourgeois followers which are, by definition, interested to defend their own elevated position. The dominated classes which comprise more or less four-fifths of the total population, are only treated in a short chapter which hardly differentiates sub-groups. Here, Bourdieu's argument is pessimistic and is opposed to the naive intellectual idealizations of working-class consciousness and rebellion put forward by leftist and orthodox Marxists in the 1970s. Rupp (1995, 1997), instead, offers a more hopeful account of the emancipatory potential and dynamics of the skilled working classes, as the development of cultural capital. Here, Rupp also formulates a missing link relating Bourdieu's class analysis to a central field of his research, the sociology of education, which we seek to develop further here. It is this more fluid orientation that we seek to use in our German case study, in which I am particularly concerned to show how a more central role can be accorded to the working and popular classes than is provided by Bourdieu's focus on the French cultural elite (1984), as well as his rather bleak assessment of "La misere du Monde".

Research questions and methodology

The basic research project,[1] was designed as an empirical test of the hypotheses on the dis-solution of class and class culture, as presented by Ulrich Beck, Anthony Giddens and post-modern sociology. In its qualitative parts, we concentrated on the new social movements and milieus which were supposed to exemplify this dissolution by a habitus of humanistic values "beyond class" (Offe 1985). In further steps, we widened our scope to West German social space as a whole which was analyzed with the help of the national occupational statistics as well as our own representative survey of 1991 and subsequent studies and secondary data analyses.

The research questions and the design of the project followed the multi-level field concept of Bourdieu by first exploring how habitus was changing, then assessing how habitus was related to occupational change, and finally considering the social and political implications of this change. This involved a different kind of inquiry to that in conventional employment aggregate work, including Bourdieu's own. Like Goldthorpe (1987), Marshall *et al.* (1988) and Wright (1996), Bourdieu mainly started with the *occupational group* and then asked what life style attributes and practices it's members preferred (see generally, Goldthorpe and Marshall 1992 for a defence of this approach). From these, he inferred their habitus. Interviews were mainly used to *exemplify* these habitus patterns. This procedure certainly contributed to Bourdieu's alleged economic determinism. Our main starting point, instead, were the *attitudes* themselves which we examined through the interpretation of large samples of non-directive biographical interviews. Having found the habitus type, we then asked which occupation, social relations and so on were "typical" or "not typical" for it.

The main part of the project asked how habitus might be changing, and in particular whether it was true that alternative milieus and the new social movements represented a new "universalist" habitus and practice which was not linked to particular class milieus? Our sample of new social milieus were recruited according to a specific "scouting" procedure in the three selected regions, choosing people with distinctive attributes and practices of the life style of the new social milieus (ibid.: 328). The sample consisted of 24 interviews for the initial non-directive biographical interviews (which had a length up to five hours) and the subsequent 220 semi-directive interviews, ensuring that the basic fields of experience were covered. For the detection of habitus *change* we interviewed two generations. Considering the gender differences of habitus, the female half of the sample was interviewed as compared to the mothers and the male half as compared to the fathers.

The habitus types were reached by the *syndrome concept*. By an intensive procedure of text interpretation, the "schemes of valuation, classification

and action" (Bourdieu) and their interrelational structure in a comprehensive habitus syndrome were extracted. The procedure followed the
rules of sequence analysis, that is the hermeneutic interpretation of
only a few lines of text at one time by a selected interpretation group
which had to discuss and note all variants of interpretation. In later stages,
special attention was given to the balance of these patterns according
to dimensions like "ascetic vs hedonistic", "dominance vs partnership"
(also in gender relations), "isolation vs cohesion", "popular vs distinctive
taste" and so on. Finally, the single habitus traits found in the interpretation had to be analyzed for their syndrome structure: How were the
single traits related, which traits had priorities (or a status of goals) and
which traits were representing competing goals or mere means and so on?

Habitus structure can be understood as organized like the ethics of
everyday life, defining which values should come first in social practice
(e.g. work before leisure) and which should come later. In the milieus
of skilled work, for example, personal autonomy is the primary goal but
embedded in a context of dispositions for learning, good work performance, solidarity, mutuality, social justice and so on. By this contextual
interpretation the classification of the working classes by isolated
properties can be replaced by a better, more elaborate account of their
milieu. Those properties, such as physical work or a collectivist outlook,
which often lie at the base of the intellectual myth of the proletariat,
can be seen by this approach to be traits which only occur under special
conditions and are not essential for class identity. The complete syndrome structures are exemplified in the typological descriptions, later in
this chapter.

The attitude syndromes were analyzed for each case separately. In a
second step, the individual cases were grouped to into one of five types
according to their different syndrome *structures*. For each of the five
types a portrait was formulated (2001: 331–363). Later, the types could
be identified as the youngest and most radical parts of already existing
parent milieus.

The next part of the study linked habitus change to changes in the
occupational and economic position. The changes of the occupational
field since 1950 were analyzed by processing the available occupational
data according to the "ascending method" of Geiger (1932: 17–18) and
Bourdieu's concept of social space. Geiger's method was designed to
avoid a main fallacy of the employment aggregate approaches. Geiger
did not start with the larger occupational categories but split them
into smaller, elementary and more homogeneous groups, with similar
professional situations, income, tradition, organizational status and

so on. After this, Geiger regrouped them one by one into larger, more homogeneous units, thus "ascending" from the single, elementary group to possible larger units. By analyzing 163 occupational groups this way,[2] we could map a selection of important occupational fields, especially in the sectors of the educational, health, technical and agricultural occupations – also divided by gender cleavages (Vester *et al.* 2001: 413–422).

The principal result of this part of the study was that, according to the data since 1950, there was a historical drift towards more cultural capital on all vertical levels of society. These findings had important consequences for the theories of the tertiary knowledge society (Bell 1973). On the one hand we could see clear evidence for the rise of post-industrial work, with a rise of tertiary occupations from about 20 to almost 60 per cent up to 1990. But this growth mainly remained a *horizontal* movement which did not basically change the vertical relations of domination between social classes – and also the gender, age and ethnic classes. As a consequence, it could be seen that classes, whether occupational or cultural, did not erode but only moved to a different zone of social space. This implies that social conflict, too, did not disappear but moved towards a new level of class conflict, based on the higher competences and aspirations for autonomy in the popular milieus.

The third part of the study was dedicated to the logic and patterns of the change of everyday culture and of political camps by considering how the milieus of the new social movements developed cohesion and identity since the 1960s. Case histories in the three regions showed by which logics, especially dynamics of conflicts and coalitions, the new movements and milieus had developed in the regional field of socio-political camps. The main finding of this part of the study was that protest action primarily did not arise according to a logic of repression, material or moral deprivation or marginalization, as the conventional hypotheses will have it. Also, the new identities were not only linked to occupational change, as the employment aggregate approach suggests. Almost half of the persons interviewed in the survey who shared the new, more qualified and modernized occupational profiles did *not* share the new habitus dispositions. This supports the hypothesis that habitus change was due to a more general change in the societal field of forces, that is the *opening of social space* for hitherto unrealized or unrealizable "designs of life" (according to the theory of Merleau-Ponty 1965 [1945]: 503–508) and to the social and political *conflicts between the generations* (see Hall and Jefferson 1975) since the 1960s.

The last part of our research aimed at a synthesis, that is the changes of the class configuration as a whole. We considered how the dynamics of the different fields, studied separately in the first parts, correlated, and how representative the selected milieus were for social structure as a whole. These questions were studied by the representative survey of the 1991 West German population.[3] Constructing the multi-dimensional questionnaire according to the Bourdieu approach (see Table 4.1 and Vester *et al.* 2001: 222–244, 546–557), each interviewed person could be located on all field levels simultaneously. For each level we could

Table 4.1   Tradition lines of class cultures (milieus) in West Germany[4]

Vertical class pyramid and its horizontal differentiation by tradition lines	**Differentiation of the tradition lines by sub-groups resp. generations in West Germany (1982–2000)**
1. *Dominant Milieus* (subdivisions corresponding to (a) "upper service class" and (b) lower service class/middle class)	
1.1. Tradition line of *power and property*: milieus of the economic and state functional élites (c. 10%)	1.1. The Conservative Technocratic Milieus (c. 9–10%) (a) The Grand Bourgeois Milieu (b) The Petty Bourgeois Milieu
1.2. Tradition line of *Higher Education and Services*: milieus of the humanist and service functional élites (c. 10%)	1.2. The Liberal Intellectual Milieus (c. 9–10%) (a) The Progressive Élite of Higher Learning (b) The Milieu of the Higher Socio-Cultural Services
1.3. Tradition line of the cultural *vanguard* (c. 5%)	1.3. The Alternative Milieu (c. 5–0%) The Post-modern Milieu (c. 0–6%)
2. *Milieus of the "respectable" popular and employee classes* (subdivisions corresponding to generations [a,b,c])	
2.1. Tradition line of *skilled work and practical intelligence* (c. 30%)	(a) The Traditional Working Class (c. 10–4%) (b) The Meritocratic Employee Milieu (c. 20–18%) (c) The Modern Employee Milieu (c. 0–8%)
2.2. Tradition line of the *petty bourgeois* popular classes (between 28 and 23%)	(a) The Petty Bourgeois Employee Milieu (c. 28–14%) (b) The Modern Petty Bourgeois Employee Milieu (c. 0–8%)
2.3. Vanguard of *youth culture* (c. 10%)	2.3. The Hedonist Milieu (c. 10–12%)

3. *Underprivileged popular classes* (between 8 and 13%) (subdivisions corresponding to orientation towards the three "respectable" popular milieus)	3. The Underprivileged Employee Milieus (a) The Status (b) The Fatalists (c. 6%) (c) The Hedonist Rebels (c. 2%)

construct independent maps – and then see which types of habitus were related to which types of occupation, social cohesion, ideological camp and so on.

A central prerequisite was to find a possibility to identify the class milieus by their habitus types. For this we were permitted to use the 44 statement milieu-indicator developed and validated by the Sinus Institute (ibid.: 546–548) which allowed us to assess what proportions of the population might fall into the habitus types we had detected on the basis of our qualitative interviews. We were further able to define the sample for qualitative research in those parts of social space about which we did not yet have sufficient knowledge. This latter procedure was especially used in our studies on the target groups of trade union adult education and of the Protestant church (Bremer 1999; Voegele *et al.* 2002).

From the habitus types we proceeded to the second level, the *occupational field*. Thus, we could identify the typical occupational profile of each milieu. It is important to note that none of these profiles followed the distinctions of the official statistics, that is between production and services, secondary and tertiary sectors, blue and white collar and so on. Instead, according to the data, the occupational profiles of the milieus rather followed (in a loose but clearly significant relation) the capital dimensions of Bourdieu. When we locate the milieus in Bourdieu's map (Figure 4.1) we see that no milieu is exclusively limited to a single occupational aggregate. Instead, each milieu spreads over a certain zone of social space which covers occupations with similar combinations of cultural and economic capital.

The field structure of social space

The most straightforward way of discussing our research findings is to show the overall map of class milieu that we uncovered. Figure 4.1 locates each milieu in Bourdieu's social space according to the occupations of

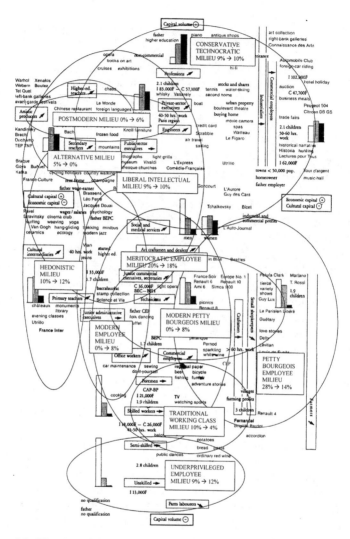

Figure 4.1 The map of West German class milieus

its members. The elliptic lines surround the field zones in which
the majority of each milieu have their occupational position. There is
a certain spreading but also a centre of gravitation in the field. Three of
the milieus are dividing the upper part of space among themselves. One
of the milieus is confined to the lower pole of space. Five of the milieus
share the middle. They are highly differentiated on the horizontal axis,

from a shrinking petty bourgeois employee milieu in the right half to growing modern employee milieus in the left half.

Figure 4.1 clearly show a relative homology between economic and habitus position. The positions the milieus take in the division of labour are corresponding to a sort of functional division between the other activities of life as structured by the habitus. Apparently, life style and habitus, as distinctive signs and practices by which milieu members find a common identity and distinguish themselves from other milieus, are the expression of a field of structured social relations and tensions which are based on complementary positions of the milieus.

Table 4.1 groups the milieus synoptically together to show their historical tradition lines as well as their internal differentiation. In the case of the "respectable popular classes", the data allow to show a habitus metamorphosis manifested in a sort of family tree. The tradition line of skilled work (no. 2.1 – the offsprings of the classical working class) consists of three generational groups: the vanishing old generation of the "Traditional Working Class", the big, but stagnant middle generation of the "Meritocratic Employee Milieu" and the growing younger generation of the "Modern Employee Milieu". This pattern of generational modernization does also show, in different degrees, in East Germany, Britain, France, and Italy for which we have the Sinus milieu data (see Vester *et al.* 2001: 34–36, 50–54). Table 4.1 reports not the occupational positions but habitus types. For this positioning we used the implicit principles of distinction by which each group delimitates itself from the other groups. The top is taken by three milieus around 20 per cent who distinguish themselves from the ordinary or popular milieus below them by their valuation of higher education and culture and the competences of taste. Below this *line of distinction* we find the popular classes (about 70 per cent) for whom qualified work or a secure and respected social status is the base of self-respect. Below them, we discover the milieus of the "underclass", with poor education and skills (about 10 per cent). They are less respected also because of their cultural habits adapted to a situation of insecurity and powerlessness. They are below what we may call the *line of respectability*.

Curiously enough, this vertical proportioning of society (20:70:10) supports what Goldthorpe and Lockwood found out in the 1960s about one of the images of society: a strong respectable middle, topped by the rich and powerful and substratified by the underprivileged. In the same map, we can also see a horizontal division of three zones separated by two cleavage lines. A *cleavage line of authoritarian status orientation* delimits the petty bourgeois and conservative groups at the right margin. In the horizontal middle, we find the milieus for whom work is the base of self-reliance and self-consciousness. At the left margin, the *cleavage line of the vanguard* separates the hedonistic or cultural vanguard with its idealistic orientations, distinct from the balancing realism of the middle.

Finally, the axis of time is shown by the inner differentiation of the tradition lines. A particularly important feature of our findings is that while Bourdieu (1984: 372ff.) treated the popular classes in a rather short and summary way, we were able to differentiate the popular milieus. Each tradition line resembles a family tree, the younger branches mainly distinguishing themselves from the older by modernized cultural capital and habitus. (As the younger branches are distinguished by modernized cultural capital and habitus, they are located a little higher and a little more to the left, symbolized by a thin diagonal distinction line.)

The dominant class milieus: power, property and education

The upper social space is divided into five sub-milieus united culturally in their distinction from those who have little academic education and are less propertied and influential. This corresponds with their occupational concentration in the fields of the larger employers, of higher corporate and public management and of the professions. At first sight, the dominant milieus as a whole remind of the "service class", as defined by Goldthorpe (1980). But Goldthorpe's approach cannot differentiate the factions which lie at the roots of the dynamics of change in the upper milieus.[5] Thus, it is certainly not true that the service class is united by the trust in the employer. Like the research of Savage *et al.* (1992) on the middle class, our empirical evidence in principle supports Bourdieu's identification of sub-groups as distinguished by their different strategies of social action. These factionings, which are essential for political and generational change, cannot be identified by the Goldthorpe approach, due to its confinement to vertical differences.

On the horizontal axis, we could identify three formations which, in tendency, correspond to the differences found by Bourdieu and by Savage *et al.* The first two formations are the tradition lines of power and property and of higher learning and higher socio-cultural services. In addition, in each of the two lines we found an upper and a lower faction. These are somewhat similar to the findings of Herz (1990) who, in West Germany too, distinguished an upper and a lower service class by levels of competence. But there is more to these differences than occupational competence. Especially, the two upper groups play a culturally hegemonic rôle for the two lower groups. Their cultural and social capital has been handed on for many generations and is the highest in the society. The first of the two hegemonic groups follows the grand bourgeois tradition and the second group follows the tradition of humanist higher learning. The two lower groups are less endowed, the first being on the way downward and the second on the way upward. Below the "grand bourgeois" faction we find an aged "petty bourgeois" faction stemming from medium employers, civil servants and farmers with outdated endowments of cultural capital. Contrasting with this is the group we find below the humanist intellectual élite. It is a modern and relatively dynamic service élite, which made its way upwards from the intellectual factions of the milieus of skilled workers and employees below them.

Concerning career patterns, the Bourdieu criterion of "social capital" is very helpful to explain the dimensions of historical class reproduction and class reconversion as a whole. If we consider the specific dynamics to reach and to maintain occupational positions, this can be better specified by the asset approach of Savage *et al.* (1992) paying specific attention to the organizational resources and relations in the occupational world. A third horizontal formation is found at the left margin of space. It is a milieu of the socio-cultural vanguard which is not simply to be explained by the same intergenerational accumulations of cultural, economic, social and/or organizational capital. As a cultural or political vanguard group, it is a result of the periodical secession from the core milieus of the top, waged by younger candidates for symbolic élite functions.

The tradition line of power and property (1.1)

The tradition line of the *Conservative–Technocratic Milieus* (now about 10 per cent) is united by a habitus of an explicit sense of success, hierarchy and power, of a distinctive taste and of the exclusivity of their social circles and networks. They are the milieus of property and of institutional domination. To them belong the best-established parts of the employers, the professions, of the private and public managements and administrations, and of science and culture.

Since 1945, the old authoritarian capitalist, state and military upper-class factions of Germany have lost their dominant positions to more modern and and democratic younger factions legitimating their hegemony as an élite of merit, education and technocratic modernization and by cultivating a political discourse of "social partnership" with the employee classes, supporting the new historical compromise of the "institutionalized class conflict" (Geiger 1949; Dahrendorf 1957).

The dominant group follows the grand bourgeois tradition of erudite and tolerant conservatism. It's members mainly consist of higher private and public managers, the owners of medium and big enterprises and members of the most privileged professions (especially in the medical and jurisprudence sectors). They belong to these groups at least in the third generation. This implies a long accumulation of social and cultural capital. Thus, the sub-milieu has one of the highest quotas of cultural capita: 37 per cent have *Abitur* (the secondary school diploma attesting the maturity to study at a university), 31 per cent have a university diploma.

In contrast, the the dominanted "petty bourgeois" faction of the milieu has surprisingly modest standards of cultural capital (very near to the survey averages of 13 per cent for *Abitur* and of 5 per cent for the university diploma). Most of them completed their educational careers in professional schools and then enter the career ladders inside private or public managements. This pattern is connected with specific family traditions. The parents, too, had reached only average educational diplomas and, like the grandparents, were employers, civil servants and farmers of the medium level. This petty-bourgeois pattern of medium resources and sustained career efforts corresponds to a cultural tradition of a rather strict and less tolerant conservatism. The socio-historic explanation of these specifics are evident when we consider the age of the milieu members. Two-thirds are over 65, the rest largely over 55 years of age (Wiebke 2002: 304). This indicates that the group is largely identical with that faction of the bourgeois class which was not able to join the reconversion towards or reinforcement of strategies of education which the majority of the bourgeois milieus made in the 1960s (see Bourdieu and Passeron 1977) and consequently is leaving the historical stage, by and by.

Despite of these differences, the factions are united in their policies of "closure", rarely admitting newcomers and up-starts to their circles. These policies, in Germany, are implemented mainly by subtle habitus and cultural selection (Hartmann 1998) working also as informal access barriers in the educational system.

The tradition line of higher education and higher services (1.2)

The second tradition line distinguishes itself exactly against this power conscious exclusiveness. Its milieus do not occupy the very highest but the "higher" ranks of administration and civil service, of the professions, the cultural, social and educational sectors and the arts. Being not at the very top, they tend to call themselves "middle class", while Bourdieu defines them as the "dominated faction of the dominating classes".

Opposing the "materialism" of its rivals, the *Liberal-Intellectual Milieu* (about 10 per cent) prefers distinction in cultural terms, combined with the assertion that everybody could achieve higher intellectual standards if he or she only wanted. The milieu legitimates itself as an enlightened vanguard, responsible for the universalistic values of justice, peace and democracy and for the social and ecological problems caused by economic progress. Their claim of cultural hegemony over society is somewhat mediated by benevolent or caritative condescension. Moreover, there are differences between the two sub-groups of the milieu.

The first sub-group, the *Progressive Elite of Higher Learning* (about 5 per cent) follows older family traditions of humanist orientation. The grandparents already belonged to the well-educated upper stratum of mainly professionals, higher civil servants and self-employed. Today, they unite the majority of the academic intelligentsia in the occupations of natural and engineering as well as the social and cultural sciences, in the sectors of publishing, the media and advertising and in the pedagogical, psychological and therapeutical services. As already their grandparents, they have high standards of cultural capital, that is 41 per cent have an *Abitur* and 23 per cent have a university diploma. Their élitist progressism combines ascetic work ethics with an ethos of high professional performance and often with very distinctive cultural practices, expressive self-stylization and a sense for unconventional ways.

The dominated faction is the modernized *Milieu of the Higher Socio-Cultural Services* (about 4 per cent). It concentrates in higher administration (often connected with new information technologies), especially in public administration, financial departments and publishing sectors. Women, in addition, often work in advisory, medical-technical and educational occupations. Their cultural capital is high only on the *Abitur* level (27 per cent) and lower in university diplomas (11 per cent) as, after school, most of them pass a professional school before starting a career in their occupation. Most of their parents and grandparents were skilled blue- or white-collar workers as well as small employers, that is mainly part of the tradition line of skilled work (2.1) with its appreciation for education. Their way into the upper milieus was facilitated by the expansion of new qualified occupations in the economy and in the welfare state, after 1950. The heritage of the skilled workers' culture of modesty explains why this milieu keeps a certain distance to the expressive and distinctive self-stylization of the dominant faction.

The tradition line of the cultural vanguard (1.3)

In the early 1990s, the place of the vanguard milieu was still taken by the old *Alternative Milieu* characterized by the life styles and ideals of the 1968 movements. Its members were mainly academic intellectuals working in the educational, research and cultural sectors as well as in the medical, therapeutical and social services, or preparing for these activities as students. They have a high rate of *Abitur* diplomas (28 per cent) and a rate of university diplomas which, with regard to the fact that many are still students, is also high (18 per cent).

Culturally, the group professed the post-materialist values of personal emancipation, individuality, authenticity as well as the universalistic or "class-less" values in the the fields of gender, ethnicity, ecology, peace and participatory democracy. Since the early 1980s, when the respective movements succeeded to form the Green Party, the milieu had found increasing public acceptance. In turn, the "alternative" values were practiced in less "class-less" and increasingly realistic forms. Many former protesters had reached their tacit biographical aim to become part of the élites. In this process, the milieu, which in 1991 was already down to 2 per cent, was gradually re-absorbed by its parent milieu, the progressive élite of higher learning.

Meanwhile, its place has been taken by new and younger vanguard milieu, the *Post-modern milieu* (about 5 per cent). It combines esthetic vanguardism and a self-oriented ambition to get to the top of life style, consumption and social positions. Mainly, its members are up-starts, often younger than 35, with higher education and still living as singles. They are students or young academics working on a medium employee, profession or employer level, preferredly in vanguard occupations of symbolic services, culture, the media, the new technologies, the arts and architecture, but also younger barristers, accountants and surveyors. (This composition is very near to the "postmoderns" found by Savage *et al.* and partly to the new petty bourgeoisie described by Bourdieu.) Meanwhile, the dreams of the new economy have given place to an increasing realism, and the milieu may well be re-absorbed by its parent-milieus in order to be replaced by the next vanguard.

The respectable popular and employee classes

The difference of the Bourdieu and the milieu approaches, as compared to the employment aggregate approaches, is especially evident when we turn to the popular classes. Here, we find a horizontal differentiation between rather static and traditionalist milieus of employees (which largely consists of the offsprings of the former small owners), a group of rather dynamic employee milieus combining the search for education and autonomy with a sense of solidarity (being the offsprings of the former working class) and, finally, a vanguard of life style (which mainly turns out to be a transitional stage of the children of the two other groups)[6]. It is important to note that, contrary to the ahistoric myth of proletarian collectivism, the key value of the new working or employee class is *autonomy* – which it already was when the working class was made (Thompson 1963; Vester 1970), and which Savage (2000) also argues characterises British working-class identities.

Work orientation: the self-reliant labouring classes (2.1)

An additional remarkable result, confirmed by our survey data, is that the milieus of the skilled working class which historically formed the core of the labour movement has not been eroded. They continue to represent one-third of the population (see Table 4.1)[7] although they changed their appearance. Contrary to Beck and Giddens, taking part in the structural change towards more tertiary and white-collar occupations did not mean giving up the basic dispositions of personal autonomy, ascetic work ethics and mutual help, though increasingly this is balanced by a moderate hedonism in the younger generations. Their main groups are the self-reliant and skilled blue and white-collar workers in modern occupations and a smaller faction of the small owners. The value system is opposed to that of the petty bourgeois popular classes whose central value is social status, derived from hierarchical relations. Instead, for the milieus of skilled work and practical intelligence, *autonomy* is the central value, and it is primarily based on what a person can create independently, by his or her work and practice. This striking parallel to the diagnosis of Savage (2000) is well illustrated by the small portraits included in the text.

The other values are more or less derived from this. Education and culture are seen as an important means to develop personal competences of work, autonomy and orientation. Different personal achievements of work and learning may legitimate a certain *differentiation* or *hierarchy* in the social order. But this hierarchy of skills does *not* legitimate any *class domination*. Accordingly, "natural" or "power" inequalities as well as deference towards social, religious or political authorities are abhorred. Work orientation founds a meritocratic sense of equality. The value of a person should depend on the practical works, independent from gender, ethnic or class-belongings.

Solidarity is not a value in itself but a necessary condition of personal autonomy which is thought to be dependent on mutual help and co-operation. It does not mean collectivism but is following the older tradition of neighbourly help and emergency ethics (Weber 1964), which is manifestly mobilized only on special occasions and for special cases. If somebody is in distress without being personally responsible for it, help is the neighbours' duty. This principle is also transferred to the political field. The welfare state should not support any feather-bedding. But it should help everybody who is in need without being responsible for this situation.

Work and life style are largely structured by a special variant of Weberian "protestant ethic", a rational and realistic method of conducing life. In this variant, however, work and self-discipline again are not values in themselves, which lead to the proverbial puritan morosity, but combined with the conviction to be entitled to *enjoy* the fruits of the own and common efforts and to receive social justice.

This general value pattern may articulate in many different ways, according to the field situation. In situations of declassment and humiliation it may motivate militant collective action. In a situation of occupational change it may motivate reconversions for new occupational fields by strong educational efforts on a family level. In a situation of prosperity, personal acquisition may come to the fore. Historically, the habitus pattern itself may shift the balance of its different traits as new generations with new formative experiences are developing their own ways. Our data permit to distinguish three milieus each of which is mainly centered around a different age cohort.

The *Traditional Working Class Milieu*, a sort of "grandparent generation", is still identified with the necessities of physical work and scarcity. In West Germany, it melted down to about 4 per cent. Here, the distance to the powerful is felt most while the relations with friends, work mates and neighbours are still highly valued in the sense of the old working-class culture. The old "proletarian experience" of want, of insecure and limited incomes and of more traditional work skills is still remembered. At work, the milieu members follow the disciplined ethos of good, responsible skilled work. At home and in consumption, they modestly adapt to the necessary. Participation in social standards has to be earned by one's own work.

"all in your own responsibility"
(A Traditional Worker)

Karl, aged 48, after secondary school and an apprenticeship as a carpenter, works at Volkswagen as a toolmaker. With his wife, a nurse, he lives in his own house in a small town. They have a son of 25. Karl's father was a carpenter, too, his mother was a housewife.

Going to Volkswagen was not only "the financial way" to fulfil his "youth's dream" to "build my own hut, here", but also a struggle for autonomy at work. First working in a department with degrading work and "catastrophic emissions", he risked severe personal conflicts to be promoted to his present working place which is "rather good", "a surrounding (of workmates) that fits": "You work independently, one is allowed to decide by oneself how it is done and so, is all in your own responsibility."

In his leisure time, Karl is rather active, as a hobby photographer, going to the theatre, doing carpenter work in his house, acquiring his yachting certificate. He meets his friends for card playing but does not like to be a club person: "I'd rather be independent." However, this does not limit his political activity, in the trade union and also the Social Democratic Party where he contributes to a magazine being challenged to activate his talents to write: "These are things to keep you going, mentally, in order to have something different, a very different *metier*." Karl actively participates in the courses of workers' education, distinguishing himself from the young frustrated workers "interested in nothing", with their "assembly line faces". He likes the courses to be well organized and socially useful, for example relating his hobby photographing with the presentation of societal problems.

Meanwhile, Karl says, "I have got myself everything I wanted to have" (a house, a sailing boat, a computer, etc.), but always caring that "I really earned it, first." At the sametime, he is severely worried about the unemployment of his son and his wife: "There, I don't have a perspective." Although active in labour politics, he is critical: the trade union is "too much a closed bunch blocking unfamiliar ideas". (Bremer 1999: 104–106)

The "parent generation" already grew up during the economic growth decades since the fifties, with the experience of rising social rights and standards. They grew to a new milieu of about 20 per cent which Goldthorpe and Lockwood called the *Affluent Workers*[8] and which we might call the *"Meritocratic" Employee Milieu* – as they strongly believe in hard skilled work which, then, legitimates participating in the standards of consumption, leisure and social security of the welfare society. Their skills, education and social standards are better than those of the grandparent generation, but not extravagant. Their occupations are those of modern employees, the men mainly in skilled blue-collar work, the women mainly in skilled white-collar work.

"that I reconciled myself with work"
(A Meritocratic and former Hedonist Employee)

Christiane is aged 43. As her mother, she is an employee in public administration, while her father is an engineer. After secondary school she "hanged around at schools for quite some time", before her parents ("now it is enough") made her go to a training for an office occupation. However, she started her professional carreer only after the five years of her first marriage, when she was alone with her little son. Now, she lives together with her second husband, a dental technician, and her son.

"Interest in my occupation has grown by and by as years passed" and as family obligations became less absorbing. She acquired additional education and a more interesting post in her office. However: "It could be a little more responsibility." Consequently she put up with the additional strain and costs of a correspondence course to prepare for a further advancement. At her age, she is "glad to have found my warm place, that I reconciled myself with work and even find it interesting".

The pragmatic orientation of usefulness is also valid for her interest in adult education. She prefers purposeful programmes, not "chatting clubs... where everybody tells what he is doing and possibly returns home as stupid as he came". She wants to "get something into her hand", while the surrounding does not have to be luxurious.

This all leaves her little time for her leisure activities (photographing, movies, museums and exhibitions) which she shares with her husband. "Material things should not be put to the front" although they are not unimportant. Most important, however, is the reliabilty of social relations for which "you have to do something not only make use of it unilaterally... We have lived to be there for others." Her present husband is a good and equalitarian partner, still interesting after 12 years, despite different opinions on education.

Political education is important to be informed and to understand articles in the press. But: "You can read much, but it is better to discuss it with others." As already her mother, she is active in the works council, without considering this as "political". Trade unions are "indispensible as representatives of the interests of the employees", but their structures have become too rigid and immobile. Therefore, she would not become a union militant: "I would probably be fed up, soon." (Bremer 1999: 128–130)

The generation of the "grand children" mainly grew up since the end sixties, in the context of educational reforms, new work and communication technologies, new social movements and a wider variety of life styles. This *Modern Employee Milieu*, first described around 1990,[9] is growing rapidly, yet comprising more than 8 per cent. They are "individualized", however, in a strong sense of personal autonomy and competence which, at the same time, is balanced with a rather high level of social cohesiveness, responsibility and employee-consciousness.

The milieu reminds of the old cosmopolitan culture of the curious and creative artisan, with a passion for learning and wandering. They work in the most modern branches of technical, social, and organizational work, in academically specialized practical occupations, ready to learn new arts and languages, and convinced of the necessity of good skilled work – and of participating in the decisions at work as well as in politics. However, this work ethic does not operate as an incentive for endless careers and acquisition. It is, in their time schedules, balanced by a caring for their friends, neighbours and parents. Although horizontal solidarity did not disappear, their autonomous habitus makes them difficult members of trade unions and other organizations with a rigid hierarchical style. However, their openness for non-conventional life styles differs from that of the Hedonistic Milieu described later because they share the sceptical employee realism of the older milieus of their family tree. Hedonism and personal emancipation are adapted to the frame of the possible.

In all three generations of milieus, trade union affiliation is still substantial although gradually weakened: around 32 in the grand-parent milieu, around 28 in the parent milieu and 24 in the youngest milieu. In their majority, all three milieus are highly disappointed by the neo-liberal tendencies in the political parties.

"not to do always the same thing"
(A Modern Employee)

Sabine, aged 31, is a dental technician, living with her mother, a cleaning lady living separated from her father, a painter.

After Abitur, she became dental technician "because I am a tinkering soul". She went to a small firm where "I can organize my work independently" and work is not monotonous: "For me it is tremendously important not to do always the same thing." Studying is not her way as she likes "to have a result on the table", "something useful and

> (Continued)
>
> meaningful". "Money was not that important for me." However, she dislikes the increasing stress on the job.
>
> Sabine is a committed trade unionist, member of the works council and often with a full schedule all the week. Therefore she needs distance from work in the rest of her time. She likes to read or "let the soul dangle" in the garden of her boyfriend (a full-time works council member) or to make walking tours with the "Friends of Nature", a labour youth organization. For her, as an active and interested person, beach vacations are "boring". Similarly, she likes educational courses, organized not like school teaching but in a modern and inspiring way, on an equal footing. The surrounding does not have to be luxurious.
>
> Politics often don't meet her demands, being connected "much with lulling" and "redundancy" and with annoying forms of conflicts. But: "If you want to move something you must commit yourself." (Bremer 1999: 119–120)

Hierarchic orientation: the petty bourgeois labouring classes (2.2)

The second tradition line goes back to the old deferent popular classes working in hierarchical relations. Today, it unites small employees and owners in traditional occupations. With their modest material and educational resources, they are likely to be the losers of economic modernization. They are looking for security in the hierarchies and duties of work, politics and the family. This corresponds with a conventional and authoritarian habitus. Solidarity is mainly limited to the core family – and combined with the hierarchical loyalty between patrons and clients.

However, outspoken authoritarianism has somewhat been modified by modern life styles. The classical *Petty Bourgeois Employee Milieu* which had 28 per cent in 1982 lost 13 per cent who now are mainly to be found in the *Modern Petty Bourgeois Employee Milieu* of 8 per cent. This younger milieu has more solid occupational qualifications and incomes and can modernize the petty bourgeois life style by elements of individual hedonism and of modern comfort. It can satisfy its striving for security better than the parent milieu, balancing authoritarianism by tolerant styles. But the fundamental belief in occupational, familial and ethnic hierarchies is still dominating.

Politically, both milieus have strong conservative and rightist leanings. However, up to now four-fifths of them give their votes to the big conservative or social-democratic parties, still viewing them as a more reliable guarantee of security interests. Parts of the milieus are important for labour. They are the "authoritarian workers" who are a membership group that trade unions have to count on. Union membership is around the average (20 per cent in the older, 26 per cent in the younger milieu). The conservative pattern of patron and client does not mean unconditional obedience. It also implies that the patron has duties which he can be reminded of. Of course, this disposition will be articulated differently, depending on field conditions. When there is strong fear of declassment – and disenchantment concerning the Employee Society, significant minorities of the milieu might turn to reactionary or racist resentments, today especially rightist populism.

Life style orientation: the hedonist popular classes (2.3)

On the left margin of the middle, we see a formation which defines itself as a sort of vanguard of life style. The members of the *Hedonist Milieu* (12 per cent) profess conspicuous anti-conformism, individual autonomy and spontaneous enjoyment of the exciting possibilities of modern life style and consumption. These peculiarities not rarely are seen as a proof of the dissolution of traditional class cultures. Indeed, they reject the petty bourgeois habitus of duty and order as well as the skilled employees' work orientation and self-discipline.

This delimitation may be interpreted differently when we consider the data. The milieu mainly consists of young people under thirty whose parents and grand parents belong to the occupational groups of the "respectable" tradition lines. The rejection of conventional values, then, may also be seen as part of the generational conflict with their parents who are belonging either to the the petty bourgeois or to the skill-oriented tradition lines. The strong negative identification disguises the internal differences of the young hedonists. The milieu is a transitory formation constituted by the prolonged adolescent rebellion against the narrow perspectives of necessity, harmony, security and thrift. About four-fifths of the milieu comply to the usual everyday routines of school, work and social obligations, and about one-fifth professes to go to church on sunday mornings. Thus, for most milieu members hedonism means little more than a leisure time compensation.

Moreover, since the golden years are over, hedonism has got into difficulties. According to their age, many milieu members did not yet leave the phases of education and transitional jobs behind them. Others are in the situation of low qualified blue- and white-collar work or unemployment.

Thus, medium and small incomes are the rule, and hedonism touches its material limits so that the group is segregated into winners and losers.

Orientations of powerlessness: the underprivileged popular classes

The third main group of the popular and employee classes differs from the two "respectable" tradition lines above them which, in "normal times", enjoy an integrated economic and moral status. The third tradition line, instead, is not stably integrated into this nexus of giving and taking and the repective traditions of internalized social control, thus seemingly justifying its "underclass" position below the invisible border line of respectability.

However, the underclass of the *Underprivileged Working Class Milieus*, about 12 per cent, is not different in all respects. Like the self-reliant labouring classes they give high priority to their family, friends and peers. But they differ in the means. For them, work is not "fulfilment" (as it is for the self-reliant milieus) nor a "duty" (as it is for the petty-bourgeois milieus). It is a necessary burden, especially as they mostly occupy the less skilled, less secure and less paid jobs.

"I live through the day, seeing what comes."
(An Underprivileged Worker)

Kalle, a Volkswagen worker of 28, still lives in the house of his parents, constructed through hard work. His father was an unskilled worker who is now pensioned after unemployment, his mother is a housewife.

After primary school, an apprenticeship as a motor mechanic and a period of changing jobs, he went to Volkswagen. "The step into the factory was the money." Here, too, he changed the department several times because of conflicts with the foremen. He is not content to work in a material supply department: "you feel like a hen in a big factory". But he does not see a way out. To make his master craftsman's diploma is too risky: "It costs 10,000 Marks." And: "Without influential relations you don't have a chance."

In his leisure time, Kalle mainly wants to have fun, meeting friends in a pub or discotheque, motorbiking or drinking. He likes to be independent, with "no big obligations". "I live through the day, seeing what comes. I enjoy simply, I cannot make big plans." He does not want "to work all my life" and dreams of a "winning lotto ticket" to buy a house, "in Canada or Australia or everywhere".

> He takes advantage of his right of an annual workers' education course, mainly to get off the job and "to meet other people". It is important to "talk a little", with a beer. He likes people who "like big talking" and not those who "come with a briefcase, sit down and swot". However, in the courses, "a little education is okay".
>
> Politics is not one of Kalle's hobbies. Politicians are much alike, thinking "how they can best fleece the little man". The results of politics are best seen "in my wage packet". Talking politics "is no use". (Bremer 1999: 110–111)

For them, the world is deeply divided into the powerful and the underdogs. Intellectuals often misunderstand this *polarized power image of society* as a source of clear proletarian class-consciousness and militancy. Empirically, however, their confidence in their own forces is realistically limited. With little own resources of economic and cultural capital, the future of their employment and well-being is insecure. Being very conscious of the risks to be destabilized and stigmatized, they prefer to develop strategies of *keeping up* with the standards of the well-to-do classes and of *leaning on* to stronger actors – the unions, the boss, a good marriage or lucky occasions of many kinds. In this, they follow the old tradition of the pre-industrial underclasses. With them, they share the belief that *investment in personal relations* (horizontally as well as vertically) is most important for social recognition while educational achievements or legal equality cannot be trusted.

These strategies vary, according to the three sub-milieus they belong to. The *Fatalist* sub-milieu (about 6 per cent) sticks to the underdog philosophy that all personal efforts are futile. But they see the unions as their voice and almost one-third of them are union members. The same is true for the *Status-Oriented* sub-milieu (about 3 per cent) although it is not so "progressive" in other respects. Its members adopt the petty-bourgeois strategies of conformity with patriarchalism in the family, discipline and reliability on the job and conventionalism of life style. Instead, the *Hedonist Rebels* (about 2 per cent) follow the libertarian philosophy of the Hedonistic Milieu, practising distance towards the authorities of the state, the churches, higher education, patriarchalism and so on. Although this is the most "individualized" of the three sub-milieus, its union affiliation is the strongest: 44 per cent.

Our data show that the strategies of *leaning on* of most of the underprivileged workers were partly successful although they did not participate mainly in the educational revolution since the 1960s.

Their school achievements are still low although more stable. However, the post-war Fordist model of social integration allowed them rather secure low-skill jobs in the pits, on the railway, in the shops or the assembly lines of big industry and also rather stable incomes. But this model is now eroding, as the less skilled jobs are exported to cheap labour countries and the social guarantees of the welfare state are increasingly reduced. Today, the underprivileged blue- and white-collar workers are dividing into several parts. Many now are among the main losers of modernization, forming the largest portion of the permanently unemployed. Others return to the old milieu strategies of combining small jobs and opportunities and of activating their networks in the informal economy. Politically, parts of the milieus may also enter into actions against ethnic minorities or into right wing populist protest.

Conclusions

In this chapter we have shown how an account of German milieu can be developed. We do not need to choose between the emphasis on stability and no-change advocated by Goldthorpe and his associates, or the theorists of the third way, such as Giddens and Beck. We can, at the margins, detect some trends towards social change but by the analysis of milieu these can be placed in a broader context of enduring processes of social cleavage and division. Thus we can avoid the seemingly static consequences of Bourdieu's theory as long as it was only applied to French society of the 1970s. Indeed, we have suggested that the changes and shifts in social structure as a whole can be understood better when culture is understood not only in its use as an instrument of symbolic domination used by the privileged classes, but also as a movement of social innovation from below. The introduction of this axis, in combination with the axis of time, may turn out as one of the most consequential innovations of Bourdieu's work. While in the upper echelons of society the drift towards more cultural capital and generational change may mainly serve the reproduction of class domination, there are also middle-class factions with "indistinctive" cultural patterns which may be possibly open for more participatory tendencies from below. Understanding the upper milieus as a dynamic field of forces, helps to understand social change better than the rather static concept of a service class. Also, the increase of cultural capital in the popular milieus strengthens their position in the struggles for more participation in social chances and decisions. In other words, the movement of classes to the left pole of social space constitutes a contradictory development. On the one hand, classes and class society are not dissolved but on a horizontal movement which, by itself, does not change vertical structures of domination. On the other hand, while class domination remains, at the same time the potential for social and political emancipation which may challenge this domination are growing.

The habitus types of the younger generation were not completely different from the parent generation, as the individualization thesis supposes, but variations of the same basic patterns. This confirmed our initial hypothesis of a generational habitus metamorphosis which had been inspired by the Birmingham cultural studies (Hall and Jefferson 1975). To find the generational similarities was mainly possible because each type could be formulated in rather general terms of the "moral" and "symbolic" meaning – and not by the surface attributes and practices of life style which expectedly differed between the generations.

Finally, I hope to have shown how we can develop Crompton's critique of "employment aggregate approaches". When class-belonging is based on a common habitus and on common biographical strategies transmitted mainly in the families and milieus, it is also connected with the preference for specific zones in the occupational field – but there is no simple relationship between occupation and class. Furthermore, when class-belonging is based on habitus, the discussion whether the belonging of women is given by their occupation or by their husbands can be seen to a "pseudo-discussions" (Crompton 1998) since there is no need to prioritize either male or female habitus, and in many respects the household becomes the key unit. The difficult task to integrate complex societies cannot be tackled by organizing policies around supposed single trends, mechanisms or dominant groups as theories of post-materialism, of individualization or of the service class tried to recommend. If Ralf Dahrendorf's vision of the coming of a new authoritarian century shall be disproved, a better knowledge of societal dynamics is needed, including theories and an empirical diagnoses which allow to distinguish the dimensions of complex societies by a new approach which differentiates as well as integrates these dimensions. Building on Bourdieu's work offers the best way of developing such an account.

Notes

1. The project "Social Structural Change and the New Socio-political Milieus", carried out at the University of Hannover from 1988 to 1992, was especially supported by the Volkswagen Foundation. The study and its methodology are documented in Vester *et al.* 1993/2001. East German society was not included because the German Democratic Republic was not accessible

when the project began in 1988 and, moreover, it constitutes a different variant of social structure, which we studied in a separate project (Vester *et al.* 1994).

2. Each group was assessed according to a catalogue of eleven socio-economic properties: size and change of size since 1950, gender, age, educational and occupational diplomas, occupational position, economic sector, main activity, weekly working time, net income of full and part time employed, immigrant quotas and incidence of unemployment (Vester *et al.* 1994: 381).

3. The interviews were made in June and July of 1991 by the Marplan Institute, with a random sample of 2699 German speaking inhabitants of 14 years and older, representative according to the demographic structure of the 1988 micro census.

4. The allocation of the West German milieus is based on our own representative survey of 1991 (Vester *et al.* 2001). The percentage data concerning West Germany were taken from "Sinus" surveys (SPD 1984; Flaig *et al.* 1993; Spiegel 1996).

5. Analysing the West German service class according to the Goldthorpe approach, Herz (1990) started from mainly the same occupational groups as we arrived at. Consequently, the sizes are rather similar, that is between 20 and 23 per cent (Herz 1990: 234) and between 18 and 20 per cent (Voegele *et al.* 2002: 275–309). However, Herz remains confined to the limits of the "employment aggregate" approach which cannot give differentiated information on milieus as "action aggregates". He can give only wholesale information on the criteria of socio-cultural class cohesion, stating as common a high concentration of cultural capital, of privileges, of intergenerational continuity and of a common cultural identity.

6. This is shown below, in the portrait of the woman who reconciled herself with work after a period of refusal.

7. Bismarck (1957) named the same percentage for the 1950s, and there are indications for a log historical duration of this quota.

8. Strictly speaking, Goldthorpe *et al.* (1968a,b, 1969) studied a specific group of "affluent workers", that is those in de-skilled work and urban living conditions which is only partially identical to the milieu described here. For a detailed discussion see Vester (1998).

9. This type was first explored by mentality researchers in Heidelberg (Flaig *et al.* 1993) and Göttingen (Baethge 1991).

5
Local Habitus and Working-Class Culture

Mike Savage, Gaynor Bagnall and Brian Longhurst

For much of the 19th and 20th centuries, the study of class was inextricably tied up with understanding space and place. The 'classification' of population involved the moralisation of space, with classes being zoned into specific locations and spatial boundaries acting as social markers (e.g. Katznelson 1985; Poovey 1995). During the 20th century this approach took an increasingly critical turn, as academic researchers within the burgeoning community studies tradition sought to show how local studies could be used to illuminate the nature of power relations and structural inequalities (e.g. Frankenberg 1966 and more recently Allan and Crow 1994). The rise of this critical perspective was also related to the trend for official studies of class to take a different focus, centring on class as defined by occupation rather than by spatial location. Szreter (1996) has shown how the occupational approach to class developed at the end of the 19th century in association with developments in statistical science, medical eugenics, and sociology (see also Yeo 1996). By the last thirty years of the 20th century this occupationally based approach to class had become dominant in public research spanning academic and government sectors, to the extent that Crompton (1998) could talk about the power of what she termed the 'employment aggregate approach'. The occupational approach entailed the dominance of the national random survey over the local study, and entailed a fundamental break from older traditions of stratification research. Yet by the 1990s this occupationally based approach was itself under attack for being reductive (see the overview in Crompton 1998), and many sociologists either abandoned class analysis altogether or sought alternative perspectives (see further, Chapter 1).

This redefinition has not, hitherto, led to a full reassessment of the value of 'local' studies, largely because such local studies have been thought to be outdated in an increasingly globalised context. The aim of this chapter is to explore how local case study research can help to recharge class analysis, not by reinstating community studies, but as a means of developing Bourdieu's approach to class analysis.

Our case study examines how a long-standing subject of interest – the extent to which the working class endures as a distinctive social entity in de-industrialised conditions – can be looked at afresh through a local case study approach. We briefly examine arguments pointing to the decline or fragmentation of the working class, noting that such arguments are often unsubstantiated by detailed research. Most of this chapter reports the findings from our study of Cheadle, in Greater Manchester, drawing on forty-three in-depth interviews carried out in 1997/98. Here we show that despite the diversity of occupations and employment relationships found in the area, it is possible to detect dominant local lifestyles and shared dispositions, sustained by local neighbouring relationships as well as common experiences. These can be seen as rooted in manual skills and can be defined as a 'practical' habitus. We show that this finding does not entail reifying the culture of the local area, since we point to differences amongst residents, but that people's sense of belonging to the area is related to the way that they share these dominant values. We also go on to explore the complex relationship between this kind of locally embedded habitus and discursive forms of identity and class awareness.

The first section sets the scene for our research by exploring recent views about the changing nature of working-class formation and considers how Bourdieu's work, and in particular the concept of habitus, can be used to address these debates. The second section explains our research strategy and methods. The third section examines the occupational structure, family relationships, leisure and lifestyles of Cheadle residents, to show how despite their occupational diversity there are common forms and styles of local attachment and interaction. The fourth section examines the nature of local embeddedness in the area, and the fifth considers how Cheadle residents talked about themselves and their neighbourhood. Here we show their complex recognition and misrecognition of class, and certain common formulations, for instance in their nostalgic, utopian or fantastic desires and hopes. Our conclusion relates our findings to debates about working-class formation.

The working class in British society

Until the 1970s it was largely agreed that the working class was characterised by distinctive cultural values and practices which stood outside,
and in opposition to, those of the middle and upper classes. A series of
landmark studies of working-class culture, especially those carried out
between the 1950s and the late 1970s (see Savage 2000) emphasised the
distinctive values and solidarities seen as characteristic of working-class
life. Examples include studies such as Thompson's *The Making of the
English Working Class* (1963), Hoggart's *The Uses of Literacy* (1957),
Williams's *The Long Revolution* (1961), Dennis *et al.*'s Coal is Our Life
(1956), Goldthorpe *et al.*'s *The Affluent Worker* (1968a,b, 1969), and
Willis's *Learning to Labour* (1977).[1] These were not merely empirical studies
of the working class in particular milieux, but helped define core issues
for sociologists, historians, educationalists, and those interested in
cultural studies. These studies differed in how they understood
working-class culture, but in each case it was seen to be of fundamental
significance: for understanding the development of democratic institutions (Thompson), forms of communication (Hoggart, Williams), political
change (Goldthorpe and Lockwood), and educational attainment (Willis).
Questions have been raised, both when these studies were written and
subsequently, as to whether some of these studies romanticised working
class culture, and the dominant view today is that the working class was
always fractured on multiple axes such as gender, ethnicity, and reputation.[2] In some respects, however, this is not the key point. Perhaps the
main point of interest is the way that such studies were seen as matters
of key concern, to academics and a larger audience. Class seemed to
matter, and debates over class came to be seen as of central importance
to public political concerns.

Over the past twenty-five years, this sense that the working class
'matters' has ebbed. It is now difficult to detect sustained research interest
in the nature of working-class culture. Some recent studies define working-
class culture merely as an absence, a stigmatised position that is defined
in terms of its social undesirability. For Skeggs (1997: 95), 'Who would
want to be seen as working class (perhaps only academics are left)?' The
young working-class women she interviewed in the Midlands in the
early 1990s had little identification with working-class values, and instead
they sought actively to 'dis-identify' from class, by trying to demonstrate
their respectability and femininity. For Charlesworth (2000: 13–14), the
gentrification of the Labour movement and the restructuring of higher
education have meant that 'there is no interest in class within the

university and among publishers...There is no symbolic profit to be had from being a working-class intellectual or scholar which means that one cannot simply be what one is, say what one has to say, without constant verbal and non-verbal violations.' Charlesworth's study of Rotherham presents a portrait of despairing people whose lives have been undercut by de-industrialisation. There is no place for the working class. Being socially recognised involves the refusal of a working-class label, with middle-class membership becoming an unspoken assumption of full citizenship and entitlement (see also Savage 2000). The working class continues to exist structurally but, in the words of Charlesworth (2000: 289), 'it is the paucity of the working people to render the world that leaves many feeling there is something missing from their lives'.

These writers draw critically on Pierre Bourdieu's distinctive sociology of practice in framing their arguments. Well known over two decades for his argument that cultural capital secures middle-class advantage in educational attainment (e.g. Bourdieu and Passeron 1977), it has become clear that this conceptual framework allows a robust and flexible, but also controversial, way of grounding class analysis (see further, Chapter 1). Skeggs (1997: 161) uses 'Bourdieu's metaphors of capital and space' to show how 'a group of white working-class women were born into structures of inequality which provided differential amounts of capital which circumscribed their movements through social space'. Theirs was a 'social and cultural positioning (which) generates denial, disidentification and dissimulation' (Skeggs 1997: 75). Charlesworth focuses more on the significance of habitus, the internalised dispositions that govern social action. This is not to be seen mechanically as defined by social or economic indicators of class (such as occupation or income), nor by attitudes (such as class identity). Habitus is embodied, and thereby more deeply rooted than people's attitudes or identities (see also Giddens 1984 on the similar distinction between practical and discursive consciousness), and hence reveals social identities not just in statements or beliefs but in embodied social practice. For Charlesworth (2000: 107), 'there is no more profound adherence to the established order than that pre-reflective conformism that emanates from one's sense of possibilities being the internalization of the opportunities inscribed in one's position'. The working-class habitus, not one based on the written word or discursive communication, is therefore limited and stigmatised, and is itself a marker of social marginality. 'From conditions of absences people do not know the feel of a brighter culture' (Charlesworth 2000: 293, and see more generally 203–204).[3]

This account of the stigmatisation of the working class can be related to wider sociological research. Scott (1996: 243) draws on Weber's distinction between class and status to argue that 'the collective identity of manual workers...is no longer consolidated by status conceptions rooted in factory production and cohesive communal relations.' The declining size of the manual working class and the end of mass production is one key feature of this change. Another is the differentiation within the working class between those who were able to take advantage of demand for their manual skills and those whose skills are increasingly redundant. In this way Pahl (1985) and Saunders (1990a) argued that there was an increasing division between the 'middle mass' and the underprivileged within the working class. Affluent workers have become increasingly privatised as they were able to afford the lifestyles of the middle class, manifested especially in being able to purchase their own homes and private cars. In addition, there is evidence that some skilled manual workers were able to gain access to the kinds of internal labour markets and core employment status that had previously largely been reserved for the salaried middle class (see Savage 2000, Chapters 3 and 6). In the process, they became increasingly distinct from those members of the working class who were subject to unemployment, casualised work, and who were unable to afford privately owned housing.

These views have been contested. Goldthorpe argued that although the working class became smaller, it was still likely that its members were recruited from working-class origins and hence its demographic coherence was likely to be strong. Building on this point, he drew on the arguments of Heath *et al.* (1985) to argue that there was no long-term tendency for class dealignment in voting to occur (Goldthorpe 2000). A further variant of this argument is by Devine (1992a) who re-interviewed the kind of affluent working-class households in the 1980s that Goldthorpe (1968a,b, 1969) had studied in the 1960s. She showed that in many ways these affluent workers did not conform to the picture of instrumental individualism that Goldthorpe (1968a,b, 1969) had emphasised in their study. Rather, she emphasised that 'working class lifestyles and values have not changed as much as the Luton team suggested' (Devine 1992a: 209).

In addition it proved difficult to sustain the view that there were fundamental differences between the affluent working class and the unskilled working class. Even those studies which have tried to specify a distinct underclass with separate lifestyles, attitudes and behaviours have at most shown that 5 per cent of the workforce belongs to it (Buckingham 1999), meaning that only a small proportion of the working class can be seen as part of it. Other studies argue that it is difficult to find any clear differences between skilled and unskilled workers, and show that the working class is still demographically coherent compared to the middle class. A variety of studies testify to the persistence of fundamental class divisions in a variety of relevant social indices, such as the consumption of food (Warde 1997), and voting patterns (Evans 2001).

It is also possible to dispute the argument that working-class identities are stigmatised. Working-class identification remains relatively strong in Britain, and there is evidence that class identities continue to be keenly felt. Devine's research on class attitudes amongst her sample of affluent workers indicated that although significant numbers of the workers she interviewed had become cynical about the Labour Party, clear class identities still existed, especially manifest in political discourse. 'The interviews of this study had a strong collective class identity' (Devine 1992a: 210). This point is also made by Marshall *et al.* (1988) on the basis of his national survey carried out in 1984 on class divisions in England and Wales (see Savage 2000; Savage *et al.* 2001).

How then, do we understand the working class? One view would be that the working class has always been a vehicle for academic researchers to advance their own cause (see generally Goldthorpe 1988). As universities have become more fully incorporated into an audit culture characteristic of neo liberal governance (Rose 1999), and also as the substantive findings of academics have less purchase in a society organised around seduction (Bauman 1982, 1988), so the working class becomes less salient to academics. The famous studies of the working class mentioned above were all interesting in that they used the working class as a means of countering academic orthodoxy and developing new disciplinary perspectives in the claim that they could interpret how the working class 'spoke' – in social history, cultural studies, and sociology. Perhaps the apparent invisibility of the working class in current research is due to the 'normalisation' of academic disciplines within an audit culture, rather than to changes within the working class themselves?

In this context, Bourdieu's work is distinctive in focusing on both the conditions of the production of academic knowledge and the class relations more generally as the research object. His work (along with other arguments regarding reflexivity) makes it clear that there is no way in which working-class culture can be understood transparently. Rather, we need to think about strategic sites in which research can not only develop new findings but also pose new questions. It is our contention that local studies continue to be important as a means of recognising the uncertain interface between academic research and 'other' cultures.

It is not incidental that the pioneering studies of the working class were either local studies (Dennis *et al.* 1956; Hoggart 1957; Jackson and Marsden 1962; Goldthorpe *et al.* 1968; Willis 1977) or were sympathetic to understanding class in local contexts (Williams 1961; Thompson 1963). In important respects, working-class culture was seen as related to forms of local identification and interaction. The fact that arguments regarding the weakening of class in general, and working-class forma-tion in particular, usually rely on other kinds of evidence, which do not systematically draw on local ethnographies or community studies, is itself a problem. As we argue elsewhere (Savage *et al.* 2002) it is possible to re-energise local studies through a greater attention to issues of habitus and capital, through their relationship to place and space – rather than through occupation or the division of labour, as has been the standard approach in class analysis. Bourdieu sees social distinction as being inherently spatial in character: the powerful depend on being spatially distinct from the powerless, and situations which bring these classes into interaction are dealt with through the ritualisation of encounter, in which the structuring of interaction usually allows the powerful to retain control (see especially Bourdieu 1999a). Conflicts over space are in fact rare, a point which can be related to the power of the habitus to act as a regulating device. Where people feel comfortable in places, they tend to populate such places, either through permanent residence or through revisiting, but where they do not, they tend to avoid them. Hence, a complex process of the sorting of people's habitus to certain kinds of zones allows a social *which is also a spatial* structure to be defined.

There are reasons for thinking that residential space plays a particularly prominent role in the spatial and social structures of contemporary cap-italism. In an increasingly unregulated housing market, there are relatively few pressures forcing people to live in particular houses,[4] and instead a high degree of residential sifting as people move (and move again) to find locations where they feel comfortable. The fact that such residential clustering is socially important is attested to by many indicators: the persistence of ethnic segregation; by the development of market research place-based social categories used by advertising agencies and the like; and by the accentuation of significant place-based variations in health, poverty and wealth and other salient social outcomes, as well as in voting and political alignments. We need to retain certain elements of 'community' studies by recognising the importance of studying how local belonging is generated or challenged. However, rather than oper-ationalising these questions only through the nature of local social ties or local interaction, the Bourdieuvian perspective suggests the importance of relating how an individual's habitus enables them to feel at home in a particular place, in ways which may not depend on significant physical interaction (indeed in some cases, the ability of people to avoid interaction may be important for them to feel comfortable). This thereby avoids the possibility inherent in community studies of defining community normatively and through drawing fixed boundaries.

Research methods

We now turn to our substantive research, funded by the ESRC,[5] which examined the lifestyles of residents in four contrasting areas around Manchester in 1997/98. This project was not designed to explore working-class formation. Rather, we intended to see whether there was a distinct clustering of lifestyles in different types of local areas, and to see how homogeneous such lifestyles were. Our research design sampled four distinct types of middle-class areas. The four areas were:

1. *Wilmslow*: This was a market town twelve miles south of Manchester, which was located in the desirable north Cheshire suburban belt focusing on Macclesfield and Altrincham. We expected to find high-status, affluent middle class. We interviewed in areas of detached housing, where properties were valued in 1997 at between £250,000 and £750,000 (see Savage *et al.* 2002).
2. *Ramsbottom*: This was an old Lancashire mill town twelve miles north of Manchester and close to Bury. The area had been subject to considerable new building and had emerged as a popular commuter belt location. We interviewed in large older terraced and newer detached and semi-detached housing which sold for between £50,000 and £150,000.
3. *Chorlton*: This was an area of urban gentrification close to the centre of Manchester, clustering around an area with new cafes, winebars, restaurants and specialist shops. We expected to find large numbers of academically well-qualified public-sector workers, and interviewed in 'desirable' streets where properties ranged in price from £50,000 for small terraced houses to £200,000 for the largest terraced houses.
4. *Cheadle*: This was selected because it conformed to the stereotype of an inter-war suburban estate of three-bedroom semi-detached housing. In 1997/98 houses were valued at between £50,000 and £65,000, and we expected to find large numbers of intermediate-class white-collar workers.

In each location we aimed to obtain fifty in-depth interviews, which were tape-recorded and transcribed. We took a one-in-three sample from the electoral roll, using a quota to obtain similar numbers of men and women. The response rate in Cheadle was 29 per cent, yet because all the interviews were carried out in one relatively enclosed estate, and our respondents are relatively similar to the social profile of this area, we are confident that our findings are generalisable.

Cheadle as a working-class locale

It rapidly became clear as our interviewing began that the respondents in Cheadle did not conform to the lower middle-class stereotype that we expected. It became clear that Cheadle was not a fashionable place to live, certainly as compared with our other case study areas. The housing stock, of inter-war three-bed semis, looked somewhat dated in style. The estate itself had experienced little re-development from either public or private sector: there were no new café bars, shops or leisure facilities (as in the other three areas). Respondents frequently complained that roads were busy with traffic and that Cheadle was affected by aircraft noise resulting from being directly in the flight path of Manchester airport. Surrounding areas of parkland and low-density housing had recently been the subject of office and housing development.

The most immediate sense gained from the interviews in Cheadle, certainly compared to those in our other three case studies, was that life was pretty tough. Admittedly, there were only two unemployed respondents in our sample, and only four households with incomes of under £10,000. In this sense, there was little absolute deprivation in the area. However, the moderate incomes of most residents were clearly hard-earned. Only three households had incomes above £40,000, and three quarters were earning less than £30,000. Only two men earned more than £30,000 whilst 26 earned less than £20,000. Only four women earned above £20,000, and in general their paid employment was seen as subsidiary income to that of the male breadwinner. There were only four cases where women were the main earners in the household. Working respondents worked long hours, with many households having complicated shift arrangements to allow both partners to work whilst covering childcare responsibilities. In most cases there were strongly demarcated gender roles, with women being primarily responsible for domestic work, shopping and caring.

Initially, the respondents seem diverse in terms of their class profile. If one classifies households according to the social class of the main earner, 13 (30 per cent) were manual working class, 11 (26 per cent) were intermediate class, 10 (23 per cent) were self-employed, and 9 (21 per cent) were in the service class.[6] However, this apparent diversity actually masks a strong culture of manual labour which predominates in most households, and which gave the area, as one respondent put it 'a practical flavour'. No less than eight of the self-employed were involved in manual labour in building or other outdoor work, and the other self employed were also involved in manufacturing activity. Some of these were involved in franchising arrangements that to all intents and purposes made the workers dependent on the franchising firm.

Six of the nine service class respondents also were strongly steeped in the experience of manual labour. This was most true for Edward, currently a further education lecturer in carpentry and joinery, whose work history exemplified many of the difficulties faced by manual labourers since the 1980s. His story is worth relating at length.

Yes, I had my own business for a number of years and for one reason or another it failed, probably my own fault more than anything else, I had a period of unemployment, I then out of the blue just went to the Job Centre in Manchester, for no reason, I just felt that I wanted to go that day, and there was a job advertised for a youth training supervisor in carpentry. I went for the interview, they called me up the next day saying you've got the job, and I found myself having half a dozen lads round me without any real experience or knowledge of how to train. So I was then encouraged by my wife to go and get some training, which I did at Manchester Poly, I did a one year course in further education for teachers, which was a City & Guilds, which I achieved, whilst I was working. At the end of that I was recommended to do the Certificate in Education. I then went to the boss at that time and said I need to go on this course one day a week, what about letting me go for day release on it and after a lot of hesitation he said yes you can go on it. So I got on the first year of the course in Manchester, I had the second year of the course at Bolton Institute of Higher Education and I became a CertEd at the end of it. Towards the end of that course the job was advertised that I'm in now, I applied for it, got it and I've been there ever since.

Q: *And how long is that?*

M: Twelve years.

Q: *And before you had your own business, what did you do?*

M: Well if you want to start from when I left school, from leaving school at 15 and a half, without any qualifications I went into an apprenticeship as a joiner, living in Northwich. A year after I started there they closed down, I then spent the rest of my apprenticeship with a building company. I served my time there. I went to college for four years and got advanced crafts in carpentry and joinery, building science, and about six months after coming out of my time we moved from where we were living in Northwich to Sale. I got a job with a building company, just as a joiner, worked my way up to chargehand, from chargehand to foreman, I was then asked to become general foreman on site. So at the age of 32 I worked my up to general foreman. From there at that point we were just about to get married and I had an argument one day with the contracts manager and I walked off the job. My mother and father at the time were on the markets and said, instead of going back into the trade, come into the markets with us. I didn't do that but we opened up a shop, a mini supermarket. From there I ran that for about three and a half years and then sold the business and moved into something else which failed completely, then had a period of unemployment. We then started moving around the country a little bit because of the problems that we had. I actually had a job as a newsagent manager for a while, which moved us round the country, we were living in the north east for a while, and we moved to Middleton, from Middleton we left the newsagents business and moved into a flat in Stretford and had a job as a milkman. From there, because I was home half nine, ten o'clock finished for the day, I thought I'd do a few jobs, joinery from Iris Hill, put adverts in newsagents windows, and it led to getting quite a bit of work. I finished up doing two jobs and I thought I'd give my milk job and go joinery full time as my own business. And that's how I started off in business doing joinery and from there, just all of a sudden going out with some friends one night, he said just in conversation, I said I had to go out and buy window frames and he said, what about if you had a place to make your own frames, would you be able to make money out of it. I said probably, so he said I've got an empty warehouse, look at it. So I decided after looking at it to set up in business, we got money out of the government to set it up and I was then making window frames, working six in the morning til nine at night and getting very stressed. I became very ill with it, it's the only time I've ever been on tranquilisers because I was so ill and I gave that up. It was making window frames in kit form for the DIY market and it was also an idea that was just about to be sold abroad because of the easy way of transporting window frames to other parts of the world and we were getting all sorts of specifications in to have me make window frames for places where they could be transported in containers. It was at that time I became ill because of the pressures we were under and I gave the business up. At that point I became unemployed, I then got a job with a building firm, John Lawlers, and it was six months before Christmas. I was alright til then, after Christmas the work dried up, they made me unemployed again. And that's my life story!

In one sense, Edward's work history was very turbulent, as he moved between different sectors of employment, into and out of self-employment, into further forms of training and finally into professional employment. In another sense, however, his work had been rather stable, as he sought different kinds of outlet for his skills in joining and carpentry. The important point here is that the experience of manual labour allowed fluidity between occupational classes. A different kind of example of this point is the experience of Stuart, who worked on tarmac, reinstating roads and footpaths, for his brother-in-law's firm.

Q: So how did you get involved in that kind of work?

M: I just got asked when I married Michelle, her brother was doing a job and he wanted someone else to take over some work and I started from there really.

Q: So you didn't have any particular skills, you just picked it up did you?

M: Not with that job no, but I did work with him when I was seeing Michelle, before we got married, over a weekend, for a good couple of years, every other weekend and I got to know a lot about it then.

Q: And how many hours do you work, it sounds like you work a hell of a lot?

M: I usually get up about half past five in the morning and get in for about six o'clock, depending, summer times we might not roll in til half past nine at night, it depends what work you're doing and what kind of money can be earned, the more metres you put in the more your pay packet is at the end of the week.

Q: But you can be working ten, eleven, twelve hours every day?

M: You could be yes, you could be working eighteen hours a day, seven days a week, depending if you need the money or you want the money. You get used to it, it's just one of those jobs, it is physical work, it is graft. I like being outside anyway, I couldn't have an inside job.

Q: Do you work nationally?

M: All round Wales at the moment, we're doing north Wales.

Q: Do you drive there each day in the morning?

M: Yes, I start from here and I pick up the lads up on my way through from Fallowfield, and then Stretford and Northingden then up to Northwich to pick up the tarmac and then from Northwich into Wales.

Q: Do you want to carry on doing this job for a long time, is it your future?

M: Yes, I wouldn't lose interest, I like doing the job, unless something better come along, but the money'd have to be right. I can't see any change in the near future.

Q: And would you say you had a good social time at work?

M: Yes, we've got a good rapport, we can have a good laugh together, one of the lads is a bit mad and we do have a good laugh, it's very rare that we have a bad word.

Most service- and intermediate-class respondents had manual skills which were now being used in a professional or managerial context, as production managers, or lecturers teaching forms of manual skill. Most workers had similar kinds of educational histories, having been to local schools and all having left school at or before the age of 16. Around half of the men had picked up a 'trade' through apprenticeships and/or City & Guilds qualifications, whilst a number of women had also had vocational training, for instance as nurses. There was only one respondent who had a degree in a 'pure' academic subject, such as were common in Chorlton or (to a lesser degree) Wilmslow. This was not an area, therefore, where households had much 'cultural capital'. Whilst education was in general highly prized, this was nearly always seen in terms of interest in manual, physical skills. John was a driving instructor and an enthusiastic member of the Territorial Army. He joined, because,

M: I wanted to learn to drive a lorry, I wanted my HGV. The idea was I'll get my licence and then I'll leave and get something out of them, and I found I enjoyed it so I stayed, like a lot of them.

Our point, then, is that the apparent occupational diversity of the area actually masks a strong shared culture of physical labour. Altogether only eight households (18 per cent) were not steeped in some form or another in this experience of manual labour.[7] Even though there was very little employment in large factories, there were striking similarities in the skill profile of local households. In this respect de-industrialisation has led not to the collapse of manual skills as such but to their dispersion to diverse kinds of outlets.

Locality and embeddedness

Most residents in Cheadle are strongly embedded in the area. Twenty-three (53 per cent) had been brought up locally, either in Cheadle or in an adjoining area within one mile from their current house.[8] All the other manual workers, except one,[9] had been brought up elsewhere in the Manchester conurbation, mostly in more central areas of Manchester such as Levenshulme, Reddish, Ancoats, and Rusholme, from which they had migrated out. It follows from the relatively local origins of these manual worker respondents that they tended to have close family ties in the area. A very large number are in regular contact with their extended families, who live within a relatively short distance. Two-thirds of the sample (28) had either their parents or the majority of their non-resident children living close by, at most within a fifteen-minute car journey.[10] This degree of local family connection is similar to that found by Young and Willmott (1957) in Bethnal Green in the 1950s and in other working-class 'community studies' such as Hoggart (1957). Although Cheadle's housing stock – 1930s semi-detached houses – is different from the small-terraced houses that are iconic to the classic working-class community, the actual social character of the area seems largely consistent with them. There were only two manual workers whose immediate kin did not live locally. One had parents living in Stafford, and the other in Bury – neither of these being a very large distance away. In both cases, these respondents had been brought up in the Manchester area but their parents had subsequently moved away. Every manual worker was thereby characterised by having strong Manchester roots or connections, and most had strong and enduring local kin ties.

Cheadle residents shared a strong culture of neighbouring. Two-thirds of respondents said they had regular social contact with neighbours; and in the majority of households, neighbours 'popped in' without making arrangements in advance. Many respondents spoke about their neighbours as a positive feature about living in the area, and the power of neighbouring is testified by the fact that a few respondents felt that they had been locally ostracised. Respondents spoke in similar ways to the views elicited by Abrams in his 1970s studies of working-class streets (Bulmer 1986). It was important to respondents that neighbours were not too intrusive, and residents generally looked first to kin for support, but with a sense that neighbours would help out in times of need. Neighbouring involved

> The occasional popping round for a drink, asking them to look after the cat when we're away, that kind of level of socialisation, not in

and out of each others' doors every day, but from time to time just popping round and having a chat.

In some cases when it became known that neighbours had particular skills, they were sought out. Edith had done some work in prisons, and said that:

Well I've done little bits (of work in prisons, and), a few people in the neighbourhood would come to me who had sons or husbands who were in prison and thought I should find something out about this,...I've always been concerned about people in prison, at one time I contemplated going into the prison service, in the back of my mind I was feeling...I think there are too many people in there that shouldn't be there. I'm not soft, but I think there are people whose sentences are too long. I think by and large when they get there... I don't know how to express myself on that really, I just have this gut feeling that there's something...

This culture of neighbouring overlapped with a strong sociability, especially for men, in local pubs and clubs. Around half of the men belonged to either a local social club or the local Conservative Club, and most others had a 'local' pub that they visited on a regular basis, at least once a week and often more frequently. Women's social lives were more likely to be organised around their local family connections. Residential and familial stability went hand in hand, however, with the instability and spatial dispersion of workplaces. Unlike the classic working-class occupational community, most of the respondents did not work locally. A considerable number were mobile in their work, especially those in the building trade, whilst others worked in Manchester or Stockport. The majority had lived at some point of their lives outside Cheadle, with quite a few choosing to move back to their area of upbringing following some time spent elsewhere. Several had worked abroad. One hospital porter had worked in Bahrain, Denmark and Papua New Guinea. An engineering manager had worked 'all over Europe and the far east'. A road layer, currently travelling all over Wales in his work, had spent two years erecting garages in New Zealand. Yet none had spent any time working in the south of England.

The eight non-manual households were distinctive in being much less rooted in the area. Only two of the eight were brought up close to Cheadle. However, some of these professional households had become domesticated into the area. Stella for instance was probably the most affluent respondent we interviewed and was very unusual in having done a degree in drama and a Masters at Bristol before training as a teacher. She was also unusual in moving from the upper middle-class security of Didsbury because she felt the house in Cheadle was better value for money. Unlike most other Cheadle residents she thought there were few attractive features about the local area and all her social life was based upon going into Manchester and other urban centres. However, she had no immediate plans to leave (although she could easily afford to). Indeed, Stella seemed to have taken on the localism of her area. Interestingly, although she had been brought up in the Midlands, her mother had moved to be close to her when her husband died and now lived within walking distance. Her partner had been brought up in Cheadle and his parents also lived nearby. She amusingly referred to what might be seen as her domestication to the Cheadle culture

How do you regard yourself, given that you brought up in the midlands, do you see yourself as a northerner, midlander, neither?

You see my mother would always say, you northerners, she thinks I've gone totally native, but I'm not 100 per cent sure that I have really, because when we go back to the midlands it always feels quite nice, very familiar and pleasant.

However, the general pattern was for the non-manual households to feel that they did not belong to the area, with five of the eight feeling they did not belong or being ambivalent about their attachment. Bill was a CCTV installer who moved to the area having no prior knowledge of it. He had originated from Lincoln and many of his family contacts remained in Yorkshire and Lincolnshire, with the result that he wished to move back there at some point.

So do you feel like you belong round here?

I don't, no. Even though we've lived here ten years, we've been in this house since 1986, so that's now eleven and a bit years. When did I move to Altrincham, that must have been summer 1985. No, not really.

Do you feel that there's a community round here that you're not a part of?

No, I don't feel excluded, it's just people are a bit different aren't they, it's something that we've noticed, that a lot of people that we come into contact with, they seem to have stayed in the area, and their parents are from a few streets away, their brothers and sisters, all the close family, are relatively close. We're not well travelled, but we seemed like outsiders when we come from fifty miles away. So we felt a little unusual in that didn't we?

It is then possible to detect differences between the dominant group of manual workers (broadly defined) and a smaller group of professionals. Within the manual workers there were further distinctions between those who had been brought up in, or very close to, the area, and those who had moved to Cheadle from Manchester with the locals being more ambivalent and negative about living in Cheadle than did those who had moved into the area. This difference reflected the sense of the migrants that their move to the area was a sign of upward mobility, whilst the locals felt more keenly that the area was socially in decline. However, in general, the manual majority felt comfortable in the area, with a sense that they were familiar with its routines.

Class identities and working-class formation

We have argued that despite the diversity of occupations evident in Cheadle residents there are common themes: embeddedness in locality, training in practical, manual skills, and a culture of 'hard graft'. One can in this sense detect a dominant local habitus. This is not to say that everyone shared in it, but it was more likely for those who did not share it to feel 'out of place'. This local habitus was sustained by active neighbouring and socialising, as well as by common experience. In this section we turn directly to consider how this manual, practical, habitus is related to working-class formation in a broader sense.

In general, explicit class identities were relatively muted: 42 per cent refused to see themselves in any class, 40 per cent defined themselves as working class, and 18 per cent as middle class (see in general Savage *et al*. 2001). Only 21 per cent had a clear and definite view of themselves as a member of a particular class. Some of these were highly articulate, with a minority of respondents being proud to emphasise their working-class identities. Dave was the most explicit of those we interviewed regarding his working-class identity. He spontaneously referred to his working-class roots in a local council estate early in the interview, and later expanded on his identity

I will always see myself as working class. If I won the lottery, and became a multi-millionaire, I would still be working class. I think the class structure in this country is wrong. I am a staunch socialist, people call me a capitalist, if you work the system you've got to be like that because socialism is based on everybody helping each other, the difference is that you can't help somebody unless you are in a situation to be able to and to be able to do that you have got to have the finance to do it.

This class awareness was linked to a strong pride in his independence and craft training, which led him to claim pride in his lack of academic qualifications.

None, I'm daft as a brush! I served my time as a bricklayer and I sat my Craft Certificate and I became a tradesman. That's all I have ever done, I have worked all my life.

It is interesting to note in spite of Dave's views, he actually owned a small building firm and was one of the wealthiest households we interviewed. Dave's sense of working-class pride in independence was echoed by a number of other respondents, who saw their claim to be working-class as allowing themselves to demonstrate that they were independent people.

I suppose. I don't owe anybody anything. Never had anything off the State, never had any Social Security, touch wood!

These kinds of responses, however, were unusual. What seemed to matter was people's concern to assert that they were normal, respectable people, able to claim to be fully part of the social mainstream through their work, family and consumption practices. Naming a class identity was not a central part of this endeavour. Respectability is a theme that is implicit in some of their testimonies, but was rarely explicitly mentioned, and unlike the young women interviewed by Skeggs's (1997) did not appear to be associated with being middle class.

James and Deidre's testimony is worth reproducing at some length since it indicates some of the complexities in how the term 'class' was used by respondents.

M: I think we're just like the majority of people, everybody goes to work to earn their living and then you have whatever treats you can afford, but like I say, we never sacrifice our holidays for anything, even though we don't have tons of things throughout the year, like big flash cars, but we always have an excellent holiday every year, or else there'd be no point in anything really, if you were just constantly getting up in the morning and working, because we really do work hard, I'm not just saying this...

Q: *Would you say you belong to any particular social class?*

M: Social class, we only discussed this the other day didn't we? I always look at myself in a sense as being a working class person, but I had it thrown back at me from my family saying no we're not working class, we're really middle class. At one point I would say five years ago our standard of living was a lot better than what it is now. I think one of the reasons at that point, up to five years ago, pay increased quite well and then it came to a halt. We've not had any real pay increases for the last four or five years. So the standard of living has dropped, the bills have kept going up but the income has dropped.

Q: *So would you still say you were working class?*

M: I've always looked at myself as a working class person, but I'm not now. If I said lower middle class again I'd probably get disagreement from the family.

Q: *What would you say?*

F: I think you're middle class, approaching upper, because you're on a salary, you're not on a wage. Anybody that is on a wage, and there are people who are still on a weekly wage, are classed as working class because the majority of them are doing manual work, whereas in your case you're doing a skilled work and you've got a lot of responsibility and you're getting the appropriate salary for it.

M: Yes, I'm getting a salary and I will get a reasonable pension at the end of it. But at the same time, I don't think I've ever felt ourselves as being in any particular class. We are a typical family in the sense that you used to say a typical family was 2.4 children, so in that sense we're a family, we own two vehicles, we have a three bedroom semi-detached house, we've got three televisions, a reasonable standard of living, we can go out and buy food, we can pay our bills, but it's a case of just being able to do that.

There are a number of cross-cutting themes evident in this interview. First, both James and Deidre were able to talk about class identities, and were able to reflect on what the terms 'middle class' and 'working class' might mean, and how they are related to their own situation. Secondly, they did not feel that either of these terms fitted very well, and at best saw them as external benchmarks that would allow them to position themselves, rather than as fully fledged identities that mattered to them. Their class identity was a matter of debate and reflection, with internal family disagreement about whether they might be middle or working class. Thirdly, what seems more salient to them is their sense of being 'grafting', typical families who work hard to maintain an average lifestyle, as measured by certain kinds of consumption practices, and can pay their way. This 'core' identity could be compatible with either a working-class or middle-class self-definition, depending on which seemed resonant with their main claim to 'ordinariness' and 'typicality'. The following respondent, who settles on a middle-class self-identity, does so for reasons that may not be very different from someone else who would proffer a working-class identity.

Q: *If you had to describe yourself as belonging to any particular social class, what would you describe yourself as?*
M: I suppose the popular answer to that would be middle, but I would say the bottom end of middle class, if that's not a daft answer. It's not an easy question to answer.
Q: *Do you think of yourself in those terms really?*
M: I don't know, I don't look up to anybody, but I don't look down to anybody. I'm quite happy for everybody to be equal..., but I'm quite happy, I would certainly not be afraid of meeting anybody and I would certainly not be afraid of talking to people, in whatever aim of life, whether that be so called higher or so called lower. I'd certainly go and talk to the bloke in the street, I've no airs and graces about that, which might contradict my first answer really, but it wouldn't bother me (C46).

This respondent is not happy with the idea of being middle class, and prefers to be thought of as 'bottom' of the middle class, but then warms to the theme where she clearly indicates that what matters to her is the idea of equal treatment. This final quote indicates this further.

Well I would say I was working class, in that I had to work for my living, but some people would say with your attitude and so on I'm middle class, I don't particular look at putting people into a class, I try and be classless. I think I really feel that goodness and intellect and brightness and humility are more important.

What we see here is a dissociation between the language of class, and people's identities. In part, this is due to the fact that class boundaries do not map onto people's experience of manual labour, exactly in the way that similar types of people are differentially located in manual, self-employed, intermediate and service-class positions. In part, there was no rallying cry of class from institutional forces. Few respondents felt any association with the traditional Labour movement, whether this be trade unions or the Labour Party itself. Those workers who were in trade unions tended to be critical of them, and showed little loyalty or commitment to them. Many of those workers in the building industry worked closely with small employers and in general were on good terms with them. For many of these workers, their main chance of 'getting on' lay in starting a small business themselves.

This ambivalence regarding class identity can be related to the fact that the discourse of class is largely detached from people's practical awareness. It is more in people's everyday awareness that modes of class awareness are revealed, often implicitly. A good example of this is the remarkably frequent sense of nostalgia. For some, this was linked to a feeling that the area was 'going down'. But several respondents worked up this perception into a deep nostalgia for what respondents saw as a lost world, in part linked to a widely shared sense that Cheadle had lost status. James recalled that:

I think years ago, I was brought up in Stockport schools where I was called a snob because I came from Cheadle, I think that label has now left us, but I remember, not being bullied, that's not the word, but as soon as you said you came from Cheadle, it was like oh right, posh. That label's definitely gone.

Sheila was in her early eighties and had moved into her current house when it was first built in the 1930s.

It was the most snobbish place you could have wished to come to, and of course me – not so much now because you haven't noticed it – but me with my cockney accent I stuck out like a sore thumb....I thought what a place, and in Cheadle if you went shopping you went with your hat on, your gloves on, it was the most toffee nose place...Even going to the shops.
Really?
Oh, yeah.
When did that begin to change?
Oh, after the war because a different sort of class of people were moving in, you know, and then of course as my children sort of came along...I had a very good neighbour next door here. She came from

the Isle of Man. I mean, they lived in Wythenshawe and they lived in a council house in Wythenshawe.

James was an administrator who had been brought up in the area, though he had also lived elsewhere. He clearly articulated a sense of unhappiness about the area and linked it to its changing status.

And what do you like and dislike about Cheadle?
I couldn't say there's anything I like about it, I don't really like it at all.
So it's different from where you were before?
Yes. It's changed beyond recognition really. You probably look back to when you were young and imagine it all right, but I think it's going downhill...

In many respects, then, the nostalgia is about social decline. However there is more to this issue than observations about social deterioration. What is evident in the above is also the sense that respondents feel personally implicated in such changes. They feel deterioration personally, as if it cannot just be about the place, but also themselves. Their own identities become bound up with their feelings about the area, with people's sense of personal ambivalence being inter-related to their interpretation of Cheadle itself.

F: I'm sure we were happier, they were happier times. We don't like living in this age do we? It could be our age, you think when you look back times were happier, I don't know, but I do think life was nicer than it is now.
Q: *It's quite a common perception isn't it?*
M: It's a bit dog eat dog now I find and in the days we're talking about you could walk out of this house and walk across the road to talk somebody and go and visit them for reason, and leave your front door wide open, you can't do that these days. A lot of people our age are frightened of going out at night, this was never the case at one time. I mean the number of times my wife as a single person has walked through Manchester late at night, there was no fear at all of being accosted. You can't do that now.

Stuart's story is a fascinating example. Stuart had enjoyed a remarkable life. He was currently working as a manager for a small engineering company, and had worked in engineering in many parts of the world. In between times he had also been involved in his wife's flower business.

He had enjoyed highs and lows, at one time having the finances to send two of his children to private school, but had recently fallen on harder times, and his current position, working in a friend's firm, involved very hard work for little financial reward. Although he had only lived in his current house for eight years, and he had previously lived in a much grander house, his current house had belonged to his family since it had been built in the 1930s – indeed he had been brought up in it. He was not happy about his decision to move back to his own child-hood house.

> I realised it was a mistake because it's like not moving forward, but moving back. I've always said to my wife that it was a bad move on my part, I didn't give it a lot of thought, but we'd spent a lot of money on the house because, at the end of the day, with respect to my mum, it's an old lady's house, so we gutted it, literally. So moving back to Cheadle, Cheadle's changed, like everywhere else, it isn't that I've never been away, I've lived abroad. I had a fantastic childhood here, but it's changed, it was a beautiful area at one time, there was a load of wide open spaces, yes it probably was looking through rose tinted glasses...

But you feel like it's gone down?

> Yes, it's lost the villagey feel. We still call it the village, Cheadle village, but anybody that's moved in here fifteen years ago call it the village. Everybody knew everybody, I was brought, because my parents come from a two up two down environment, it was still neighbours over the fence. The lady who unfortunately has now died, but moved away and retired, I used to call her aunty. I could wander into her house, my mum and her always had a cup of tea at 11 o'clock in the morning, it was the old values and that's how I was brought up. That's changed, everybody keeps themselves to themselves now. In my teenage years I used to go drinking in Cheadle, I would never drink in Cheadle now.

> ....

The next question is would you be sorry to leave this area?

> No. I suppose it's where you're going to, I wouldn't be sorry if it was going down, but no, I feel as though I could move anywhere in the world.

And do you feel part of the community here?

> No. I think that's what I think I was trying to explain before. I know everybody, or my mother knew everybody in this drive, it's weird because it's unusual as all the old neighbours had died, and I've not

bothered to get to know new neighbours. That may be my fault, we keep ourselves to ourselves, we have very good neighbours either side, I probably know four families in this drive, whereas at one time when I was a kid, I knew everybody. It's probably quite unusual, because I'm literally living where I grew up.

This kind of nostalgia is of course a commonplace in accounts of working-class community – it is evident in Richard Hoggart's account of growing up in Leeds or Raymond Williams's in the Welsh Borders. What seems to be at work here is the retrospective projection of hope into a lost world, given the impossibility of an individual transcending their day-to-day environment with its insecurities, difficulties and problems. A corollary of this backward looking sense was also an interest in how chance may change their lives. When asked whether they thought they would carry on living in the area, one-third of all respondents replied that they would unless they won the lottery. This very revealing way of answering the question allowed respondents to state that they had no intention of leaving, and sometimes that they were quite happy living in the area, but then to acknowledge that this was linked to the fact that their only real prospect for change lay in unforeseen circumstance. It was a part of acknowledgement that in a fantastic world they would live somewhere else, but in their day-to-day world they had little choice.

Q: *What might make you move?*
M: The lottery! Who knows, circumstances can change any time.
Q: *But you've no sort of set plan?*
M: No. You don't know what's round the corner do you?

In some cases this mention of the lottery was related to a statement that respondents simply were not able to practically bring about any hopes they might have.

Q: *So you're generally pretty happy here, you'll carry on living here and you can't really see any circumstances where you would move?*
M: No, unless I won the lottery. I do have ambitions, but at the moment I can't fulfil them.
Q: *So do you think in reality you'll be staying here for a while?*
M: Yes, I can see us staying here for a while. There's no possibility in the near future of us moving. Unless we win the Lottery.

We can see in these references a complex interweaving of necessity and fantasy into a vision of a possible world that actually will never transpire ('unless we win the lottery'), which reaffirms the lived world of everyday, pragmatic life. This manual worker majority is then one embedded in place. The stories of their own lives were related to the places they had lived and to the changing standing of Cheadle. This led to a degree of emotional identification (both positive and negative) with Cheadle that tended to be absent in the other places where respondents' relationship to place was rather more 'external' and detached.

Conclusions

It is not the aim of this chapter to argue that Cheadle is in any way a typical kind of place (though nor is there any reason to think that it is unrepresentative of other similar estates which exist in and around British cities)[11]. Our case study of Cheadle is used for strategic analytical reasons, to explore how we might conceive the association between place, class and habitus, and reflect on what our study entails for understanding the contemporary working class. In addressing these issues, we discuss the relevance of our findings for debates about working-class formation raised in the first section.

In some respects Cheadle could be seen as the location for the kind of affluent middle class seen by Pahl and Saunders as becoming increasingly separate from more disadvantaged parts of the working class. Indeed, we have noted that most households here do get by and enjoy at least moderate levels of income. Nearly everyone was a home-owner, most owned cars, all had the usual kinds of consumer durables that are seen as preconditions of modern life. In addition, the relatively suburban location meant that these households are well apart from inner city Manchester and respondents report few ties, or much interest, in the more deprived population found there. However, on the other hand, most households recognise the precariousness of their position, with redundancy being a frequent possibility, and many have had the kind of insecure job histories that are characteristic of the manual labour market. Households continued to rely on the kinds of support networks of kin and neighbours that defined them as part of a larger group. More importantly, the 'practical' habitus evident here has few real points of contact with the habitus of a middle class characterised by possession of cultural capital. There is no real sign that these residents are part of a broader culturally privileged middle class, and it is not incidental that the few professional households in the area felt out of place (even when their levels of income were similar to those of other residents). We can at best, therefore, speak of a fracturing of the working class rather than any thoroughgoing embourgoisement process.

In developing this point, we argue that occupational approaches to class miss the fact that this practical habitus is actually consistent with numerous different occupational class positions, and focusing on the mobility between class positions may understate the persistence and stability of the habitus itself. However, we also argue that the focus on habitus allows us to avoid the problematic conceptual framework of 'community' that has been applied to many studies of the working class in the past. The idea of community carries with connotations of the power of face-to-face interaction, shared normative understandings, a sense of homogeneity and solidarity. The respondents in our study have varied biographies and lifestyles, tend to be fiercely defensive of their independence and autonomy, and do not use the language of 'community' in talking about the area. Furthermore, it is possible to use the concept of habitus to explore processes of residential sifting and change. We have seen how professional households may find the relatively low-status nature of the housing stock and residents against their taste, and will therefore tend to move (though we have also seen how some professionals may come to terms with this). We can also detect a complex interplay between the long-term Cheadle residents and those moving out of Manchester. The latter view moving to Cheadle as a sign of upward social mobility, but their movement to Cheadle tends to confirm in the long-term residents their belief that the status of the estate has declined (see generally on the significance of internal boundary drawing within working-class area) (Elias and Scotson 1985). It is thus quite possible to explore dynamic features within the practical habitus we have identified, and to recognise tensions with other kinds of habitus that some residents bring.

Let us now turn to a second, broader, issue concerning our understanding of the 'practical' habitus on display in the area. Contrary to the rather bleak portrait painted by Charlesworth, most respondents were not desperate or hopeless. This was not just due to the fact that they were not in absolute poverty. It was also due to their moderate pride in possessing manual, practical skills that earned them not only a living but also degrees of self-respect. Cheadle respondents were remarkably resourceful in 'getting-by', drawing on the resources of manual skills, hard work, the social support of neighbours, kin and workmates, and had adapted to Post-Fordist economic arrangements with remarkable perspicacity. The issue here is the perennial difficulty of understanding this practical habitus through the lens of intellectualised (and thereby culturally privileged) academic research. We have emphasised the lack of clear fit between discursive class-consciousness and class identities and people's practical feelings and values. Most individuals' sense of themselves is detached from ideas about class which they see as external and as pertaining to political and public discourse, but which are the staple of academic inquiry. It is precisely this lack of fit which has allowed academics in the past to use the working class as vehicles for their (often very challenging and important) intellectual projects. Even though we regard Bourdieu's approach as the most valuable in recognising this issue (e.g. Bourdieu 1999b), he can also be criticised for viewing the popular classes from the lens of academic reflection and not being attentive to the real cultural significance of practical, skilled, lives (see Chapter 4).

Whilst we have argued that the practical habitus is not a desperate or hopeless one, it is the case that respondents recognise it as a culture of unending work and toil. The respondents here do not feel stigmatised, in the way Skeggs finds for her sample of young women (1997), and are frequently proud of their achievements. There is plenty of evidence for the 'inverting' of middle-class cultural frames amongst our sample, with local residents making a moral virtue out of their reliance on practical skills and their capacity to 'get by'. At the same time, in their utopian and fatalistic belief that the only way out comes from the chance workings of the lottery reveals a deep rooted view that life could be better.

Finally, in conclusion, we have to emphasise the indeterminate nature of our findings. One rendering of our research is that the practical habitus we have detected in Cheadle has a long history, and may also have a long future, given ongoing needs for ongoing manual skills. Another interpretation, however, would argue that we are perhaps picking up the last generation of craft-skilled workers, and that this habitus may be in decline (see Savage 2000). It is perhaps not incidental that building work, which still requires handicraft skills, dominates in the area, but that there is very little demand for skills from any kind of industry or service.

Notes

1. These are only a selective list of some of the key work of this period: other possible candidates for inclusion would include Jackson and Marsden's (1962) *Education and the Working class,* and Beynon's (1975) *Working for Ford.* It might also be argued that at about the same time British literature, television and film also gained their international reputation through equivalent kinds of narratives of the working class (see Hill 1986; Rowbotham and Beynon 2001).

2. A good discussion of these studies is still Johnson 1979.
3. It is interesting to note that Skeggs's emphasis on capital allows her to see the difficulties of working-class women in terms of their relationships to those with capital, whilst Charlesworth's emphasis on habitus leads him to focus on the limitations of the dispositions and values of the working class itself. Against his own intentions, perhaps, Charlesworth's account could be appropriated by those arguing that the working class cannot help themselves and need to be coerced back into mainstream social values.
4. This marks significant changes from even the 1970s when the action of urban gatekeepers (local authority officers, mortgage lenders, etc.) was a crucial device in the creation of urban segregation. Such forces continue to operate today, but in a much reduced way due to the de-regulation of financial lending and the declining proportion of the housing stock in public (or other social) hands.
5. 'Lifestyles and social integration: a study of middle class culture in Manchester', Ref number R 000 23 6929.
6. ONS Social Class classification is adopted here. Employment is taken for last occupation if the respondent is retired or unemployed. There are 36 conjugal households (composed of male and female partners) three sole female households, two sole male households, and two other types of household.
7. These include one male teacher living by himself; a household of two civil servants; a household with a male research radiographer and female carer; a household with a male computer software worker and a female employee in medical services; a household with a male local authority housing manager and a female part-time nurse; and a household with a male electronic engineer and a female education officer. Also included here is a household with a male university lecturer in biomechanics (but whose background is in mechanical engineering) and a woman teacher, and a household with male CCTV engineer and female part-time worker. Both these latter cases have strong engineering elements which might be deemed to give them something in common with the manual culture of the area, but they are included here because they have no direct experience of manual work.
8. This means that they stated that they were brought up in Stockport, Gatley, Cheadle Hulme, Edgeley, Davenport or Hilgate.
9. Who had been brought up in Birkenhead.
10. Depending on the age of the respondent, they tended to have either living parents or children no longer living at home.
11. On some occasions more than one household member wanted to be interviewed, and we went along with this, taking care to record the views of both household members. Here *M* refers to James and *F* to Deidre.

6
Memory Magic: How a Working-Class Neighbourhood Became an Imagined Community and Class Started to Matter when it Lost its Base

Talja Blokland[1]

Introduction

Only two people waited in line at the butcher's shop. A third man ate a local speciality that only small, traditional butchers carry. Since the ethnic minorities arrived in this neighbourhood, business had declined, the butcher explained: "The migrants don't want my meat because of their religion." Born and raised here, the butcher had taken over the shop from his father-in-law over 20 years ago. The chewing customer used to be a shop-owner here, too. He had given up after "twenty burglaries and three robberies". The neighbourhood decayed so much, it drove him crazy. He now had a nice house in a suburb, where he "withered". Everyday he returned to the shopping street. It used to be a good place to live, they agreed. "You never locked the front door. People popped in and out each other's houses. There was trust. Everybody knew each other. No one could rob you at daylight without anybody helping you, back then."

This encounter took place in Hillesluis, an inner city neighbourhood on the Southern bank of the river that cuts right through Rotterdam, The Netherlands. Hillesluis was built for migrants that came from surrounding towns and villages to work in the expanding docks and shipbuilding in the early 20th century.

One can hear such conversations in many urban areas where social problems concentrate. The notion of a working-class community that older residents retrospectively construct often suggests that they derived a sense of being working class, and being this *together*, from the neighbourhood as such. When these residents address change, they smoothly move from talking about *similar* to *shared* norms, values and life styles, and find explanations in class: "we were all working class". That the move from *similar* to *shared* is sociologically problematic reveals the discussion on objective social situations and their subjective perceptions.

When we fill out surveys, we are often forced to think about ethnicity, class and race as pre-given boxes in which we fit or don't. But when we classify ourselves in the "practical sociologies" (Lemert 1995) of everyday life, class and social identity are not as simply linked as the phrase "please tick the box what is your social class" suggests. That people identify themselves as members of a certain class, ethnic or religious group cannot *a priori* be equated with how they socially engage with others. In other words, a sense of community, belongingness, togetherness or solidarity is not an *automatic* result of how people categorise themselves.[2]

Naturally, this debate in its broadest form has received attention ever since Marx (cf. Williams 1976): Is class a matter of "broad aggregates of people which can be classified together by an objective criterion" (Hobsbawm 1984: 15) or does class in "the full sense only comes into existence at the historical moment when classes begin to acquire consciousness of themselves as such" (Hobsbawm 1984)? To sociologists, Lockwood's well-known "Sources of variation in working class images of society" (1975) has triggered much discussion on how workers can be differentiated. Lockwood contrasted several types of workers according to what he saw as their situational interpretations. Williams' (1976: 66–67) explanation of the origins of the term "class" discloses how class has an inherent duality as category and formation. Class formation where categories become collectivities raises questions as how we know collectivities exist (Savage 1996: 65–66) and how "socio-cultural" class formation and "political" class formation are linked (idem: 67–70). Urban areas like Hillesluis are sites of making and unmaking class (cf. Savage 1996: 65), both culturally and organisationally but, as we will see, always partially.

The image of decaying neighbourhoods as once local, close-knit, working-class communities is often inaccurate (Lis and Soly 1993; Scherzer 1992) and reflects the representations of those who dominated discourses at the time and are now used as sources (Behagg 1986). Increasingly, historians show that no one "working class culture" existed by the very fact that culture does not have unambiguous meanings (Kirk

1991: 211) and that divisions characterised such neighbourhoods along lines of ethnicity (Walton 1987: 183, 254), gender (Davies 1992: 2, 30–54) and religion (Moore 1975; Walton 1987: 184–188), so that "the relationship between neighbourhood loyalities and class feeling is difficult to establish" (Davies *et al.* 1992: 15–16). Sociologists also demonstrate that "the working class" is and was far less homogeneous than the label suggests (Dennis *et al.* 1956: 17; Beynon and Austin 1994: 187–188; see for an overview Devine 1992a). They discuss its "internal" differences (cf. Lockwood 1975: 16–18; Frankenberg 1966: 262; Bulmer 1975a,b; Devine 1992a; Crompton 1998) and reflect on why the vision of homogeneous, clearly bound classes is so powerful and political (Williams 1976: 62; Cannadine 1999: 139–193).

This chapter discusses social constructions of the neighbourhood Hillesluis as one working-class community when people collectively remember. It confronts this with their individual stories about ambivalence, social distinctions, and categorical divisions. The latter indicates that this neighbourhood hardly was one community of shared beliefs and values that all identified with.

Everyday life, Wright remarks (1985: 14), is full of stories: "these are concerned with being-in-the-world rather than abstractly defined truth [...] [E]ven when they are told of times past, stories are judged and shaped by their relevance to what is happening now, and in this sense their allegiance is unashamedly to the present." As we will see, listening to people recalling the past reveals the magic in memory: memories turn colours, change their features, all depending on who tells them and whom they are told to. What accounts for this magic? Why do magicians adjust, change and recreate their stories?[3]

I suggest that collective remembering is a process of social identification in which the notion of one working-class community serves as a foundation for inclusion and exclusion along lines of race, ethnicity and generations. I discuss this against the backdrop of social changes, and argue that class started to matter when it lost its structural basis to the people involved.[4] Through empirical examples, I hope to argue that this is linked to exclusion and inclusion and symbolic power over space.

This chapter draws on data collected in Hillesluis, Rotterdam, The Netherlands, in 1994–95. I moved into the area for a year and collected material by participant observation, interviews with (former) residents and professionals, and archival research.[5] From the late 1960s to the 1990s, Hillesluis slowly became an ethnically mixed area (Table 6.1), with a low average income, high unemployment rate and low level of education compared to the rest of the city. It became known as a multi-problem

Table 6.1 Residents by ethnic classification, 1995 (percentages)

	Slaghek neighbourhood	Rieder neighbourhood	Walraven neighbourhood
Surinam	14.9	11.5	12.2
Netherlands Antilles	4.1	4.5	4.1
Cape Verde	3.3	1.7	1.5
Turkey	28.7	20.2	10.5
Morocco	13.9	8.7	11.4
Other non-Dutch	14.7	20.4	23.9
Dutch	20.4	33.0	36.4

Source: Centrum voor Onderzoek en Statistiek, 1996 (COS 1991–6).

area. One of its problems was its lack of cohesion – politicians, policy makers and some residents said so. In their view, the ethnic heterogeneity lay at the roots of this lack of cohesion: whereas people used to identify with their neighbours as a "real working class" community (*lit. "een echt arbeidersbuurtje"*), the basis for such sense of community had been challenged once the migrants came.

Telling stories: some preliminary notes

Social identifications

Telling stories is central to social identifications. I follow Jenkins in his *Social Identity* (1996) that, first, social identities of individuals exist in continuous processes of establishing, maintaining and changing them. Therefore, I prefer social identifications over social identities to stress the processual character (cf. De Swaan 1995: 25). Social identifications, then, are processes in which people experience and express that some are like them, and that some others are different. These similarities and differences render the base for affective connection with those people whom one experiences as similar (ibid.).

Secondly, I follow Jenkins' link between social identity and community. "Who we are" is not so much a matter of "objective" categorisations – ticking that box in the questionnaire, finding your occupation in the list of eight categories – but of *doing* community:

saying this or that, participating in rituals, mounting political protest, fishing together, or whatever. It is in and out of what people *do* that a shared sense of things and a shared symbolic universe emerge. It is in talking together about "community" – which is, after all, a public *doing* – that its symbolic value is produced and reproduced. (Jenkins 1996: 106)

Collective memory

Telling stories *together* is not merely recalling the past. What people tell about the past at least as much about people nowadays construct a meaningful social reality (Leijdesdorff 1987: 27; Thompson 1988: 102; cf. Gans 1962: 73; Fentress and Wickham 1992: x). We can view collective memory simultaneously in two ways. First, collective memory can be a *shared* memory: a tale of past events that members of a social group construct. Not the event, but the process of together recalling it makes it collective. Secondly, collective memories can form a collective "mind": a container of stories about the past that one does not need to have lived through personally (Van der Ree 1995). Such a container positions its possessors as group. It contributes to cultural group cohesion (Merton 1949: 370), especially when what is cherished is related to objects and places that the group has lived with for long times (Wright 1985: 230). As such, the container helps to include and exclude.

Tales of community: how "we" were all "the same"

Hillesluisers often said to each other that "It just all changed around here." What changed was "the unity", "being together among each other". "The neighbourhood used to be *gezellig*". *Gezelligheid* is a common Dutch term for a combination of sociability and conviviality.

In specifications what they meant by *gezellig*, residents stressed the socio-economic equality of past times ("everybody was poor"), the cultural homogeneity ("everybody was in agreement" or "you all more or less had similar ideas"), the solidarity ("people were kindly disposed to one another", "people helped each other out") and the lack of moral ambiguity ("everybody knew how to behave"). The *together remembered* neighbourhood was, in other words, a socio-economical, cultural and moral homogeneous and solidary community.

Even relative strangers could be encountered constructing such a shared past. Two elderly women who met regularly over coffee at McDonalds usually started telling each other how badly deteriorated the area was and how nice it used to be. They watched the shopping street, sipping their coffees. A drug addict drifting about, teenagers boisterously impressing each other, girls in short skirts and tight shirts mooching, or a newspaper story of a robbery triggered the key sentence "you didn't have that in the past". Generally, three elements informed the conversation:

bad behaviour of today's youth, little they could expect from children and grandchildren, and the dangers of going out. After stating that in the past everybody was poor but supportive, stories followed. One lady told the other how her neighbour helped her when she was seriously ill, the other told at her turn how she helped the next-door family when her neighbour died. They recalled that "everybody" blinded the windows with sheets when a neighbour died ("Remember? But if we drop dead tomorrow, we can lie there dead a couple of days and no one is going to notice") and talked about the Second World War when it was hard to make ends meet but people "always" helped each other.

Such conversations carried an implicit notion of class, combined with gender and generation. When sharing stories about the past, such as at McDonalds, people who did not know each other otherwise, and had never met each other's family, been to each other's houses or interacted in other parts of life, assumed an equal position or *Lagerung* (Mannheim 1996: 120–123) within the economic and power structure of a society. The stories' focus on care, support and survival strategies of working-class housewives in harsh times reinforced such gendered similarity. One does not need to have belonged to the same network then to be part of a *Lagerung* now that connects a class position with positions of age, gender and stage in life cycle.

Differences mattered a lot in everyday life when one was younger no longer weighted heavily in finding partners in remembering. One seemed keen to assume that the walk of life of the conversation partner had been roughly similar. Collective remembering then contained a lot of "binding power". But individual stories showed another picture.

Tales of distinction: how "we" compared to "them"

Hillesluis always contained diverse socio-economic categories. Before the Second World War, income differences were spatially expressed. A monthly rent required a monthly salary, as paid to white-collar workers: clerks, accountant assistants, the school's headmaster and some railroad foremen. Certain self-employed people (a hairdresser, a corner shop-owner, a housepainter, a woman with lodgers, some license-holders of pubs) lived in houses with monthly leases.[6] Skilled and unskilled workers and the unemployed lived in streets with weekly rents. Local shop-owners did not necessarily earn more than labourers and depended on them for clientele. They did not stand out much.[7] As a woman who runs a diary shop said: "we were simple, working class, just like the whole lot".

But what was "working class"? A category or also a formation? And only *one*? Did class-based *catnets* (categories×networks, White quoted in Tilly

1984) of people who shared local shops, pubs and workplaces evoke the experience of community?

Differences on the shopfloor

Historians argue that the division of respectable and rough working class has incorrectly been associated with a labour aristocracy (Walton 1987: 249–251; Davies 1992: 2–4), although contemporaries involved in charities or housing for workers liked to classify this way (de Regt 1984; Kidd and Roberts 1985; von Saldern 1990; McKenna 1991).[8] Hillesluisers who worked in docks and shipyards made similar distinctions.

At the shipyard Piet Smit, adjacent to the neighbourhood, former workers said "everybody was a worker", but not everybody was "the same", as has been reported in other studies. Manual workers separated themselves from the "little offices" (*kantoortjes*). People in the office were "a different kind of people".

Nor were "blue overalls" all equal. Status differences coincided with job descriptions. Better-paid "craftsmen" like bench workers saw themselves as different from riveters. They exported their job status to wider life style classifications. Riveters had tough work, and therefore they were "rough men" (*ruwe mannen*) or "coarse people" (*grof volk*). One needed strength for this job. A "thin little lad" (*schriel ventje*) could not do it. Outside the factory, riveters were coarse in their speech, liked a fight and tended to bring their wage to the pub instead of to mum.[9]

Moreover, all might have been workers, religious differences separate them in everyday socialising on the shopfloor, a retired employee recalled:

> On Monday morning, you saw cliques on the shopfloor, from this church or that church, or a few football supporters. Over there, they stood talking about the [zoek op: preek] of this [dominee], on the other side you had another group talking about their [dominee], and then the lads who discussed the match of the Sunday. As long as we've had the factory, it has always been like that. As soon as they got a chance on Monday morning, they looked for their own kind.

Religion was an important category for differentiation in individual stories far beyond the shopfloor.

Differences in categorical practices

How people formed their social networks *and* a "we" in opposition to otherness depended on *categorically organised practices*. As class, so was religion an organisational category.

Hillesluisers' religious affiliations were always diverse. Pre-war parish records show in the 1930s an estimated 30 per cent Protestants (Calvinist, Reformists, Dutch Reformed) and approximately 10 per cent to Catholics. In the national elections of 1935, 47 per cent voted social democratic, 6 per cent communist, 15 per cent Catholic and 20 per cent Protestant.[10]

Regional backgrounds accounted for these differences (Van Dijk 1976; Valten 1988). Orthodox Protestant Zealanders typically wore black dresses and white caps or black suits. Men specialised in specific jobs. The little shop-owners who sold hot water and utilities for laundry (the "boilerman"), and men who kept carriages often came from Zealand. Migrants from Brabant were typically Catholics. Initially they worked manual jobs. Gradually they too opened shops. Up to the late 1950s it was said to be common practice to shop "at one's own faith". In the newsletters of the Dutch-Reformed Church only Dutch-Reformed retailers advertised. When Catholics organised a fair, Catholic shopkeepers supported.

These all related to the specific Dutch socio-political organisation in which coalitions across religion were made in the upper layers of society, but in which vertical integration was maintained through a system of "compartmentalisation" (Lijpahrt 1968). Difference organised social life: from clubs, voluntary organisations and schools, to newspapers and radio channels (Bosmans 1988: 399). *Catnets* got among people of one denomination, who had similar life-rhythms and met each other on all sorts of occasions. The *catnet* thus was organisationally and culturally cohesive.

In the early 20th century, maintaining this cohesion seemed more important than keeping people inside the church. When the daughters of a Calvinist had cycled on Sunday their father got an official warning: would it happen again, then he would be expelled (Van Zuylen 1966). Charity helped reaffirming this cohesion. Poor people who read a Catholic newspaper got clothing coupons and those who did not did not get. To receive food aid with Christmas, poor Catholics must attend Mass regularly. The networks provided support beyond the church. When Mr Hoogeboom (born 1916) left school, he was unemployed:

> Well, if you didn't have a job, you went to the minister. We had heard about that. He would take care [...] There was someone, Mr. Wit, he was a church member, and a foreman at Piet Smit. [The minister] said, "are you without a job", I said "yes". "Make sure to be at Piet Smit tomorrow morning at 7. And wait for Mr. Wit'. So the next morning I went off to Piet Smit. Mr. Wit came. He said, "what are you here for?" You see, you knew them from the church. I said, "the

minister said I had to come down here this morning to see you." I said, "and here I am". He said, "go inside. Go to the storage room, I'll be right with you." So I went. He came and he said to the man there, "register this boy, will you. He can start working right away."

For some, networks consisted exclusively of people of their group. Others were strangers, and a little exciting: young Protestant boys went to "watch the communists" when they were striking and rioting with the police. Mrs Vranken (born 1910) told about her Protestant youth:

> You were raised protectively. You remained in your own circle [...]
> [A]t that time the Calvinist interpretation was the only correct one
> [...] So everything that wasn't Calvinist wasn't necessarily weird, but
> they didn't fit...that wasn't pure (*zuiver*).

So the categorical organisation of those practices, from all walking to church at the same time to playing in the same football team, influenced people's network formation. Class then was not the only, and may be for some not even the most, salient category for social identifications.

Differences in respectability

That differently oriented religious and political groups in the neighbourhood did not form one community in the compartmentalised Netherlands might hardly be surprising. But not all social distinctions run along categorical lines.

Knowing your neighbours was more common than today. But knowing them does not imply social identification. Knowing one's neighbours resulted from time spent locally.

One walked to factories, pubs, churches and leisure-societies. For the weekly bath when few houses had a hot water tap, one went to the "boilerman" for hot water or to the public bath. Local shops were frequented every few days in times without refrigerators. Door-to-door vendors brought women out in the street on fixed moments. So people came across the same people frequently at the same spots. These meetings did not result automatically in friendly contacts. They led to *public familiarity*: mutual recognition of others as neighbours with visible, specific ways of living. This public familiarity fostered social identifying *and* disidentifying, creating communities, as examples will illustrate.

Distinctions, based on tidiness and hygienics, "respectability" of poverty, hanging out the window and sitting on doorsteps, all draw on some distinction of "good" and "bad" people that sometimes coincided with slight socio-economic differences.

Mr Van Vliet, born 1936, was a grocer's son. His family always bathed at home. His mother disliked the public bath:

> Those who went to the public bath were looked at as a bit wrong. Not just by us, but by the more decent people in the neighbourhood, those who did not go to the public bath. People of less social standing went to the public bath [...] We were grocers. And although we felt very much at home in the working-class district, we didn't really belong to it. Or let me put it differently, we went along OK with the neighbors, and all went very well, but for our own feeling we belonged to a different standing, the ones who did not go to the public bath. Let me put it that way.

So did Aunt Liesje (1922), married to a worker of a milk plant:

> It was no fun there. You did not know what went in there, you see, you better scrubbed it thoroughly before you could take a shower. No, no, we were not that kind of people.

The weekly laundry was hung out drying on balconies, roofs or backyards. Good housewives had snow-white laundry. A mother remembered neighbours joking amongst each other about her not-so-spotless children's clothes.

Clean and intact clothes were very important, regardless of poverty. Poor people did not have to drink, gamble, make debts, cheat one's partner, curse or be unclean. In this way, residents who considered themselves poor but respectable differentiated their community from people of lesser standing. A man remembered he felt "lower" as a child than neighbourhood kids because they lived "decently", while his father drank. A woman whose husband was an alcoholic remembered she was uncomfortable going out on Monday, after her husband had hit the bottle a bit too much in the weekend, as "everybody would gaze" at her and gossip behind her back. Mr Van Gastel, born 1930, illustrated his family was "respectable poor":

> There were people who got welfare benefits but didn't provide for their families. They were rough, they only [...] drank away their sorrows, and their children were bums, naturally, they went stealing

at the market. It started off with their situation at home. 'Cause even being poor didn't mean you could not live respectably.'

People who gossiped too much had less standing than people who minded their own business. Negative gossip cannot be separated structurally from praise-gossip (Elias and Scotson 1985), but Hillesluisers differentiated gossip from slander. Slander was associated with hanging out of the window all day, trying to find out about everything, popping in and out of people's houses and sitting on the doorstep, practices considered "not decent".

In histories of working class, boundaries between the private home and the public sphere are sometimes said to have been blurred or non-existing. But Hillesluisers spent much time outdoors motivated by a strong sense of privacy. People who allowed others "into their whole business" were seen as less respectable than residents who only discussed private problems with intimates.

As these examples illustrate, in a sphere of public familiarity many residents knew quite a lot about the visible everyday practices of their neighbours. They used this knowledge to delineate their own imagined community in opposition to others' communities.

Change: the end of work and community as "we" knew it

Both in individual and in collective stories, broader changes lured in the background, although they were rarely addressed explicitly. Immigration, economic restructuring, de-compartmentalisation and technological advancement resulted in more mobility, less local public familiarity, and a fundamental change in the notion of "working class". There is much to be said about all these changes, but only some short remarks can be made here.

For all the divisions and cleavages, Hillesluis had seen a few big employers, with Piet Smit's shipyard as the central one, and the closure of factories and displacement of harbours closer to the seashore and further removed from the residential areas, had changed the *localness* of being a working-class person. Economic globalisation had effects on Rotterdam as international transit city. Both job growth from 100,000 in 1947 to 338,000 in 1966, with 20 per cent employed in industry and construction, and decrease to now 294,750 jobs with 15.5 per cent in these sectors reflected global developments in trade and industrialisation (Wiggers *et al.* 1975: 564). There is, for example, hardly any shipbuilding left since Japan became the world's leader in this industry (cf. Roberts

1993). Rotterdam is not a "standard" postindustrial city (Mollenkopf and Castells 1991; Sassen 1991), because there is not a large group of rich people and underpaid workforce in the service sector to attend to their needs (Burgers 2000). Even though the harbour still is a major source of employment, technological innovations have altered the nature of this work, and of the identity of workers, fundamentally over the past 100 years. Indeed, due to economic restructuring of the employed residents many still worked in low-paid jobs, but service-sector jobs had gained importance, factory work was less often skilled work of craftsmen and more often temporary work at the running belt.

Immigration (see Figure 6.1) has made "ethnicity" a factor of importance that it historically never was. Regional differences could hardly be said to define "ethnic groups". As we will see, ethnic diversity is critical to how people presently constructed the image of a community-of-all in the past.

Religion lost its significance from the 1950s onwards. The Netherlands has become one of the most secularised countries, so that this dividing line no longer mattered to most current residents.[11] This also resulted from the de-compartmentalisation and professionalisation of community, health and social services (Hueting 1989; Neij 1989; Oudenaarden 1995). *Forgetting* or *omitting* the history of compartmentali-

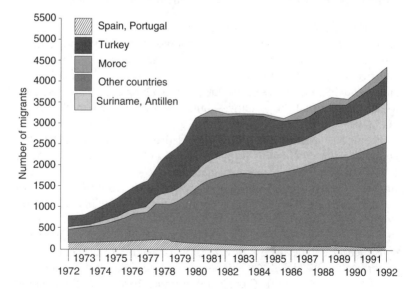

Figure 6.1   The changing ethnic mix of Hillesluis, 1972–92

sation in collective memories had become easy now that the relevance of such compartments for everyday life practices had eroded.

That such changes matter, even though they remain unspoken, is obvious. "Experience of the social structure is mediated through the individual's attitudes and expectations, based upon his own historical experience", Roderick and Fryer argued (1975: 114), "Explanations [...] in a-historical terms, whether the structure of the work-place or of the community, are inadequate. Images of society are not only a product of present milieux, but of present milieux interpreted in the light of past experience and expectations for the future, individual and collective."

One of the results of changes has been that social identifications take place in a different framework. Through the lens of this present situation socially identifying has become hard for those who once belonged to "the working class" and are now retired, redundant, and living in a renovated but changed neighbourhood where native Dutch are now one of the many minorities.

Tales of marking borders: how class matters versus ethnicity

When they then together constructed their image of the past neighbourhood, the power of bonding was stronger than the power of differentiation. O'Byrne (1997: 73–74) argued that the identity of "being working class" is only constructed in reference to; first, an objective structure of material conditions, physical location and flows of people; second, a normative structure of values and traditions; and third, the interaction of people and cultures within the locality.

This is illustrated in the reception of an exposition in the 15-year-old "neighbourhood museum", an initiative of the residents' organisation. The exhibition focussed on the migration of the first residents from Zealand and Brabant. It drew comparisons to today's immigrants to create understanding for cultural diversity within the community worker's discourse of tolerance. It stressed that in the early days the neighbourhood also had a variety of customs and habits, and that everybody had been a "stranger" at some point.

Several elderly interpreted this differently. They applied this migration history to argue that the newcomers of today needed to adapt to the dominant Dutch culture, *as we all did*. Instead of socially identifying with a tolerant multi-cultural and inclusive community, they used the exhibition to stress how diverse people of the past had all quickly "become one and the same" of this "working-class neighbourhood" and how migrants today failed to do so.

When people imagine the working-class community in contrast with their contemporary environment, these are not "false representations", but "part of the process of constructing an operative symbolic and social reality" (cf. Cohen 1992: 80). Especially women who used the neighbourhood space intensively for socialising saw their localism particularly challenged, so they felt, by new residents who used the same space. Local power relations make localism "the result of (class) cultural practices which, in many cases, produce a conscious resistance to external forces and a mistrust and rejection of globalist values in favour of defence of local activity" (O'Byrne 1997: 74).

A conflict over a square showed that here women framed their experiences in a juxtaposition of class against ethnicity, and connected to a localism and notion of "ownership" of space. The women who lived at the square did not appreciate that Moroccan teenagers played football there. A community worker and youth-worker noticed complaints. They organised meetings for all involved to re-design the layout of the square, assuming that bringing them together could solve the problem. The women wondered why the boys should have a say at all: They did "not belong to the square". They felt entitled to adoption of the boys to *them*, the powerful and symbolic owners of the space. Meanwhile, they also had a sense of powerlessness.

They did not believe that the "social control" could be "re-established", as the professionals hoped to achieve. While we were out on the square, some Moroccan children reacted more than once rude when one of the women, Tonnie, corrected them for vandalising. They told her to get lost, and wait for the day "you have to listen to *us*". Such incidents made Tonnie fear that "eventually the Dutch will have nothing to say anymore":

> There are a lot of things that I think, they should root those out, because we will have nothing to say. They will have the power [...] because they themselves go around screaming, in a number of years, then we will be in power and you will have nothing to say whatsoever.

TB: What do you have now that you think you might loose?
Tonnie: "In the past, I did not have anything to say either, *but the culture was different, isn't it? It was more one, really.* Nowadays, when you are waiting in a shop, they give you a bloody prod with their shoppingcart, because they want to go first. [...] The foreigner wants to reign over us by putting us aside, because they need to be served first. No! We all

politely wait our turns, as we all learnt that. They don't need to act like I want this, I want this. Because we all have to wait, *and we all have to work hard for our money.* (my italics)

As in the reactions to the exhibition, we see here that Tonnie expresses a belief in a lost cultural homogeneity, and indicates that migrants, in her opinion, think of themselves as *better*, and act as if they deserve better than others. By her statement "We all have to work for our money" Tonnie seems to suggest that eventually the immigrants are not anything else but working class, something "ordinary" and nothing special, but that they exclude themselves and thus disintegrate any possible local community by their very ways of living. More strongly, this can be found in the words of a socially mobile woman, whose father never held a regular job, who married the son of a school's headmaster who had his own plumbing firm: "Then they say, they come from a simple milieu", and then I think, "Oh well, thank you very much, I come from a simple milieu, but I have never *acted so stupidly.*"

Thus the recalled past when "we were all labourers" juxtaposes a similarity of class versus a dissimilarity of ethnicity, while the cultural differences of immigrants – rather than any of the broader social change – became a cause for the fact that this community is lost.

For residents with the most localised life styles, this creation of symbolic defences or boundaries "to replace the structural boundaries now transformed or undermined by social change" (Cohen 1986: 7) was most important. The together constructed notion of the lost community served as a means "to contrive a sense of collective self" for these residents "in response to penetration or subversion of their structural boundaries" (Cohen 1986: 8).

Practice of exclusion: how a working-class neighbourhood became an imagined community

Having spent their younger years in the neighbourhood connected the remembering people *more* than the social distinctions that kept them apart in times past. In a neighbourhood under change they developed a mutual social identification of a *Lagerung*, formulated in opposition to immigrants and youngsters.

Everyone who cannot participate in the collective enterprise of remembering is an outsider, as Lash (1991: 104) argued. At community events, such as the fortnightly bingo in the community house, talk about the past and recalling memories of shared experiences was a secret language to those who had not been present at those times and a powerful mechanism of exclusion.

Small stories about the neighbourhood in which one person added to the story of another and "everybody" knew what it was about were overarched by the myth of the *gezelligheid* based on equality and similarity. Implicitly, such references to the lost *gezelligheid* were exclusionary mechanisms in the presence of outsiders. It suggested that: "*we* who have lived here all our lives and *who own this neighbourhood* had a better time amongst each other when it was 'only us'. *You*, new arrivals, are, in other words, the cause why it is no longer as *gezellig* here as it used to be, and you don't know how *gezellig* it was, because you were not around."

Through such mechanisms, newcomers such as migrants remained outsiders, and the memories of the good old times did their magic in not only creating a collective history of a working-class community, but also constructed a *contemporary* imagined community to whom some belonged, and some could socially identify with, while others certainly could not.

Conclusion

Several Hillesluisers thus gave detailed accounts in individual interviews of how, up to the late 1950s, they did not interact with certain other residents because of their habits, religion, or social status, constructing a historically divided neighbourhood. Meanwhile, the same people used local facilities as meeting points to produce new local networks and to search for social identifications with others that they presumably would have ignored fifty years ago. They hence imagined a community by developing a sense of "we all are working class".

Rather than in opposition to middle class, this articulation of the neighbourhood as a working-class community reconstructed working class in opposition to immigrants. The immigrants came and our working class disappeared: observing those two changes, class and ethnicity became, as bases for identifying oneself, one's community and "others", intertwined within that space called "neighbourhood".

Notes

1. This is a revision of "Where class does not unite" presented at the ESRC-seminar, Manchester, 16 April 1999. I thank Fiona Devine, Rosemary Mellor and Tim Strangleman for their helpful comments. The first drafts of this paper were prepared while I enjoyed a fellowship of the Niels Stensen Stichting.
2. In Merton's framework (1949: 299–300), a group is not a collectivity.

3. The question *how* people construct such memories is discussed in Blokland 2001.
4. Due to space limits, I will need to take shortcuts in the presentation of the empirical material that supports my argument. More material is discussed in Blokland-Potters 1998. This study was published in English by Polity in 2003.
5. See Blokland-Potters 1998 for methodological details.
6. Source: Adresboek Algemene Beroepen en Bedrijven, 1920, 1924, 1928, 1940, Gemeente Archief Rotterdam (GAR), and interviews.
7. Cf. Davies, who argues that such shop-owners had to conform to neigh-bourhood life dominated by "working class customs and attitudes" (1992: 3). Walton points out that for labourers a shop, or work in a co-op – Hillesluis had two co-ops – often was the first step of social mobility (1987: 307).
8. Roberts (1995), using oral histories, finds a connection between job status and respectability, whereas Davies (1992), using similar methods, denies such a connection.
9. Compare similar findings of extrapolation of difference on the shopfloor to differences in life styles, Warner *et al.* (1949: 108).
10. Sources: Schreurs (1962: 45), KAKSI Parochistatistiek, *Ons Kerkblad*, 15^e jaargang nr.2, *60 Jaar H. Kruisvindingsparochie 1923–1983*, Archief Meertens, ADR, inv.nr.84. Other sources used in this section: *Gereformeerde kerkbode*, 1936–58, Bouman & Bouman 1952, Van Zuylen 1966 and interviews.
11. Secularisation had not just resulted from the urbanisation. As Hobsbawm (1984: 45) has pointed out, the city might have eroded formal religious practices, but much industrial development took place in small-scale communities where religion was, and remains strong.

7

Middle-Class Identities in the United States

Fiona Devine

Critics of 'class analysis' have frequently argued that the absence of class consciousness, and specifically working-class consciousness, undermines the view that America is structured by class. The most recent exponent of this view is Kingston whose book, *The Classless Society* (2000), has been much admired. Kingston argues that class sentiments are weak since evidence indicates that people's objective class position and their subjective class identification are poorly related. He notes that when Americans are asked to identify their class positions using a fixed choice format which includes the category working class, Americans divide themselves almost equally between the middle class and working class. These findings indicate that self-identification with the working class is strong. Kingston casts doubt, however, on whether these findings are indicative of a high degree of working-class consciousness in any meaningful sense. In contrast, when people are presented with an open-ended class identification question where they have a free choice on their use of class labels, most working-class people identify with the middle class. These findings suggest that Americans tend to place themselves into an all-embracing middle class. Kingston concludes that membership of a class does not generate similar class sentiments either through the workplace or in the wider community. America, therefore, is a classless society.

Kingston's style of argument is brash and assertive which makes the book, initially at least, an engaging and challenging read. A close reading of the book, however, reveals it is a polemical reinterpretation of mostly old evidence. More importantly, the argument is rather out-dated in the way in which it attempts to close down sociological interest and research into class subjectivities and class more generally in America.

Class location does not generate class identity that does not, in turn, sustain class action. Thus, there is no story to tell about class in America, full stop! It has, of course, long been known that working-class identification is low in the US in comparison to, say, Britain. What Kingston fails to consider is that Americans use the language of class when they identify themselves with the middle class. Drawing on a comparative project of American and British doctors and teachers, this chapter considers how middle-class Americans use the language of class, the label of being middle class (and other class labels) and what they mean when they identify with a class. The next section reviews previous debates on class consciousness and class identification in the US. In contrast to Kingston's narrow discussion of class identification in the US, there is a body of theoretically and empirically informed research on class subjectivities which has examined working-class and middle-class identities. The interplay between, gender, racial and ethnic identities with class identities is also addressed. The evidence suggests that peoples everyday experiences in school, in jobs, in the communities in which they grew up and the ones in which they now live generate and sustain class sentiments and the lived experience of class shapes people's cultural values and practices.

The second section discusses the empirical material on which the rest of the chapter is based. The research involved in-depth interviews with doctors and teachers in the US and the UK as part of a wider comparative study of how middle-class parents guide their children through the education system into 'good' jobs thereby reproducing intergenerational class stability. How the research was conducted is discussed in the context of the long-standing controversy that sociologists' predispositions about the salience of class in people's lives has influenced how they have questioned ordinary folk about class and the conclusions they have reached about class identities (Grusky and Sorensen 1998: 1196). Discomfort and unease with an explicit discussion of class in pilot interviews in Britain led me to drop a direct question about the interviewees' family class position when they were growing up in preference for an indirect question requesting a description of their childhood standard of living. Many of the British interviewees from seemingly middle-class origins were silent about their class position although some used the language of class. All of those from working-class origin made reference to their working-class backgrounds. In sharp contrast, virtually all of the American interviewees discussed their family standard of living explicitly in class terms whatever their class origins. Such frequent use of the language of class is very surprising since it is the British who are supposed to be obsessed with class. What is unsurprising, however, is that most of the American interviewees described their family background as middle class although distinctions within the middle class were made.

The third and fourth sections focus specifically on how the American interviewees used the language of class to describe their family standard of living when they were growing up. It also draws on other explicit references to class by the interviewees when they discussed their own education, their work histories and how they were helping their children through the school system into good jobs. The third section focuses on the interviewees who categorized themselves as middle class. While most of the informants considered their family background as middle class, distinctions were made between an upper middle class, middle class and lower middle class and the meaning of these distinctions is explored. The fourth section examines the identities of those who identified themselves as something 'other' than middle class and how the use of labels such as working class, blue collar and poor described their lives. In both of these sections, it is argued that the language of class is not merely used as a shorthand label to describe standards of living. The interviewees used the concept to capture their experience of life and those of other people around them in the communities in which they grew up, the schools they attended, the jobs they occupy and the suburbs and towns in which they now live. It is also used to explain how the lived experience of class, as well as those of their parents, shapes their own cultural values and lifestyle practices be it their choice of where they live, how they choose to spend their money and their concerns about their children's education in school and beyond. That their life histories are told through the lens of class suggests that Americans think they live in a society characterized by such divisions. America, in this respect, is not a classless society.

Class consciousness and class identities

Early sociological interest on the subjective dimensions of class in the US (like Britain) focused on Marx's theory of class consciousness and the extent to which members of a class have a sense of shared interests which might be mobilized by organizations in pursuit of those interests. These big theoretical issues invariably translated, somewhat prosaically, into empirical research on class identities which included the study of popular perceptions of the class structure, people's willingness to place themselves in a class category and the extent to which these class identities shaped their political proclivities (Devine 1997: 75). Not surprisingly, given the debate with the ghost of Marx, interest focused primarily on the salience (or otherwise) of working-class identities over time. Over a period of 50 years, protagonists occupying positions at each end of the spectrum held sway. Thus, in response to a series of studies carried out by *Fortune* magazine in the early 1940s which found that almost 80 per cent of the population defined themselves as middle class, Centres (1949) conducted a survey which allowed people to identify themselves as working class and found that 51 per cent of his respondents did so as opposed to 43 per cent who considered themselves middle class. In turn, other sociologists (Kahl and Davis 1955; Hodge and Treiman 1968; Coleman and Rainwater 1978) criticized Centres for their research indicated that an all-embracing middle-class identity was dominant in America.

This view was dominant between the 1950s and the 1970s (the period of the long post Second World War boom of course) until Jackman and Jackman's (1983) research reasserted Centres' position regarding the continued salience of a working-class identity in the US. They found that 43 per cent of their survey respondents identified themselves as middle class and 37 per cent identified themselves as working class. Identification with the middle class was stable across Centres' survey and their own. The drop in working-class identification was explained with reference to those who identified themselves as being poor (8 per cent) who drew away from identifying with the working class (although it must be said that bringing these two categories together would still leave an unaccounted drop (6 per cent) in working-class identification). Be that as it may, other researchers also argued that the distinction between the middle class and the working class is widely recognized and largely understood in the US (Vanneman and Cannon 1987). Similarly, Wright (1985: 450) found 'class location and experiences do systematically shape consciousness' and proletarians endorse working-class attitudes while the bourgeoisie endorse pro-capitalist attitudes (albeit less than in other countries like Sweden). Kingston's (2000) (re)assertion that the findings on working-class identification are highly problematic and most Americans see themselves as middle class represents a swing of the pendulum once again.

Kingston (2000) is undoubtedly correct when he argues that there are considerable methodological difficulties in the study of class consciousness. The fixed choice option does not tell us very much about the salience of identities, class or otherwise, in people's lives (although it is still an interesting sociological question why people are willing to label them-selves as working class in such surveys). Nevertheless, Kingston fails to acknowledge that people still use the language of class when identifying themselves with the middle class and the context in which they do so and how they talk about class is worthy of further sociological consider-ation. While Kingston seeks to close down this avenue of investigation, fortunately others have explored middle-class identification further. Halle's (1984, see also Halle and Romo 1991) now rather old but still widely cited ethnographic study of chemical workers in New Jersey is helpful here. Halle's (1984: 203) blue-collar workers held three identities. First, his blue-collar workers did not self-identify with the working class although their workplace experiences generated a strong sense of being 'working men' reflecting the reality of their position 'in the system of production'. Second, outside work, they identified themselves as being 'lower middle class' or 'middle class' in that they saw themselves as a set of people 'at a certain income range and standard of living' shared by blue-collar workers and white-collar employees alike. Finally, in the sphere of politics, Halle's workers subscribed to the all-inclusive identity of being American and living in the United States. Halle's blue-collar informants, therefore, had multiple identities that were context specific and their middle-class identity derived from their everyday lives and preoccupations outside work.

Zussman (1985) also argued that people derive different class and other identities from their experiences in the different contexts of work and home in his study of 'middle-level' engineers.[1] Again, his study is now rather old although it is still widely referred to by contemporary writers (and, indeed, his discussion of the intersection of biography and social structure with reference to the concept of career is as contemporary as they come). Zussman (1985: 221) found that the engineers' experiences at work, mostly notably persistent conflicts between them and manual workers on the shopfloor in the factories of his research, meant that they certainly never saw themselves as the members of a working class. That said, they could not lay any claims to a professional identity as a 'collective mobility project' in the same way that medics and lawyers had done. Rather, the concept of career – an orderly work history that progresses towards more responsibility – was central to these 'middle-level' employees. Be that as it may, Zussman argues that the workplace is not the only source of the engineers' views about politics and society. Their private lives and their concerns as parents, home-owners, consumers and so forth also shape their identities. It generates a sense of a 'working middle class' that they share with the affluent working class who live in the same residential communities. People's lives outside work shape their views of society and politics and explain the ubiquitous identification with the middle class.

The way in which Americans employ an all-inclusive conception of the middle class, aligning themselves with other ordinary working (class) people has been discussed in more recent research on the middle classes. Lamont's (1992) study of the culture of the French and American upper middle class is a case in point. Lamont interviewed professionals, managers and businessmen about what it means to be a 'worthy person' (i.e. questions of morality) and especially the use of symbolic boundaries to define their own identities and distance themselves from others. Lamont (1992: 69) found that socioeconomic boundaries were much more salient to her American upper middle-class informants than her French counterparts who attached greater significance to cultural and moral boundaries in the process of self-identification. Money, personal income, levels of consumption and 'comfort levels' were important to the American men's view of themselves and their status in society. Yet, Lamont noted that few Americans referred to being middle class and instead emphasized how they were 'ordinary Joes' whose high-level work was no more valuable than others and who enjoyed equal relations with subordinates. In contrast to the French, who explicitly acknowledged the importance of class differences (culturally if not materially), the Americans respondents had a weak middle-class identity in that they were anxious not to distinguish themselves from ordinary working (class) people in an almost classless way.

The interviewees in each of these sociological studies, therefore, have aligned themselves, to a greater or lesser degree, with a seemingly all-embracing middle class. Historians have also begun to explore the popular view that there is a 'vast amorphous' middle class. Walkowitz (1999), for example, explores the issue of what the label or category of 'middle class' actually means. He draws on cultural studies and post-structuralism to argue that identities are historical and contingent and he shows that the meaning of middle-class identity has changed over the twentieth century by way of a history of social workers who patrol the boundaries of class. In the early twentieth century, Walkowitz argues that social workers, who were predominately lowly paid Jewish women, deployed narratives of professionalism – although based specifically around notions of a feminine professional woman – to construct a middle-class identity. This identity was challenged in mid-century by the depression and poorer working conditions and accompanied by the growth of more radical unionization. This led to a change in social workers' class identities in that they saw themselves as working class in the world of employment although still middle class in the sphere of consumption. Post-war affluence led social workers to reassert their professional identity, in terms of consumption at home. This identity also shifted in meaning, however, as the increasing racialization of social workers' clients: namely, African American and Puerto Rican welfare dependents living in the inner cities led them to reassert their respectable whiteness as part of a middle-class identity.

Walkowitz's historical study is a remarkable account of the changing meaning of middle-class self-identification that is not just a socioeconomic category of middle-income earners who enjoy an array of consumer goods. It is also a racialized and political category which separates respectable whites from the 'other' who are mostly poor Black and Hispanic people living in dangerous urban enclaves who see themselves more clearly as working class. Walkowitz's emphasis on the instability of class identity might be somewhat misplaced if the striking stability in the popularity of the category of middle class in the face of all these changed meanings is acknowledged. This quibble aside, his study shows that the study of class identities need not and, indeed, should not confine itself to questions of working-class identities and working-class consciousness. Other American historians (Bledstein 2001; Johnson 2001) have called for further exploration of how, where, when and why people identify themselves as middle class and what they mean when they represent or position themselves in this way. It goes without saying that further sociological enquiry into middle-class identities would not go amiss either. The next section goes on to discuss a qualitative study of middle-class Americans. It does so in the context of debate about some of the methodological problems that have beset sociological research on class of both a quantitative and qualitative kind.

Researching the American and British middle classes

The empirical material on which this chapter is based derives from a wider comparative qualitative study of doctors and teachers in the US and the UK (Devine 2004a,b).[2] The main focus of the study was on how the middle classes reproduce their positions of power and privilege across generations. It sought to explore, in other words, the processes by which parents guide their children successfully through the education system into 'good' jobs. One of the main findings to emerge out of a long tradition of comparative research on social mobility is that America and Britain (like most other industrialized nations) enjoyed high rates of absolute social mobility in the twentieth century (Grusky and Hauser 1984; Goldthorpe 1987; Hout 1988; Erikson and Goldthorpe 1992). Many people from working-class backgrounds experienced upward mobility into middle-class jobs. Relative rates of mobility (based on a comparison of the mobility chances of different individuals), however, remained stable. People from middle-class backgrounds still had a far greater chance of getting middle-class jobs than their working-class counterparts. Change in class structuration, therefore, had not been accompanied by a decline in class inequalities. Goldthorpe (1996, 2000) tried to explain these macro-sociological regularities by developing a micro-sociological theory of how middle-class families mobilize their economic, cultural and social resources to secure their advantages over generations. This theory guided the qualitative research reported here (Devine 1998).

The comparative research involved in-depth interviews with case studies of doctors (physicians) and teachers (educators) in Boston in the US and Manchester in the UK.[3] Physicians were chosen as an example of a high-level middle-class occupation known, in the past at least, for its high level of occupational inheritance and domination by me while educators were chosen as a typical low-level middle-class occupation known to be more open to men and women from working-class origins and still dominated by women (Bianchi 1995; Mare 1995). A total of 86 interviews were conducted with the informants and their partners (who, of course, were not necessarily doctors or teachers) all of whom had at least one child making their way through the school system at the time of the interview. The American sample (on which this chapter concentrates) comprised 41 interviewees.[4] They were aged between 32 and 63, and they had 55 children amongst them. The interviewees were predominately white Americans although many of them were second and third generation immigrants with diverse ethnic origins. The sample also included first-generation immigrants from the West Indies, the Indian continent and Asia and 4 African Americans in the sample. This overall diversity was to be expected given America's history as an immigrant country (Farley 1995). The interviewees mostly lived in houses (the majority owning their own homes) in the predominately white suburbs and small towns surrounding Boston with only a minority of respondents resident in the more ethnical city.

The methodological difficulties associated with asking questions about class and trying to ascertain the salience of class in people's lives has already been noted. The on-going debate on the issue in the US and the UK has usually focused on quantitative research and considered the pros and cons of fixed choice and open-ended questions (Kingston 2000) as well as the impact of a battery of questions on class on questions about self-identification (Saunders 1989). While in-depth interviews might be seen as the answer, it would be naïve to think that qualitative researchers do not have to confront similar difficulties. In my previous research on working-class lifestyles and sociopolitical proclivities (Devine 1992a,b), for example, a discussion about class was far from easy. It provoked considerable unease because the interviewees had strong pejorative views about class and some of the older interviewees spoke with considerable bitterness about the effects of class on people's lives. Class was frequently equated with issue of status and hierarchy and how people were looked down upon and considered inferior in the past. Many did not really want to talk about such a negative topic, often distancing themselves from it by referring to its importance in the past and its declining significance now. They denied that they made judgements about other people's worth or that other people did these days. At the same time, they were also prepared to identify themselves with a class and name other classes when asked to do so. If the interviewees had not been asked to do so, however, it is an open question as to whether they would have done so given their views about the demise of class or, at least, status. These issues are increasingly being acknowledged and its implications addressed in class analysis at least in Britain (Skeggs 1997; Bradley 1999; Savage *et al.* 2001).

The intensive interviews for this research were conducted by way of life histories. The interviewees were asked to describe their early childhood, their experiences of education and their subsequent work histories. Attention then turned to their children and how they had helped or were currently guiding them through the education system into 'good' jobs. The research was undertaken in Britain and then in the US. Some pilot interviews were conducted in Britain first of all and the interviewees were asked if they felt their families belonged to a social class when they were growing up. It was the last question in the first section on their early childhood. Asking the interviewees to discuss their childhoods and collecting some important biographical information about where they grew up, their siblings, their parents and so on along the way was, of course, a pleasant experience for the interviewees and myself. Again, however, the question on class created some unease and awkwardness as the interviewees expressed their dislike of the topic. Given their discomfort and my own concerns about rapport during the rest of the interview, I decided to drop the question. After all, an explicit discussion of class was not crucial to my research focus on class processes. Moreover, rightly or wrongly, I was already sensitive to the fact that the topic of how middle-class families reproduce their advantages across generations was hardly going to encourage potential interviewees and the research had already been described much more innocuously in terms of how parents help their children with their education.

The final interview schedule, therefore, closed the discussion on the interviewees' childhoods with a question about their families' standard of living when they were young. In Britain, most of the interviews of middle-class origin talked how their parents owned their own home, an array of consumer goods like a car, whether they went on holiday and so on. Reference to being relatively *comfortable* and not burdened by financial worries was frequently made. Occasionally, some of the interviewees made an unprompted reference to being middle class and this was probed further. Some of the interviewees were from working-class backgrounds who had enjoyed social mobility into medicine and teaching and, more often than not, they immediately discussed their standard of living in class terms and explicitly described it as working class. Thus, while the interviewees of middle-class origin were silent on the issue of class or sometimes embarrassed when they mentioned it, the informants from working-class origins were happy and often proud to talk about their background (Devine 2004b; see also Bradley 1999). Explicit reference to class by the interviewees was sometimes made in later discussions about their education, their work history and how they were helping their children through the school system and into good jobs. In total, half of the British sample made an unprompted, explicit reference to class and there were plenty of other implicit discussions of class using various euphemisms.

In sharp contrast, virtually all of the American interviewees discussed their families' standard of living explicitly in class terms and, more often than not, to describe their families of origin as middle class. In one respect, the frequent language of class was very surprising since it is the British who are supposed to be obsessed with class. In another respect, the interviewee's responses were unsurprising since the tendency to describe their class background as middle class was to be expected. What was also interesting here was the way in which the British were rather uncomfortable about using the term 'middle class' because of its baggage from the past. Arguably, the interviewees were often reluctant to acknowledge that they had an advantaged start in life although, more importantly, they were anxious to distance themselves from the idea that they were 'snobby' and regarded themselves as superior to others.

They also wanted to distance themselves from other pejorative characteristics of the middle class – of being conventional, boring, suburban
and apolitical – although Johnson (2001) has argued that this caricature
also prevails in the US among academics if not the public at large. Such
concerns did not seem to detain the American interviewees who used
the class category with apparent ease and comfort. The label middle
class did not appear to have such negative connotations – especially
around issues of status – so there appeared to be no need to distance
themselves from the term like their British counterparts.

Of course, it could be argued that the interviewees were merely using
class labels as a way of making 'the world tidier than it is' (Jencks *et al.*
1979). It could be claimed, for example, that my interviewees used the
term 'class' as a shorthand way of describing the socioeconomic background
of their parents and their family standard of living and it meant nothing
beyond that. I would know what they meant by the use of the term
'middle class', that it denoted a level of consumption and lifestyle, so
there was no need to elaborate further on these issues. To be sure, there
was an element of this in the interviews. For the most part, however,
the way in which the interviewees talked about class meant much more
than this. They used the notion of class to capture their experiences in
life and those of the people around them at home, in school, in jobs
and in the communities in which they lived. They also spoke of how
these experiences shaped their parents and their own cultural values
and lifestyle practices. The discussions of class, therefore, spoke of the
lived experience of class, of how class position shaped their life-chances,
the constraints they encountered and the opportunities they enjoyed as
well as how they, as active agents, shaped their own lives in terms of
their cultural values and lifestyle practices.

Originating from the middle classes

Most of the interviewees categorized their family of origin as middle class
confirming Walkowitz's (1999) claims about the ubiquitous character of
the label 'middle class' and how the terms has come to embrace an
increasingly wide range of people, albeit predominately white, in the
US since the 1950s. That said, my informants distinguished between
different types of middle class: namely, upper middle class, middle class
and lower middle class thereby giving a more precise meaning to their
use of the term than the more general category of middle class. A number
of interviewees, for example considered themselves as 'upper middle
class'. The label 'upper middle class' has appeared in previous research

in that 8 per cent of Jackman and Jackman's (1983: 80) respondents categorized themselves in this way. The interviewees' used the label to denote a high standard of living and one that was higher than the average. The focus on consumption rather than occupation was obviously discussed given the reference to class derived from a question on family standards of living. The only son of a businessman and his wife, Michael Reed described his upbringing as 'Upper middle class. Comfortable. Went to nice schools. Went to summer camp. Took vacations'.[5] Similarly, Alan Garrett, the second son of a government statistician and a librarian, described his family as:

> middle to upper middle class. Basically, there was a budget like everyone else but we were comfortable. They owned their own house and a summer house and two cars and we were able to go on vacations.

Like their British counterparts, the American interviewees made frequent reference to being 'comfortable' although, in a distinctly American way, comfort was demonstrated with reference to the ownership of summer houses! Some of the interviewees referred to how their parents moved from being middle class to upper middle class as they were growing up. Movement to the upper middle class was closely associated with a move to a bigger house in the suburbs. The son of a research scientist and a housewife, George Marshall recalled how he (and his younger brother and sister):

> grew up the first twelve years of my life on a post World War Two housing development where there was very small five room single family houses and then we ended up moving when I was 12 or 13 to a more upper middle-class type area.

Interestingly, George had rebelled against the 'socially isolating' white suburban living of his childhood in the 1960s and he worked in a health centre serving a low-income ethnic community in the city of Boston. He and his wife, Judy Kennedy, were the only white doctors who did not live in the suburbs. They were keen that their three sons enjoy the ethnic diversity of the city. Anxious, however, that their children do well in school they sent them to private school rather than Boston's public schools.[6] This decision was the source of some anguish to George for it troubled him that there was, in his words, 'little economic diversity. There is not a lot of scholarship so it tends to be more middle class'. Despite his efforts, then, his children were also 'socially isolated' in class terms.

Some of these interviewees went on to describe how their parents had made their way up from more humble class backgrounds. These narratives of social mobility were not surprising, of course, since the US has enjoyed distinctly high levels of absolute upward social mobility for much of the twentieth century (Hout 1988; Erikson and Goldthorpe 1992). Still, it was interesting to hear family histories being told using the language of class. David Neale, for example, described how:

> [My] family's standard of living was upper middle class to upper class. My dad had a very good job. He was a very prominent engineer and he did very well for himself even though he was from a working-class family. He kept a lid on us financially. We didn't all have cars and stuff like that. We lived in a very affluent community in a nice house.

David was somewhat unusual in making reference to his father's occupation and the fact that his father came from a working-class background. Few of the interviewees used the label 'working class'. What is also noteworthy were his comments on the way in which his father's background influenced how he and his siblings were brought up. They did not, for example, have a typically American middle-class adolescence owning their own car as soon as they were eligible to drive. His father's class background, then, had an 'effect' on David's childhood since it seemed his father did not countenance typically upper middle-class consumption in a way that it might have done if he had experienced it himself.

It was more common, however, for the interviewees to describe their family background as middle class without any additional distinctions. In some respects, the interviewees' discussions of their family's standard of living were barely distinguishable from that of those who described themselves as upper middle class. Nadia Khan was the daughter of a businessman and a housewife who was brought up in the Indian subcontinent. Somewhat ambivalently, and more like the British than the American interviewees in this respect, she said her family was 'Probably middle class I would say. We had what we needed. We didn't have extra but we were quite comfortable and we traveled.' The comfortable lifestyle of the middle class was emphasized by both sets of interviewees. That said, the interviewees who described themselves as comfortable often sought to qualify this remark by emphasizing their ordinariness simultaneously. Lamont (1992), as was noted earlier, also found her middle-class respondents keen to characterize themselves as 'ordinary Joes'. Jack Pool's father and mother were both doctors although his mother did not return to her medical career until her children were in high school. Describing his family standard of living he said:

> I would say it was middle class. We were in a pretty nice community but we lived in an average house in the community. We had new cars like every five years or so but they'd kind of be pretty average cars.

Being middle class equaled with being average and ordinary. Many of the interviewees used the category middle class to describe their family's standard of living although it became apparent that they enjoyed very different standards of material comfort in their childhood. Jack Pool, quoted above, was the oldest of four children who all boarded at prestigious private schools. He went on to an Ivy League school before becoming a doctor and two of his three siblings were also medics. His middle-class family, in other words, seemed as affluent as some of the interviewees who described their childhoods as upper middle class. That said, his perceptions were influenced how his parents had spent their income and wealth. He recalled how his parents had often joked about the way in which school fees 'took whatever luxuries they would otherwise have had'. His parents were affluent although much of their money was spent on privately educating four children and this is why they had a seemingly ordinary house and an average car. Other informants' parents were less affluent although they also described their class origins as middle class. Linda Chapman, for example, was one of two daughters whose father was a salesman and whose mother worked in a department store later in life. Her father moved jobs frequently and she did not think he was highly paid. On her standard of living she said:

> I would say middle class. I don't think we were in need of anything but I don't think we were extravagant. I think we had what we needed and probably a little bit more ... It was average middle class.

The middle class was, indeed, very inclusive as Walkowitz (1999) has argued.

A lack of material deprivation and some degree of comfort, it seemed, was the common denominator for all the interviewees who described themselves as middle class. Again, like their upper middle-class counterparts, many of these informants drew on narratives of mobility when speaking of their family background. These stories often emerged when they spoke of their parent's childhoods and their experiences of education.

Sometimes the discussion made explicit reference to class. More often than not, talk of class was implicit for the interviewees often spoke of their parents coming from 'poor' backgrounds rather than specific working-class origins. It might be that the term 'poor' was a nonodious category (Jackman and Jackman 1983: 18) in the way that 'working class' or any reference to class might have been. Kevin Bailey, for example, explained that his father, who became a professional engineer, went to college:

> [Even] though he came from a very poor family and a very poor school system. . . .Dad had to work jobs, like lousy jobs, and then he saved his money and went to college in the evenings just to get basic skills to go to college and then he got to go to a very good school.

Kevin concluded that his father 'was completely self motivated and he expected the same out of me'. His father's harsh experience, of sacrifices made in search of self-improvement, had a tremendous effect on what he expected of his son. Again, the effects of class on family biographies were acknowledged, sometimes implicitly and sometimes explicitly.

Finally, there were a group of interviewees who described themselves as 'lower middle class'. The use of this label was bewildering in the sense that the interviewees' fathers were usually employed in working-class jobs. They did not describe their childhoods as working class however. There does not appear to be any quantitative data that has allowed respondents to define themselves as lower middle class so it is difficult to ascertain the popularity of the term from previous research. That said, Halle (1984) found that many of his workers described themselves as 'lower middle class' and, in her recent study of working-class men in the US and France, Lamont (2000) also noted that some of her American working men labeled themselves as 'lower middle class'. Maria Moran, a doctor, was the eldest of three children whose father was a longshore-man (a docker) while her mother was a homemaker. She talked at length about the way in which the lack of money dominated her early family life and how she was desperate to escape from this life of economic deprivation from an early age. As she explained:

> My parents were born I think in 1926. They grew up in the great depression and you could not spend an extra penny without re-evaluating and evaluating it over and over again. To be honest, I was good at school. I was a good student and I just never wanted to live that way.

She went on to explain how her parent's experiences of the depression had subsequently shaped their caution and fear about spending money even when they had it later on.

Intriguingly, when Maria discussed her father's job, she actually described it as a 'working class job, reasonably well paid. It was just after World War Two so it was a good time to be in America. You didn't have to be very educated to make a reasonable amount.' Like Halle's (1984) informants, a reference to working class was confined to a discussion of her father's job while the term 'lower middle class' was employed in relation to a discussion of standards of living. What is also interesting to note is reference to post-war affluence so that people like her father, who was not college-educated and worked in manual job, were 'reasonably well paid' so they could afford a standard of living not dissimilar to the middle class. Others, however, very much stressed the effects of class on their everyday lives and how a lack of money shaped their existence. Bob Farrell, a teacher, came from a relatively large family of five children of which he was the oldest and only son. His father was a self-employed painting contractor while his mother was a homemaker. He said, 'I would say our standard of living was probably lower middle class. My father was a blue-collar worker. Our economic status was somewhat shaky. His economic status depended upon the availability of work which was very good in the spring, summer and fall and marginal in the winter, particularly between the times from thanksgiving though say Feb.' These times were 'sometimes difficult for the family' for although they did not quite go hungry or cold, there were a shortage of clothes and shoes.

Being other than middle class

The majority of the interviewees, therefore, described their family standards of living as middle class although distinctions within the middle class were not uncommon. It could be argued that most of them were correct in the labels they used for they were of middle-class origins. One or either of their parents had middle-class occupations: that is in non-manual professional and managerial (although sometimes middle-level or even low-level managerial) positions. Only those who identified themselves as 'lower middle class' could be said to have incorrectly described their family background in class terms although reference to their father's having working-class or blue-collar jobs did not go completely unacknowledged. The use of different class labels was evident among other interviewees. Some informants described their family background as working class although they expressed some uncertainty about the category and wondered if they had been middle class. It was if they were conscious that description of their working-class background – that is growing up in the relatively affluent white suburbs – did not sound especially working class in comparison to the working class – that is poor blacks living in urban ghettos – of today. Describing their childhoods as working class did not sound quite right. They reappraised the appropriate class labels to describe their childhood from the vantage point of being adults and knowing more about class than they did when they were young. Like the changed meaning of 'middle class' described by Walkowitz (1999), the meaning of the label 'working class' had seemingly altered too.

Judy Kennedy, for example, was a physician who had enjoyed considerable social mobility. Her father was a television engineer and her mother had stayed at home looking after six children. She said:

> It's interesting because I didn't know what standards of living were until I got older but we lived in a very small community. I always thought of it as working class but now that I've got older and looked back, it was probably considered middle class although I never felt wealthy by any means.

Ray Chapman also used the class labels interchangeably although, unlike Julie, in the context of his father enjoying promotion in his job which facilitated a move to a bigger house. Robert was a university professor, married to a teacher, who enjoyed considerable social mobility. His father was a police lieutenant who enjoyed promotion but then died young. His mother took on various clerical jobs after his death. The oldest of three children, he was the only one to go to college and his siblings did not pursue career type jobs. He said:

> I definitely, through my elementary years, would characterise our neighbourhood and community and ways as working class or working class with aspirations in education to middle class if it makes sense to separate those two at all. Once … we moved … to one of the suburbs it was still a suburb that had a strong working-class element and a strong middle-class element. There was not much professional or upper middle class there. I have sort of self-identified as working and middle class in terms of my upbringing.

While hard to disentangle, Robert's comments are interesting for the way in which he associated the middle class and not the working class with educational aspirations and the middle class in his community was not the same as the upper middle class who occupied professional jobs. Robert is worth dwelling on further for he was concerned about the absence of 'economic diversity' in his children's lives. He and his wife had moved to the suburbs for their children's education (which is one of the main reasons for white flight) (Massey and Denton 1993). The suburb had it downsides however. Robert was concerned about the consumer aspirations that his children expressed and the peer pressures they experienced from their more wealthy friends 'about the Mercedes that you get at aged 16'. The absence of working-class people in their lives also troubled him. He said:

> In fact, one of the things Linda and I find a challenge and worked consciously to do was to have them interact with people from a lower social class than we are because I am a little bit worried about attitudes that are drifting in – because of the [N] community – about what it means to be working class. I kind of self-identity having working class routes so (I have) a respect for people in the trades or who have craft skills that don't necessarily involve college.

His children's social isolation from and ignorance of working-class people had generated, it was implied, a lack of respect for other people who led different lives to their own.

There were few instances of working-class self-identification and the label was used with some ambivalence about its meaning. Again, these findings confirm earlier research such as Halle's (1984). Halle also found that term 'blue collar' was popular among his manual workers and the label was used, albeit infrequently among the informants of this research too. Jane Bennett, a physician, was the daughter of a police lieutenant and her mother was a 'stay-at-home mom'. On her family's standard of living, she said, 'By American terms, my family was a blue-collar family. We lived in a two family dwelling. My parents owned their own home and rented a second apartment in their home.' Julie made no explicit reference to class in her interview although her account of educational success and the effects of peer pressure on her educational aspirations was implicitly about class. At school, she was among the top set who were expected to go on to higher education. Her parents were very keen that she did well although she emphasized the importance of school and peer pressure on her experience of social mobility:

I would say actually my school environment and exposure to people who were, in particular, better off, more highly educated, that's what really brought me into a different prospect. Frankly, I looked at my class mates and where they were expecting to go – because my personal experiences with better schools was quite limited – and seeing what they were looking at encouraged me to look at those institutions and I then selected on that basis.

The other term that arose in discussions of family standards of living was that of being 'poor'. Jackman and Jackman (1983: 18) gave their respondents the opportunity to identify themselves as 'poor' and 8 per cent of their sample did so. Only 5 per cent of whites did so but 27 per cent of all African-American respondents classified themselves in this way. The women of colour used the term 'poor' more than any other group of informants in the sample. Susan Rogers's father was a machinist in a factory and her mother worked part-time as a postal clerk when her children were grown up. She used the labels 'working class' and 'poor' throughout the interview. Of her parents, she said 'I would say my parents were hard working so working class.' Susan spoke at length about her parents' high aspirations for her and as a bright student she got the opportunity to go to college financed by college loans and government grants. On her education, she stated:

I was able to live on campus and get a full college experience. That's a way for poor people who are not able to afford college tuition. They stay at home kind of thing. My parents encouraged me to do that. They thought that that was the total sort of experience.

Her parents wanted her to enjoy a full college experience that was untypical of the children of poor, working-class parents like themselves. Interestingly, Susan was initially encouraged by her school teachers to become an educator but realizing that she had much more potential, she subsequently trained as a physician. Earlier, more limited aspirations had been superseded.

Similarly, Kerri Clegg described her childhood standard of living as poor. As she explained, 'Well, my mother was a single parent. My father and mother were never married so she was living by herself. She worked and sometimes worked two jobs and took care of us.' Indeed, Kerri went on to recall how hard her mother worked – how she also spent long hours at her mother's workplace after school and at weekends – and how her income paid for her private college education. Her mother's considerable sacrifices could not have been more removed from the portrayal of single black mothers that circulates today. Kerri had become a physician and married a physician and they had three sons. She and her husband, like the other women of colour, lived in the city for its ethnic diversity. She sent her sons to private school to ensure their educational success but it troubled her that it was a predominately white school. As she was acutely aware, few African Americans could pay for the schools fees that she and her husband, now part of the black middle class (Landry 1988, 1991), could afford. An interesting discussion of race and class ensured. Attempts to increase the ethnic diversity of the school, she noted, had met with limited success. While most of the white families could afford for one partner not to work or to have private nannies, most minority families could send their children to the school only if both parents worked (see Oliver and Shapiro 1995 on black and white wealth). With a prohibitively expensive after-school programme, it was no wonder that attempts to diversify had mostly failed.

Many of the informants who described themselves as something other than middle class, therefore, had very different early life experiences to their middle-class, especially upper middle-class, counterparts. To be sure, they now enjoyed much higher standards of living than their parents as a result, among other things, of their experiences of social mobility. Starting from more humble socioeconomic backgrounds, however, their routes into careers in teaching and medicine had often required, without doubt, considerable sacrifice and hard work. Yuko Yeung, for example, described her childhood standard of living as 'poor'. She has been born in the Far East and, indeed, she enjoyed an upper middle-class existence in her early years since her mother's family was very wealthy there. The family returned to the US, however, when her father, an American ser-viceman, was sent to a new posting but her parents' marriage did not last long in the States. Yuko and her younger sister lived with their mother who worked in various low-paid sewing jobs. At one point, Yuko had to make the painful decision to drop out of college to secure her family's financial position. As she explained:

I had to make decisions like I didn't want us to live in the dwelling that we did so we moved to another place which was better but I still didn't like it and I had decided to retrain my mom. I actually got a job for her. I taught her how to drive. I made her as independent as possible. Then I felt more comfortable about going back to school.

Yuko completed a pre-med degree, went to medical school and became a doctor. Her story was a typical immigrant story (Farley 1995). Yuko was well aware of how different her life had been to her husband, Peter, who was a physician too. Peter's parents were also immigrants from Europe but his father was a university professor and his mother was a doctor. He was privately educated and went to an Ivy League school for his science degree before going onto medical school. In sharp contrast, he enjoyed a very smooth and uneventful journey through the education system into a high-level job. Yuko discussed their different life experiences in class terms. As she explained, 'You couldn't get a more structured upper middle-class family with all the trimmings and all that.' They had 'walked along very different roads' she said, although 'they had enjoyed similar outcomes'. Yet, she also downplayed the effects of class on her life experiences. She had, after all, escaped her humble background and now enjoyed an upper middle-class existence. It was her individual motivation and belief in herself that facilitated her improvement. As she said:

> I think that no matter where you are in life that it really comes down to the individual. You could be in a high status position financially but if you are not an empowered, self-confident, motivated individual you will not achieve anything or very little.

Her views might be described as typical of American individualism (Bellah *et al.* 1996; Wolfe 1998). Arguably, however, it is easy to see how Yuko's experiences shaped these opinions since she had reached her destination through considerable sacrifice and faith.

Conclusion

In this chapter, I have argued that the Americans who participated in my research readily used the language of class and were able and willing to identify themselves with a class and usually the middle class. The label of class was not used simply to denote a particular socioeconomic category as a short hand way of describing a particular job position or standard of living. The label meant much more than that. Rather, my interviewees used the class categories to describe themselves and their life histories. They used class to position their parents, the class trajectories that they experienced and how their parents' experiences affected their family lifestyle practices including patterns of consumption when they were children. They used class to describe the communities in which they grew up and the people around them and their shared expectations and aspirations as they were growing up. As adults, they spoke of how class shaped their cultural values and lifestyle practices especially in terms of housing choices and consumption patterns. As parents, they were aware of how class was now shaping their children's life experiences at home, in the community, at school and so forth. In sum, the context of their everyday lived experience shaped their class identity, values and lifestyles. This research also confirms earlier research by Halle (1984) and Zussman (1985; see also Katznelson 1981; Gerteis and Savage 1998) that shows that people's lives beyond the workplace, in the sphere of housing and consumption, are especially important in shaping people's middle-class identities, cultural values and lifestyle practices.

The American interviewees used the language of class and class categories much more freely than my British interviewees. They did so because they were quite comfortable identifying themselves as middle class. It was an inclusive rather than an exclusive category embracing ordinary working people seeming to exclude only those at the extremes: namely, the very rich and the very poor. In contrast, the British interviewees were uneasy with the term 'middle class' and keen to distance themselves from the label because of its associations with status. They did not want to be seen as people who thought themselves superior to the working class. Hence, they were silent about class and it was those from working-class origins who spoke of class and spoke with pride. These findings are at odds with Kingston's portrayal of America as nation of citizens who lack class identity. Arguably, the findings differ because he is preoccupied with a lack of working-class consciousness in America and, consequently, he fails to see middle-class identification as a demonstration of the salience of class among Americans. Moreover, overly concerned to show that there is no basis for collective class action, he overlooks the ways in which class identities shape peoples' cultural values and lifestyle practices in everyday life. In contrast to Kingston's desire to close down new research on class subjectivities, I would argue that there are plenty of stories to tell about class in America for it is an important way in which people understand their individual life experiences and their concerns and preoccupations with their children's unfolding lives. The study of class subjectivities, in other words, has much to commend it.

Notes

1. A similar argument about the separation of work, community, class and politics in the US has been employed in research on urban politics. See, for example, Katznelson's (1981) excellent classic study.
2. The University of Manchester funded the British end of the research and interviews were conducted during 1997–98. The Leverhulme Trust funded the American end of the research and interviews were conducted during 1998–99. The Trust funded a 6-month trip to the US in 1998 and I returned for 2 months in 1999. The financial support of both organizations is gratefully acknowledged. During this period, I was a Visiting Scholar at the Kennedy School of Government at Harvard University. I am very grateful to Professor William Julius Wilson who facilitated my institutional affiliation.
3. While the British talk about doctors, the term 'physician' is a much more common occupational title for those with medical degrees (MDs) who practice medicine in the US. The American teachers sometimes referred to themselves as 'educators' although this was a less common practice. The terms are used interchangeably in this chapter. One other term, perhaps not as familiar in Britain as in the US, was 'women of colour'. The African-American women of the sample often used this term to describe themselves and it is also employed later in this chapter.
4. The plan was to conduct interviews with 12 families (24 individual women and men) in each of the four case studies. The total number was expected to be 96 interviews. After an interview was completed, the interviewee was asked if his or her partner would be willing to participate in the research also. While there were no outright rejections, some partners inevitably proved elusive. Thus, the final tally was 84 interviews consisting of 24 British doctors and their partners, 21 British teachers and their partners, 20 American physicians and their partners and 19 American educators and their partners.
5. All of the interviewees have been given pseudonyms to protect their anonymity. Some of the women informants had kept their own name while others had adopted their husband's surname on marriage. It seemed appropriate to give different names to wives with different names to their husbands and the same surname to the wives who shared their husband's name.
6. Like many other schools in America's inner cities, the Boston school system has a poor reputation although it was better than it had been in the past. In the 1960s there were incredible racial conflicts over desegregation that have been movingly documented by Lukas (1985) and Eaton (2001). For a Northeastern city that prided itself on being very progressive, the extent of their violence in comparison to other cities like Buffulo greatly tarnished its reputation (Taylor 1998).

8
Social Change and Social Identity: Postmodernity, Reflexive Modernisation and the Transformation of Social Identities in Australia

Tim Phillips and Mark Western

Social identity is one of the central concerns of sociology in the new millennium. The most cursory overview of contemporary work across the discipline reveals the extent to which the concept currently assumes a dominant place in research and analysis. Social identity is crucial to the understanding of society advanced by leading theorists such as Bauman, Bourdieu and Giddens, which drives much of the research agendas of key areas of sociological concern such as age, class, gender, race, ethnicity and nationalism, and centrally informs thinking in disciplines that impact upon and interact closely with sociology such as psychology and cultural studies. The centrality of the social identity concept arguably reflects the analytic utility provided by various forms of the construct (e.g. individual identity, collective identity, identity politics, virtual identity), its close links with other key ideas in contemporary sociology (e.g. embodiment, difference, community, resistance) and its centrality within classical and contemporary socio-logical thought.

However, notwithstanding the recent explosion in the scope and prevalence of identity studies in sociology, there is a remarkable absence of corresponding empirical research. With the renewed focus upon social identities has come a growing body of work concerned with elaborating and refining theoretical foundations, and mapping out new areas for substantive applications (Jenkins 1996; Cerulo 1997; Craib 1998). However, much less common have been empirical studies exploring the measurement and social distribution of social identities, or reporting personal accounts of how social identities are lived or felt by the individual across divergent social contexts.

Particular forms of social identity, such as class (Devine 1992a; Gamson 1992; Skeggs 1997; Western 1999) and nation (McCrone *et al.* 1998; Phillips 1998) have been the subjects of detailed empirical consideration. But we are unaware of more general empirical studies directed towards key questions from social theory about the future of modernity and its consequences for social identities in contemporary societies. The nature and fate of the social self in contemporary societies is a key issue of contention here. While there is a consensus that change of a significant type is occurring, there are different ways of thinking about this. Many sociologists believe that the modern age is coming to an end, and that we are in the process of moving into a new period where social and cultural life is modulated in fundamentally new and different ways. For some such as Baudrillard (1981), there has been an abrupt shift to a "postmodern culture". For others such as Giddens (1990), change has been more gradual, and we might in fact be seen as in the "late" phases of the modern age.

In this chapter, we address this question by empirically analysing continuity and change in patterns of social identification among Australians from the mid-1980s through to the late 1990s. Our objectives are threefold: to describe the relative salience of different sources of social identity in two discrete time periods and across three birth cohorts or generations; to examine period and generational differences in the strength of different social identities; and finally to assess whether identities are organised in some kind of stable system which is consistent with a coherent and unified self-concept. We begin by considering two alternative accounts of contemporary social change, postmodernisation and reflexive modernisation, and their implications for social identity. We next outline a brief theory of identity before turning to the empirical analyses.

Theories of post- and reflexive modernity

One of the reasons why identity is central to contemporary social thought and to public discourse is that rapid social change potentially produces a mismatch between social understandings and new social relations (Jenkins 1996) that problematises previously taken-for-granted identities. Two major approaches are especially relevant here: analyses of postmodernity associated with the work of Jameson (1991), Lyotard

(1979) and Bauman (1992); and accounts of reflexive modernisation provided by Beck (1992) and Giddens (1990, 1991b).

Postmodernity is a highly contested term but analysts who use it typically suggest that contemporary societies are increasingly characterised by their fragmented, fissured and fractured nature. Patterns and regularities in social life have given way to flux and fluidity (Lyon 2000). For Bauman (1992) incoherence is the defining feature of postmodernity. Incoherence in society and social relationships is matched by incoherence in social narratives, with a multitude of incommensurable accounts possible, each of which has its own values, beliefs and legitimate truth criteria (Lyotard 1979, 1988). Dealing with the "postmodern condition" involves attempting to "make sense of our lives in a context of multiple, open-ended, ever proliferating narratives and language games" (Norris 2000: 29). For Crook *et al.* (1992), these processes can be summarised in two tendencies, hyper-differentiation in which spheres of social life become increasingly internally fragmented and diverse, and dedifferentiation in which boundaries between spheres progressively erode. The implication of these tendencies is that social structures of class, gender, age, ethnicity and the like break down, while subjective forms of expression associated with them are also increasingly fragmented and individualised (Crook *et al.* 1992).

With the collapse of social structures, consumption or, more particularly, consumerism comes to occupy the centre of identity formation in postmodernity (Lipovetsky 1994; McDonald 1999). The dissolution of social structures and the proliferation of acceptable social narratives ensure that society comes to be increasingly organised around individual choice and self-expression rather than structural principles of social organisation. Personal expression is manifested through individualised consumption as source of personal autonomy (Lipovetsky 1994). "Post modern individuals" thus have highly fluid and contextual identities and personalities that are entirely contingent, changeable at will and operating on the "surface" of the self (or more accurately selves) (Lipovetsky 1994; McDonald 1999). These identities are expressed through individual and idiosyncratic styles of consumerism. Social identity in postmodernity therefore exhibits a tendency away from substance and continuity towards instability, fragility, contingency and contextuality (Kellner 1992) and the links between identities and social structures are broken.

Analyses that understand the contemporary period in terms of reflexive modernisation also assert the fluidity and multiplicity of identities, but they retreat from more radical claims about the dissolution of social structures and stable concepts of selfhood that characterise postmodern analyses. For Giddens (1991a) reflexive modernisation refers to the fact that all social practices are constantly subject to examination and potential revision. The certainty of scientific knowledge and tradition gives way to the realisation that social life must be underpinned by reflexively applied knowledge, but such knowledge is always unstable and changeable. Reflexivity thus attempts to provide a rational basis for social practice, while simultaneously undermining the possibility of rational certainty. The pervasive reflexivity of modern life undercuts the four central bases of trust in premodern societies, kinship relations, localised community relations, religious cosmologies and traditional authority (Giddens 1991a). In modernity, personal relationships of friendship and sexual intimacy replace kinship relations as a means of stabilising social ties across time and space. Localised communities with identities tied to place are undermined by globalising processes which link the local and global, and religion and tradition are overturned by reflexively organised knowledge based on abstract thought and systematic empirical observation (Giddens 1991a).

Reflexivity also permeates processes of identity formation. Within modernity, social identity becomes a reflexive project (Harre 1983; Giddens 1991a), as people exercise increasing choice over the identities that they want to matter to them and those that they do not. Just as new and appealing identities are able to be selected and lived-out, those forms of social identity which lose meaning and social signifi-cance are discarded. At the same time, however, identities are not as fluid, contingent and variable as postmodernism would argue. Indi-viduals need to maintain "ontological security", that is confidence that their self-identity and surrounding conditions and circumstances have some ongoing durability and reliability (Giddens 1991a). For ontological security an individual's self-identity, as a collection of reflexively constructed personal and social identities, needs to be coherently organised, and there needs to be some predictability about the social relations and conditions of daily life which individuals encounter.

Postmodernisation and reflexive modernisation thus have similarities and differences in the way they theorise identity formation and processes in contemporary societies. Both accounts imply increasing "voluntarism" around identity processes and formation and the importance of multiple identities to self-identity. Both theories also imply that structurally based identities rooted in kinship and family relations, religion, class and work, and localised communities should be of declining significance.

Symptomatic of these developments have been debates about the decline of class as a principal feature of contemporary societies and the emergence of new social relationships linked to lifestyle patterns and individualised consumption (Beck 1992; Crook *et al.* 1992; Bradley 1996; Pakulski and Waters 1996). The decline of traditional institutions and forms of social organisation described by reflexive modernisation, and the hyperdifferentiation of postmodernisation both imply a declining significance of class, work and occupational identities.

The theories differ, however, in whether they conceive of multiple identities being coherently organised within individual subjectivities, and how they think about the socio-structural grounding of identities in contemporary societies. For postmodern theorists, identities are completely fluid, disconnected from social structures and picked up and discarded at will. Individuals have multiple selves based on multiple identities, which are not organised in any transcontextual stable hierarchy. There is no continuity of identity across time or space, for theorists of postmodernity. For theorists of reflexive modernisation, identities are reflexively constructed but coherently organised. The reflexive "self" is a coherent individual project that is not the same as the postmodern "selves" that comprise the "postmodern individual" (if that is not an oxymoron). It is also quite consistent with reflexive modernisation that new structurally rooted identities that have their origins in ascribed differences, race, ethnicity, gender, age, nationality, and the like, emerge, while traditional identities rooted in work, family, religion and locality decline (Beck 1992; Jenkins 1996). Ascribed identities, because they are widely recognised and have clear markers around physical characteristics, language, dress, accent and style provide an experiential basis for social categorisation that is highly salient for identity formation (Jenkins 1996) under conditions of reflexive evaluation of all social practices. Within theories of postmodernity, however, hyperdifferentiation and individualised self-expression undermine the formation of perceptions of identity and difference according to such social categories.

Towards a theory of identity

The primary aim of this chapter is to document contemporary empirical trends in the salience of different social identities. Before this however, we provide a preliminary statement of our own theoretical position on identity in response to the arguments just outlined. In our view postmodern claims about identity are not sustainable for two major reasons.

From the point of view of ontological security, or from the point of view of maintaining a psychologically sustainable self-identity, it is insupportable to claim that identities are entirely contingent, changeable and have no transcontextual existence. Without some continuity of identity across time and space individuals cannot sustain sanity (Weigert *etal.* 1986) or function competently as knowledgeable actors across their daily lives. Contingent, fluid and ever-changing identities not only make it extremely difficult for individuals to be in the world, they make it virtually impossible for others to know how to deal with them.

Second, the postmodern view that identities are infinitely variable and subject only to individual choice does not appear sustainable. The highly individualised hyperdifferentiated identities endorsed by some theorists of postmodernisation are not materially or socially accessible to large sectors of the population, including the young, the unemployed, and the otherwise socially disadvantaged. There are real social, material and economic constraints on the capacity to express our identities through consumption and other means that are structured by relations of age, class, gender and ethnicity (Bradley 1996). In addition, it must be remembered that identities are enacted in social situations involving rules, norms, differential resources, and other actors. The successful enactment of an identity always depends on institutional features of the situation, prevailing social relations and the dramaturgical skills of performers within it (Weigert *etal.* 1986). Actors with more institutional power, advantaged social positions or greater skill may be able to impose identities on others, despite their preferences for alternatives. Garfinkel's (1956) analyses of degradation ceremonies in which negative identities such as "cheat", "traitor" or "adulterer" are forcefully imposed on people, regardless of their will, illustrate this latter process (Weigert *etal.* 1986).

These arguments imply that the voluntaristic and asocial conception of identity associated with postmodernism is incorrect. They also imply that opportunities for reflexively constructed identities are not equally distributed across the population. Individuals who are socially, economically and politically advantaged by relations of class, gender, age, ethnicity and so on may have more freedom to reflexively construct their identities without reference to others than individuals in subordinate social positions. These individuals may also actively and reflexively construct their identities, but will typically do so with respect to dominant social relations and groups (Skeggs 1997; McDonald 1999).

On this view, identity can usefully be defined as "a typified self at a stage in the life course situated in a context of organised social relationships" (Weigert *et al.* 1986: 53). A person's social identity is constructed in reference to social category systems (Frable 1997) and reflects their different social identifications. We follow Turner (1984: 527) in defining social identification as "the internalisation by an individual of socially significant social categories as aspects of his [*sic*] self-concept". In common with theorists of postmodernisation and reflexive modernisation we recognise that individuals have multiple social identities that are available to them, but these are socio-historically specific and hierarchically and coherently organised (Weigert *et al.* 1986). The socio-historical availability of identity should be obvious to sociologists – there are many fewer Althusserians in sociology departments than there once were, and perhaps even fewer positivists.

In complex and differentiated societies people necessarily have multiple identities. These are hierarchically arranged in terms of their importance to the self, and must also adapt to the importance expected by others. Such identities must also be flexible to accommodate changing situational requirements (Weigert *et al.* 1986), but they must be coherent enough and durable enough across situations to preserve ontological security and psychological well-being. In routine social situations, organising identities is unproblematic, and knowledgeability entails being able to present a single appropriate identity in a taken-for-granted way with confidence that it will be accepted, understood and appropriately responded to.

In times of rapid social change, however, and at certain critical points in the lifecourse, the need to organise and reorganise multiple identities becomes overt (Weigert *et al.* 1986). The birth of a child, for instance, frequently brings about a reorganisation and re-prioritisation of identities for both women and men. Other significant life-events, marriage, divorce, retirement, major illness may similarly reconfigure identities. Contemporary changes associated with increasing social differentiation, rising social and geographic mobility, educational expansion and changing social and cultural norms may also bring about changes to the organisation of social identities. The empirical processes identified by theorists of postmodernisation and reflexive modernisation undoubtedly have implications for identity formation even if we disagree about what these implications might be.

Although we are unaware of systematic empirical evidence about how social identities are changing in contemporary societies, some existing empirical research on related issues provides indirect evidence that such changes may be occurring. First, public opinion research tends to suggest that in a range of societies, socio-structural factors are of declining importance in shaping opinions, attitudes and beliefs (Studlar and Welch 1981; McAllister 1994). Secondly, in Australia, and elsewhere, researchers suggest that class is of declining significance as a determinant of voting behaviour and electoral choice (Kemp 1978; Aitkin 1982; McAllister 1994; Weakliem and Western 1999). Both these sets of findings have implications for changing patterns of social identification, because the theories that underwrite these research traditions essentially assume that the manner in which class and other aspects of social structure influence attitudes and behaviour is through identity formation or "social group loyalties" (McAllister 1994: 87). For the social structure to influence public opinion and electoral choice individuals need to feel loyalty to, that is identify with, the social categories implied by their socio-structural locations. If the impact of social structural factors on public opinion and electoral choice is either declining or variable over time, it suggests that socio-structural identities are themselves either declining in salience, or that the relative salience of different sources of identification is variable. There has not been much research on the first of these issues, but recent research in Australia and elsewhere examines the relative salience of a variety of class and non-class identities (Marshall *et al.* 1988; Emmison and Western 1990; Devine 1992b), with mixed results.

In addition to this research, many cross-national, longitudinal studies provide reasonably clear evidence of values changing in a postmodern direction over time. Most obvious here is the work of Inglehart (1997). Based on cross-national survey evidence collected between 1970 and the mid-1990s in 43 countries, Inglehart argues for a broad shift from modern to postmodern orientations in advanced industrial societies. The most well-known aspect of Inglehart's wide-ranging research programme has concerned the gradual movement from materialist to postmaterialist values. Amongst the strongest evidence for this change has been the shift amongst general publics across Western societies from economic and physical security to self-expression and quality of life as their country's highest priorities. Most recently Inglehart and Baker (2000) have asserted and found evidence that traditional values emphasising religion and traditional authority have (partially) given way in the industrialised societies to secular/rational values emphasising rationality and abstract knowledge. The findings are consistent with Giddens's (1991a) arguments about reflexive modernisation and detraditionalisation. Similarly, the results of Halman's (1995) cross-national study of changes over time in moral orientations are consistent with arguments about the diminished role of religion and tradition and the increased importance of individualism and voluntaristic choice in the construction of human action. Using attitudinal data collected in 1981 and 1990 from a cross-national survey of 15 Western and Eastern European countries, Halman found strong evidence for a decline in civic virtues (e.g. living a claiming state benefits illegally, cheating on taxes) and an increase in permissiveness (e.g. married men/women having an affair, homosexuality).

This empirical research highlights the importance of taking a "generational approach" (Whittier 1997) to the study of value change. Following Mannheim (1996), researchers argue that generational differences in the formative experiences of members of different age cohorts shape these members' orientations and value preferences. Generations have distinctive cultures and traditions arising from shared experiences and collective memory (Turner 1999). Inglehart, for instance, attributes generational differences in values associated with younger people's greater tendency to prioritise postmaterialist goals to their formative experiences of material affluence, and physical security, both of which free them from the need to worry about materialist concerns, and enable them to valorise postmaterialist goals of affection, esteem and self-actualisation.

Generational explanations also have implications for identity formation in post- and reflexive modernity. Turner (1999) argues that postmodernisation may lead to greater fluidity in generational identities, implying greater fragmentation of the identities that members of different generations hold. Conversely, economic changes associated with postmodernity, such as persistent youth unemployment may entrench material differences between older more affluent generations, and younger more disadvantaged ones. The political and economic dominance of more affluent generations enables them to monopolise cultural icons and promotes the formation of separate generational identities based on cultural dominance and cultural resistance. This is manifested in generational distinctions around popular music, fashion, "style" more generally, art, literature and politics (Turner 1999). In Australia, Davis (1997) has argued that such generational differences in identity are reflected in the way an ageing baby boomer elite dominates the mass media and other means of cultural and intellectual production and marginalises and disparages aspects of contemporary youth culture and politics.

The theoretical arguments and empirical studies mentioned here suggest several broad expectations about changing patterns and processes of social identification. First almost all this literature suggests that class and work-based identities are less important than they once were. Persistent long-term unemployment excludes large numbers of people from paid work and casualised and precarious employment regimes, coupled with international trends to deunionisation problematise the organisation of collectivist work and class-based identities (Beck 1992; Pakulski and Waters 1996). Second theories associated with new politics and new social movements suggest that non-class bases of identity organised around gender, nation, ethnicity, and so on are increasingly significant (Beck 1992). Alternatively, there are some grounds for thinking that collectivist identity sources in general will be of little salience, as people base their identities in highly individualised lifestyles and modes of consumption. Finally we might expect these processes to accelerate over time and to be more evident among younger cohorts than older ones, whose identity hierarchies were organised according to earlier social and institutional frameworks.

Research methods and analytic strategy

The theoretical and empirical literature suggests some ways in which social identities respond to social change. However, as already noted, much of the evidence is indirect. To provide direct evidence on these issues we focus on three specific research questions. Is the relative salience of different sources of identity changing over time? Does it vary by "generation" or birth cohort? Does the articulation of different identities vary over time and by generation? To investigate these questions, we use data provided by two national sample surveys conducted 12 years apart, to analyse change in the social identifications of Australians that occurred from 1986 to 1998. The first of these surveys is the 1986 Class Structure of Australia Survey, which is the Australian component of the Comparative Project on Class Structure and Class Consciousness, directed by Erik Olin Wright. The second is the 1998 Australian Election Survey, a survey of electors, timed to closely follow a Federal election, and similar to the British Election studies. The Class Structure of Australia Survey was interviewer administered with a multi-stage cluster-sampling design. The Election Survey was a postal survey based on a stratified systematic sample drawn from the Commonwealth Electoral Roll. There are minor differences between the samples in terms of age and gender. Forty four per cent of the 1986 sample is female compared to 50 per cent of the 1998 sample and the average age of respondents in the 1986 sample is 36, while in 1998 it is 47. On birthplace, however, the two samples are virtually identical. In 1986, 60 per cent of respondents were born in Australia of parents who were also Australian born. In 1998 the corresponding figure is 59 per cent. In 1986 and in 1998, 25 per cent of respondents were born overseas. The remaining 16 per cent or so on both samples are Australian born respondents with at least one overseas born parent.

Each survey contains 14 or 15 Likert style items measuring the salience of different sources of social identification. Broadly speaking respondents are asked to indicate how important various provided identity sources, such as class, gender and ethnicity, are to them. In this analysis we focus on 10 sources of identification that are common across both surveys. It is important to emphasise that we are focusing on social identification with a range of possible social categories, rather than on the broader aspects of the identities associated with these categories. Identities, broadly conceived, involve labels, names and categories through which people address others and themselves. They entail typi-fied ways of speaking, thinking and acting, and they originate in socially constructed, institutionalised meanings (Weigert *et al.* 1986). We focus on only a very limited aspect of social identity, the distinct identification with a social category, but to our knowledge, this is the first time that trend data have been presented on even this issue.[1]

For most of the analysis we investigate trends in the patterning of identification by sample and by three birth cohorts or "generations". These cohorts are defined with reference to the baby boom generation. The baby boom cohort consists of those born between 1946 and 1960 (aged between 26 and 40 in 1986 and 38 and 52 in 1998). The pre-baby boom cohort consists of those born before 1946, while the post-baby boom cohort consists of those born after 1960. The baby boom generation is clearly recognised as a "watershed generation" experiencing the affluence of the post-war long boom and comparatively high levels of physical security. Inglehart, for instance, identifies this group as distinctive in the acquisition of postmaterialist values. In Australia, as already noted, the baby boom generation is also identified as an elite cultural grouping that dominates cultural production and maligns the cultural and political practices of subsequent generations (Davis 1997).

The analytic strategy for the chapter is simple. We begin by using simple descriptive statistics to examine the salience of the 10 different identity sources by cohort and by sample. Next we systematically examine cohort and over time differences in the strength of identification using logistic regression. Finally we examine sample and cohort differences in the way people combine these identity sources using principal components analysis.

Changing patterns of social identification

Table 8.1 presents data relating to the salience or popularity of different identity sources by cohort, sample, and for the combined data set. For simplicity the identity responses have been dichotomised into identifiers and non-identifiers, and the table shows the percentage of people identifying with each source.[2] As can be seen the identity items comprise a range of socio-structural categories (class, gender, ethnicity and religion), territorial/locational identities linked to nation, place and region (Australian, state, town, sports team), and public sphere identities associated with work and politics. These are all "modernist" identities linked to social categories, rather than postmodern ones reflecting the highly differentiated individualised lifestyles and consumption patterns that some theorists argue characterise postmodern identity formation. Nonetheless, as we have already seen, theorists of reflexive modernisation and postmodernisation anticipate that formerly central modernist identities to do with class, work, family, religion and local community have either declined or been replaced by others, such as gender, age and ethnicity.

Table 8.1 shows remarkable consistency in the rankings or relative salience of the identity sources across cohorts and samples. The nation is clearly the most popular source of identification with at least 80 per cent of respondents in all cohorts identifying with being an Australian and 76 per cent of respondents in 1986, and 87 per cent of respondents in 1998 identifying this way.[3] In contrast to theorists such as Offe (1985) or Beck (1992) who argue that work no longer has the centrality for identity that it once did, over three quarters of all cohorts indicate their occupation is an important basis of identification. The percentage of respondents identifying on the basis of occupation has actually increased over the 12-year period from 1986 to 1998.

Turning to the remaining identity sources there is hardly any cohort variation in their relative popularity. The salience rankings across all 10 sources are virtually identical for the two younger cohorts, with gender being the most salient structural basis of identification, and the popularity of the territorial identity sources for town and state complementing the popularity of the nation as an identity source. Ethnicity, class and religion are all comparatively weak bases of identification, with fewer than half the respondents in each cohort identifying with them.

Table 8.1 Popularity of different sources of identification across three birth cohorts in 1986 and 1998

Pre-baby boom cohort		Baby boom cohort		Post-baby boom cohort		1986		1998		Combined	
Australian	86	Australian	80	Australian	80	Australian	76	Australian	87	Australian	83
Job	76	Job	78	Job	80	Job	72	Job	82	Job	78
State	64	Gender	56	Gender	60	Town	54	Town	69	Town	57
Town	63	Town	52	Town	54	State	51	Gender	62	Gender	56
Gender	54	State	51	Ethnicity	54	Gender	46	State	54	State	56
Ethnicity	54	Ethnicity	44	State	52	Ethnicity	40	Ethnicity	47	Ethnicity	47
Religion	48	Social class	37	Town	49	Town	36	Political party	45	Religion	40
Political party	46	Religion	34	Religion	45	Religion	33	Social class	44	Social class	39
Social class	37	Political party	33	Sports team	37	Sports team	32	Religion	42	Political party	36
Sports team	32	Sports team	28	Social class	33	Social class	23	Sports team	30	Sports team	31
				Political party	27	Political party					

One relevant cohort variation in Table 8.1 is that the relative popularity of gender is higher in the baby boom and post-baby boom cohorts than in the pre-baby boom cohort. However, this principally occurs because the number of baby boomers and post-baby boomers identifying on the basis of state and town is less than the number of state and town identifiers in the pre-baby boom cohort. Place-based identities are particularly strong amongst the oldest cohort and this relegates gender further down the identity hierarchy. The objective level of gender identification does not change substantially over the three cohorts.

In terms of over time change, the main difference between 1986 and 1998 is that there seems a stronger tendency in 1998 to identify with almost all bases of identity, with the exception of gender and ethnicity. This process largely explains the drop in salience of these two identity sources in 1998.

The final column of Table 8.1 presents overall rankings of the different identity sources. This gives us an "identity hierarchy" for the entire pooled sample. What is significant about this is how strongly traditional modernist identities associated with the nation, and with work, are ranked. Over three quarters of respondents perceive these to be salient, with other place-based identities and gender also being important. This evidence undermines postmodern and reflexive modernisation claims about the declining significance of traditional work-based and community-based identities (Offe 1985; Giddens 1991b; Beck 1992), but does provide some support for claims about the re-emergence of new structural sources of identity, such as gender, and the declining significance of class (Beck 1992; Pakulski and Waters 1996). The consistency of rankings across years and cohorts also undermines postmodern claims about the contextuality and fluidity of contemporary identities and gives more credibility to the view that identities are stably hierarchically organised.

To test sample and cohort differences in identification more systematically, Table 8.2 presents the results of logistic regression analyses regressing each identity measure on variables for time and cohort. We first tested for sample and cohort interactions, implying that cohort differences are not the same across samples. If the interaction between sample and cohort was not statistically significant for a given identity we then examined the additive effects of sample and cohort. The table summarises the results of these analyses presenting predicted probabilities from the appropriate (additive or interactive) logistic model.[4]

The logistic regression analyses indicated that the only identity sources for which cohort differences themselves varied in 1986 and

Table 8.2 Predicted probabilities of identifying with different identities by time and by cohort

Identity source	1986			1998		
	Pre-baby boom	Baby boom	Post-baby boom	Pre-baby boom	Baby boom	Post-baby boom
Australia	0.81	0.72	0.77	0.90	0.88	0.82
State	0.55	0.43	0.41	0.70	0.59	0.57
Town	0.46	0.37	0.34	0.74	0.66	0.63
Job	0.74	0.72	0.68	0.77	0.83	0.85
Gender	0.57	0.59	0.63	0.52	0.54	0.58
Ethnicity	0.56	0.46	0.52	0.52	0.42	0.48
Class	0.30	0.31	0.36	0.41	0.42	0.49
Religion	0.45	0.32	0.34	0.50	0.36	0.39
Political party	0.28	0.24	0.12	0.57	0.41	0.35
Sports team	0.31	0.31	0.42	0.33	0.25	0.28

1998 were Australian, job, political party and sports team. For all other identities cohort differences in identification did not vary over time.

Beginning with Australian we can see that in 1986 over 80 per cent of members of the pre-baby boom generation identified with the nation while only 72 per cent of the baby boom generation did. The regression results imply that this is the only significant difference in 1986. In 1998, however, both the pre-baby boom generation and baby boomers were more likely than the youngest cohort to identify with Australia, although levels of identification among all three cohorts are very high. For the other two territorial identities, generational differences are constant over time, and show the same pattern for each identity. Members of the oldest cohort are significantly more likely than either baby boomers or the post-baby boom generation to identify with their state and town. In addition, identification with these regional sources is stronger in 1998 than in 1986 as was also suggested in the previous table. Together the results suggest that national and regional identities are more salient among older cohorts than younger cohorts, regardless of time period.

Turning now to the status-based identities, gender, ethnicity, class and religion we again find some systematic differences. In both 1986 and 1998, members of the youngest cohort are more likely to identify on the basis of gender, than members of the oldest cohort are. Members of the youngest cohort are also more likely to claim a class identity than members of the other two cohorts, while members of both the oldest and youngest cohorts are more likely to identify on the basis of ethnicity than baby boomers are. Finally, members of the oldest cohort are also distinctive in identifying on the basis of religion, being more likely to identify than individuals in either of the other two cohorts. Overall, with respect to the status-based identities, the youngest cohort is distinctive in its class identification, the oldest cohort in its religious identification, and the baby boomers by the weakness of their ethnic identification.

The fact that younger cohort members are identifying more with structural sources of identity such as gender and class undermines generational arguments that the postmodern decoupling of identities and social structures will be more common among the young. Certain traditional identities, most notably religion, prevail among the oldest cohort, but others do not. The finding with respect to gender is much more consistent with our arguments about the socio-historical availability of identities, than a more general postmodern claim about the erosion of socio-structural sources of identity. Feminism sensitises both women and men to gender, with the effect that gender identification is strongest among the young and least among the aged, with the baby boom cohort occupying a middle position. The finding with respect to class is also noteworthy, since the death of class thesis probably also implies that class is least salient as a basis of identification among the young. Young people have the weakest connections to institutions (trade unions, political parties, full-time employment) that might ostensibly promote a class identity and yet class identification is highest in the youngest cohort.

In terms of over time change in the socio-structural identities, there is no consistent trend in the data. Gender and ethnic identification declined over the period, but class and religious identification increased. These trends contradict postmodern expectations about the declining significance of core modernist identities associated with class and religion. They also contradict Giddens's (1991b) arguments about reflexive modernity and the disappearance of core bases of trust located in religion and tradition.

The remaining two identities, political party and sports team both exhibit interactions between sample and cohort. In 1986 members of the youngest cohort identified less with a political party than members of either older cohort. In 1998, both the baby boomers and the post-baby boomers are less likely to identify with a political party than members of the oldest cohort are. However, levels of party identification are higher in 1998 than in 1986 in all three cohorts, a finding which contradicts some previous research showing declining partisanship in

Australia over time (McAllister 1994: 41). One relevant issue here is the change in the party system between 1986 and 1998. Australian politics in 1998 was arguably more diverse than in 1986 with a wider range of minor parties (Democrats, Greens, One Nation) existing in addition to the major ones. Increased choice may be associated with higher levels of party identification as previously disenchanted electors are drawn to new parties. Party identification may also be stronger immediately after an election campaign (as was the case with the 1998 survey), than in the period between elections (1986).

Finally, in 1986 members of the youngest cohort were significantly more likely to identify with a sports team than members of the other two cohorts. However, by 1998, the only cohort difference occurs between the two older cohorts, with the pre-baby boom generation more likely to identify with their sports team than baby boomers.

The evidence to this point indicates that levels of identification with place-based and status-based socio-structural identities are comparatively high and relatively stable over time and cohort. This does not suggest that either postmodern or reflexively modern societies have distinctively new forms and processes of social identity. To conclude the empirical analysis, we next examine the ways different identity sources are structured or interlinked. Do people who believe that class is an important basis of identification also believe than gender is important, for instance, and do people who reject class also reject gender? If identities are completely fluid and contextual, survey responses will be essentially random, and there will be no coherent structure in the way identities are articulated. On the other hand, if identities are systematically organised we should find clear patterns or "structures" in the empirical associations between different identity sources. We investigate this issue in Tables 8.3 and 8.4, using principal components analysis to see if the identity sources are empirically associated in ways that make theoretical sense. In Table 8.3 we carry out the principal components analysis separately by year. In Table 8.4 we present similar analyses by cohort.

Table 8.3 shows that in 1986 the identity measures fall on two largely interpretable factors, and one weaker, and less interpretable one. In 1986, identities could quite clearly be grouped into a territorial dimension, geographically bounded, and consisting of multiple overlapping "imagined communities". This dimension comprises state, Australian, town and sports team. The second dimension comprises socio-structural or positional based identities, class, gender and ethnicity. The third dimension comprising religion and political party does not represent

Table 8.3 Principal components analysis of identity sources by year

1986	Factor 1	Factor 2	Factor 3	1998	Factor 1	Factor 2	Factor 3
State	**82**	8	16	State	**79**	20	19
Australian	**73**	1	6	Australian	**72**	−1	9
Town	**69**	13	16	Party	**69**	29	8
Sports team	**42**	17	−13	Team	**46**	33	16
Class	2	**72**	13	Religion	16	**78**	4
Gender	7	**65**	−12	Gender	10	**75**	12
Ethnicity	18	**60**	14	Ethnicity	20	**69**	30
Job	25	29	23	Job	5	10	**85**
Religion	6	2	**78**	Class	20	29	**68**
Political party	5	9	**67**	Town	**53**	6	**62**
Total variance explained	19.5	14.5	12.3		22.3	19.8	17.5

Note: Component loadings are multiplied by 100 and rounded to nearest integer. Loadings greater than 0.40 are shown in bold.

a strong association in the data, however these two identity sources represent, in particular ways, potential sites of core beliefs and values. As Bean's (1999) work has shown, there have historically been strong connections between religion and electoral politics in Australia, with religious divisions a significant source of political behaviour.

In 1998 we again see indications of the territorial based dimension (state, Australian, town and team), although it is less coherent than in 1986. Political party now also loads on this dimension, and the town-based identity loads strongly on both the first and third factors. The second factor, comprising religion, gender and ethnicity is a status-based or socio-structural dimension, similar to that found in 1986, but the third weak factor, comprising occupation, class and town is not found in 1986. This last dimension combines key factors of class-based identity rooted in an occupational community, where the coincidence of work, class and residence combine to lead to the formation of solidaristic class identities (Blauner 1964; Lockwood 1966), but such occupational communities are increasingly rare in globalised economies. In any event, the basic finding of the over time analyses is that the territorial and status dimensions to social identity persevere over the time period, but that these dimensions are slightly less coherently structured in 1998 than they were in 1986.

Table 8.4 Principal components analysis of identity sources by cohort

Pre-baby boom	Factor 1	Factor 2	Factor 3	Baby boom	Factor 1	Factor 2	Post-baby boom	Factor 1	Factor 2	Factor 3
State	**78**	9	22	State	**79**	20	State	**79**	21	-2
Australian	**73**	-1	6	Australian	**78**	-7	Australian	**71**	2	5
Political party	**62**	33	-4	Town	**70**	21	Town	**62**	19	38
Town	**57**	-3	**56**	Party	**42**	37	Party	**58**	11	27
Team	**46**	21	12	Job	**40**	37	Team	**46**	**43**	**-44**
Gender	5	**75**	8	Sports team	33	30	Ethnicity	16	**73**	2
Religion	21	**66**	-1	Ethnicity	18	**70**	Religion	11	**69**	18
Ethnicity	9	**63**	30	Gender	4	**62**	Gender	3	**65**	3
Job	5	5	**83**	Class	26	**59**	Class	26	**45**	**40**
Class	17	28	**63**	Religion	7	**59**	Job	20	15	**80**
Total variance explained	21.5	16.4	15.6	Total variance explained	31.5	11.5	Total variance explained	22.2	19.3	12.4

Note: Component loadings are multiplied by 100 and rounded to nearest integer. Loadings greater than 0.40 are shown in bold.

In Table 8.4 we investigate the articulation of identity sources by cohort. The oldest cohort shows three reasonably clear dimensions – a territorial dimension, this time including political party along with state, Australia, town and sporting team; the status-based or socio-structural dimension comprising gendered, religious and ethnic identifications, and the class and work-based identity identified previously. Among baby boomers, the identity items load only on two dimensions one comprising the territorial sources (Australia, state and town), but including party and job; and the other representing a clear socio-structural dimension (ethnicity, gender, class religion). Political party and job load weakly on both factors.

The youngest cohort also illustrates territorial (state, Australia, town, sporting team) and status-based identities (Ethnicity, Gender, Religion, Class), but these are somewhat more fragmented in that the sports team-based identity loads moderately strongly on all three factors. There is also a comparatively clear articulation of class and job – two central modernist identity sources in the youngest cohort, although class is also associated with the second socio-structural factor. This positional dimension of social identity is also clearly defined in the youngest cohort, which we would not anticipate according to postmodern arguments about the highly individualised fluidity of identity formation processes among postmodern individuals.

Discussion and conclusions

This evidence suggests that territorial and positional identities are still salient over time and by generational grouping. The territorial identities are arguably more important than the socio-structural ones for most people, but certain socio-structural identities, notably gender (especially for the youngest cohort), and religion for the older cohort remain highly important components of the self. Respondents see their gender and their religion as being important qualities that distinctively shape "who they are". Class, paradoxically, is a more important source of identity for the youngest cohort than for the older cohorts. In addition, the relative salience of identity sources is remarkably consistent over time and by cohort, as is their articulation, as revealed by the principal components analysis.

These findings suggest that there is more commonality and consistency about levels and patterns of social identification than postmodern theory suggests. We found little evidence of an absence of structure in the way identities are articulated, no evidence that work as source of identity is unimportant (indeed quite the contrary – almost 80 per cent of all respondents saw their job as an important source of identification), and some evidence that class and religion are only important identity sources for less than half the population. Although this is only preliminary research into social identification, and we do not address deeper issues about the meaning of such identifications, Australia does not appear to exhibit the kind of postmodern identity flux that theorists such as Lipovetsky (1994), Bauman (1992) or Lyotard (1979) emphasise. The evidence highlights consistency and continuity of identities among different groups, over time, and within individuals, rather than instability and discontinuity as postmodern accounts predict. There is also mixed support for theorists of reflexive modernisation. Class and religion are not salient sources of identity for many people, supporting the claims of Beck (1992) and Giddens (1991b) that these earlier modernist identities have declined in significance. However, place-based identities, which link ideologically to notions of community, are highly salient. This finding applies both to the nation, as an imagined community, and to localised places such as states and towns. Moreover, there is only limited evidence that socio-structural identities in general are unimportant sources of identification. The weakest structural bases of identity, class and religion, are still claimed by about 40 per cent of respondents.

The evidence with respect to salience and patterning therefore does not suggest that the contemporary period is one in which social identity processes are distinctively different from earlier times. But this research admittedly addresses change over time in identity processes in a limited way. What is missing is a detailed investigation of the meanings associated with the different sources of identity. Social identities are "social", they entail and construct perceptions of similarity and difference and inclusion and exclusion (Jenkins 1996; Weigert *et al.* 1986). They also have important affective components that involve emotions and feelings, such as warmth, disdain and disgust (Weigert *et al.* 1986). Important changes in the meanings associated with social identities could be occurring, even when the hierarchical ordering of identities appears stable. In addition, consistency across groups in the salience of identities does not necessarily indicate consistency across groups in the meanings associated with those identities.

Identification with Australia provides a case in point. Previous research into the symbolic dimensions of the Australian national community suggests that the boundaries defining what it means to be "Australian" can be conceptualised in terms of internal and external friends and enemies (Phillips 1996). Such boundaries identify "insiders" who are part of the symbolic community of Australia and "outsiders" who are not. The 1998 Australian Federal election was distinctive for the presence of Pauline Hanson's One Nation Party, which attempted to mobilise a national rhetoric based on populist conceptions of insiders and outsiders. "Insiders" in this rhetoric included "ordinary" Australians, "battlers" and Anglo-Australians (Ward *etal.* 2000), while outsiders included elites of various kinds, especially political elites (i.e. the established parties), members of certain ethnic communities, welfare recipients, Aborigines, academics and the mass media (Ward *etal.* 2000). The One Nation Party had little success at the 1998 poll (although elements of their highly exclusive conception of the national community have arguably since been adopted by the major political parties). Yet, the presence of One Nation in the 1998 election can be seen to reflect the extent to which the identities of Australia and Australian are contested. While our evidence suggested that national identification was widespread in 1998 following the election, the electorate was clearly divided about what such identification meant. Such dissensus in popular conceptions of the nation was also strongly evident during the Australian constitutional referendum in the following year (Charnock 2001).

This argument suggests that the research agenda for identity in the contemporary period needs to move in several directions. First, cross-national studies need to extend this research, by further investigating issues relating to the salience and structuring of modernist identities associated with place and social structures. Without cross-national research into the salience and structuring of social identities we do not know how general our findings are. Perhaps Australia is distinctive in the extent to which modernist identities hold sway. Second, postmodern identity forms rooted in consumerism and individual self-expression also need to be systematically examined. One of the characteristics of the postmodern individual may be the ability to switch back and forth between modern and postmodern identities, largely at will. We may have tapped into the modernist elements of the "postmodern self" in this research by concentrating on modernist identity sources. Alternatively, one element of the "postmodern individual" may be a capacity to hold and present modernist identifications alongside postmodern ones. In subsequent research we intend following this issue further. Finally, research needs to address seriously the meanings of social identities, the extent to which such meanings are contested, and the social structuring and implications of those identities. Deeply contested identities are also likely to be highly salient to the actors concerned, and to be significant causes of social and political action. Contested identities provide a basis for political mobilisation and action at local, regional, national and supranational levels, as recent debates in Australia around national identity and events since September 11, 2001, indicate. We cannot infer similarity in the content and meaning of social identities from broad similarities in the ordering of identity hierarchies and the articulation of the social identities that comprise them.

Notes

1. It is also important to emphasise that we focus primarily on "modernist" identity sources linked to social categories and groupings rather than more individualistic "postmodern" ones. We have information about postmodern identifications in the 1998s data, which are the subject of another paper, but no comparable data in 1986. Since this chapter is primarily concerned with examining trends and generational differences in identities we limit our analysis to sources of identification that are common to both datasets.
2. This can be thought of as the average probability that an individual will claim this identity. The ranking of identities in terms of probabilities thus bears directly on issues of their relative "salience".
3. One sampling issue is relevant here. The 1986 survey used an area-based sample, while the 1998 survey uses the Commonwealth Electoral Roll as a sampling frame. The electoral roll is confined to Australian citizens and Commonwealth citizens who were enrolled to vote in Australia in 1984. The citizenship requirement partly explains the stronger identification with Australia in 1998.
4. When we fit the interactive model, the predicted probability of identifying simply equals the observed probability. However, the regression analysis also gives us statistical tests of the regression coefficients that translate (roughly) into tests of differences between cohorts in the probability of identifying.

9
Class Analysis: Beyond the Cultural Turn

Rosemary Crompton and John Scott

It was argued in the Introduction that debates in the area of class, as is the case in many other debates in sociology, have been crucially affected by wider intellectual developments. The most significant of these wider issues has been the 'cultural turn', an increasing emphasis on the significance of cultural factors, over and above the economic or material, in sociological explanation. It was also noted in the Introduction that the cultural turn is itself 'turning', resulting in a re-evaluation of the salience of culture. In this concluding chapter we re-address each of these issues as they affect class analysis.

Classical sociologists, such as Weber and Durkheim, recognised a duality of focus in their work and explored both the 'economic' and the 'social' as elements in sociological explanation (see discussion in Holmwood and Stewart 1983). This was especially recognised in the formulation of traditions of economic sociology, which insisted that economic life is 'embedded' in larger and all-encompassing social and cultural relations (Granovetter and Swedberg 1992; Smelser and Swedberg 1994). Putting the matter somewhat crudely, the framework of economic sociology argues that it is impossible to conceive of an 'economy' independently of some sort of functioning 'society' or encompassing set of social relations. Indeed, social relations necessarily precede exchange relations, and changes in the 'social' reflect changes in the 'economic', and vice versa.

The concept of class, as developed by Weber, Tonnies, Marx and the German tradition of sociology more generally, brilliantly encompasses this 'embeddedness'. Pre-modern societies are seen as combining 'status' and 'class' in their forms of stratification, with modern societies showing an increasing differentiation and autonomisation of economic class relations from the cultural and normative framework of traditional status.[1] Given the wide range of definitions of class, however, it is hardly surprising that individual social theorists and empirical researchers have varied in the relative emphasis that they have given to the economic and the cultural in their construction and use of class concepts.[2]

In the Introduction to this book, the empirical tradition of British work on class consciousness and ideology was briefly reviewed (Lockwood 1959, 1966; Brown and Brannen 1970; Newby 1977). Some of this work might be described as British social anthropology (Stacey 1960; Littlejohn 1963, see also Kuper 1973), given its focus on the in-depth case study. Devine and Savage have criticised the debate on class consciousness and ideology for its reliance on a theoretical model of structure/agency relations that did not adequately grasp the connections between these two levels of analysis. It is important to emphasise, however, that the body of empirical research that this debate was grounded in was both sensitive and insightful in its demonstration of the ways in which attitudes, behaviour, and 'identity' are systematically related to employment, social background, and locale. It is true that this empirical work was used to develop conceptual frameworks that might be construed as determinist (see in particular Lockwood 1996). Nevertheless, we would argue that there is a continuing need for this kind of empirical work if we are to understand social change over last 40 to 50 years. We will argue that, for all their many strengths, approaches informed by the work of Bourdieu (1977b) neither replace nor significantly improve upon this older and rather more straight-forward approach in which the consequences of employment (and its absence) were systematically explored in the context of neighbourhood and family.

Methodological contrasts in class analysis

The theoretical debates in sociology that culminated in the turn to culture and postmodernism began with the so-called 'paradigm wars' that are now being recognised as having come to an end (McLennan 2000). The critical rejection of what was often, crudely and simplistically, described as 'positivism' developed from the 1960s (Giddens 1974) and was as much about methods of social research as it was about the theoretical positions that were taken up. It involved, for example, a critique of quantitative and survey methods (Glaser and Strauss 1968), which were seen as reflecting the adoption of an inadequate natural science model of explanation. Survey research (bad) was criticised for its supposed indifference to human agency and for forcing the subjective understandings of 'real' human beings into abstract scientistic theoretical boxes, out of which questionable universalistic laws could be formulated.[3] In contrast, qualitative research (good) was praised for its focus on interpersonal understanding and subjective meaning and for producing authentic descriptions of the multiple social realities that constitute social life.

Research in class and stratification was significantly affected by these methodological disputes, as much as it was affected by substantive theoretical criticisms of its central 'class' concept (see the commentary on these debates in Crompton 1998). In Britain, the dominant 'employment aggregate' approach to class (Goldthorpe 1980, 1987; Erikson and Goldthorpe 1992) was overwhelmingly quantitative and variable-oriented. It utilised a class scheme that focused exclusively on employment relations. Indeed, the rationale of the Nuffield research programme developed by Goldthorpe and his colleagues required that the scheme should be 'as sharply defined as is operationally feasible, in order to avoid any confounding of class with other factors of possible relevance' (Goldthorpe and Marshall 1992: 385). In this approach to class analysis, class was assumed to be the independent variable, with only multivariate analysis having the ability to establish the relative significance of class and a range of other variables related to status, consumption, sex, and ethnicity (see also Wright 1985).

The criticisms levelled against this variable-oriented employment aggregate approach to class have been many and various. Feminists argued that it did not adequately conceptualise the work and employment situation of women. The initial response of both Goldthorpe and Wright to this criticism was to claim that gender inequalities are 'external' to the class structure, and so need not be considered. This response was rightly rejected for missing the crucial point that, whatever their relevance for status relations, gender divisions are also directly constitutive of class relations themselves. The Nuffield approach was also criticised for being excessively narrow and as having moved away from the Weberian concept of 'social classes' which are 'the outcome of both "class" and "status" processes' (Scott and Morris 1996: 48). The changing and complex nature of structures of employment – from which the nominal categories of the class scheme are derived – was also seen as problematic as far as the implementation of standard class schemes was concerned. Furthermore, the exclusive focus on employment relations ignored the crucial importance of property divisions in the formation of advantaged class situations (Penn 1981). It was argued that, taken in isolation, the employment aggregate approach excluded any systematic consideration of the *processes* of change and development in social class formation (Scott and Morris 1996; see also Crompton 1998).

Goldthorpe (1996, 2000) has recently come back with a trenchant defence and justification of variable-oriented class analysis, dealing with some, but by no means all, of the myriad criticisms levelled at the Nuffield programme. This defence forms a part of his larger programme for a new foundation for sociology. He argues that two elements can together form a central element in a rebuilt disciplinary core: the quantitative analysis of large-scale data sets (QAD) and rational action theory (RAT). Through QAD, empirical regularities concerning social facts can be established, and through RAT they can be explained (but see Devine 1998).

Work using QAD, Goldthorpe argues, has demonstrated the persistence of class differentials in educational attainment in Britain, despite the fact that educational opportunities have been formally extended to all. A RAT-based narrative explains this persistence on the basis of the benefits that accrue from improved educational options. These are more likely to be realised for children from the more advantaged families, and the relative costs of education for such families are, of course, lower. The third stage of the QAD/RAT approach involves a test of the validity of RAT-based explanations. Here, but nowhere else, Goldthorpe recognises a place for sociological ethnography in the empirical evaluation of RAT-based causal narratives. Goldthorpe argues, for example, that a causal narrative developed in relation to the question of the differentiation of employment contracts and their linkages to his class scheme could be tested in this way. In his own work, he cross-tabulates the degree of difficulty in work monitoring with the degree of specificity of human assets, in order to identify a series of spaces (high/high, low/low, low/high, etc.) that correspond to the occupational aggregates identified by the class scheme. These spaces are then available for ethnographic exploration. It may be argued, however, that Goldthorpe's solutions to what he sees as the general 'problems of sociology' are susceptible to similar kinds of criticism as have been levelled at his approach to 'class analysis'.

We will develop this argument by drawing a sharper distinction between variable-oriented and case-oriented approaches to social research.[4] It should be stressed that this distinction is not the same as that between quantitative and qualitative research, as case-oriented research may very often be quantitative. The contrast being discussed here, rather, is between particularising and generalising strategies, between historically oriented 'thick description' and radically analytic research strategies in which cases are broken into parts that are difficult to subsequently reassemble into wholes. Ragin (1992: 5) has argued that variable-oriented comparative work, in and of itself, both disembodies and obscures cases. He argues that a discourse on variables that is not balanced by a discourse on cases can too easily result in a detachment of the investigator from real situations and events. In extreme situations, this can degenerate '. . . into arid debates about the best way to measure variables and model their relationships without concern for the empirical events reflected in the variables' (Ragin 1991: 2).

This kind of criticism could well be levelled at some of the issues that have emerged around the debates on class schemes (e.g. Evans 1996; Jones and McMillan 2001). Furthermore, the QAD/RAT combination advocated by Goldthorpe is methodologically individualist, and indeed offers little (if any) space for the analysis of institutions as wholes. We would argue that research in class analysis, and indeed in sociological explanation more generally, requires a more complex and subtle understanding of the relationships between the micro and the macro (Archer 1995; Scott forthcoming).

We do not wish to reject 'variable-oriented' approaches to the study of social class and stratification, far from it. Rather, we would argue that case-oriented and variable-oriented approaches to class and stratification must be seen as *complementary* strategies and that *both* of them are necessary in order to understand the complex phenomena under investigation. The exploration of structures, such as organisations, localities, and labour markets, which are widely agreed, by researchers of different theoretical and methodological persuasions, to be central to the investigation of class and stratification can only be achieved through an approach that focuses its attention on system integration (Lockwood 1956). Indeed, much of the empirical work drawn upon and generated by Lockwood's classic analysis of class consciousness (see, in particular, Bulmer 1975b) is case-oriented in character. Indeed, the influential work that Goldthorpe undertook with Lockwood (the 'Affluent Worker' studies) focused on the interrelation of institutions in a particular local labour market with specific employing organisations (Goldthorpe *et al.* 1968a,b, 1969).

This complementarity of methodological approaches is apparent in the chapters, which use a diversity of methods to investigate the complex topics encompassed by class and stratification.

Taking culture (too) seriously

It is important to recognise, however, that the variations between different approaches to social class do not rest upon methodological distinctions alone. In the first chapter of this book, Devine and Savage have described the 'impasse' that developed in class analysis during the 1980s. This impasse, they argue, developed because the strengthening theoretical tendency to take culture and consciousness more seriously as an autonomous, driving force in social change was not associated with any defensible theoretical linkages between structure and action or, specifically, between class structure and class consciousness. Devine and Savage see this as a positive and significant break that has reoriented class analysis and moved it on in new directions. They argue that 'Insofar as values and norms are recognised as powerful in their own terms, this involves breaking from a tradition that links them to structural foundations. You cannot have your cake and eat it' (p. 11). Thus, 'taking culture seriously involves breaking from stratification research, at least as conventionally conceived' (p. 11). They point to the reorientation of stratification research from studies of class consciousness to studies of identity, where identities are viewed not simply as 'reflections of position', but rather as 'claims for recognition'. This trend is something that, with certain reservations, we welcome as opening up new and neglected issues. Devine and Savage draw extensively on the theoretical work of Bourdieu to frame an alternative approach to stratification research, which, they suggest, offers 'a distinctive new approach to issues of class, culture and identity which focuses on the complex interplay between habitus, reflexivity, and identity' (p. 15).

Bourdieu's approach is certainly of considerable value in any attempt to understand and explain the interdependencies and connections between economic and cultural capital. We would hesitate, however, to follow our co-editors in claiming that it can completely replace other theoretical and methodological approaches that have sought to explore the economic *and* cultural dimensions of class. As we will argue later on, a renewed emphasis on identity and difference should not be allowed to obscure or to downgrade one of the major preoccupations of class analysis, which is the study of structured social inequality. To develop our argument, it will be useful to draw upon some of these other debates about the relative salience of the cultural and the economic in social life. The most fruitful way into these debates, so far as their implications for research on class and stratification are concerned, is to begin from a contrast between 'dual systems' and 'unitary' approaches to the culture and economy question.

Those authors who advocate what might, with some over-simplification, be described as a dual systems approach argue that the crucial differences between culture and economy must be respected (Ray and Sayer 1999). This approach, like that of Parsons (1937) and Habermas (1981a,b), emphasises the normative aspects of culture and the instrumental aspects of economising. Culture, they argue, involves 'a concern with practices and relationships to which meanings, symbols or representations are central: in short, "signifying practices"' (Ray and Sayer 1999: 5). Cultural phenomena are mutually shared and never simply imposed by one group on another. By contrast, '...economic activities and processes involve a primarily instrumental orientation; they are ultimately a means to an end, satisfying external goals to do with provisioning' (ibid.: 6). Although economic activities are always culturally embedded, it is possible to distinguish between the cultural or normative and the economic or instrumental activities and phenomena (see also Lockwood 1956). In respect of social class, therefore, a dual systems perspective would draw a distinction between, on the one hand, the 'objective' outcomes of class processes, such as material differences in income and wealth and the social relations associated with these, and, on the other hand, the 'subjective' and culturally mediated experiences of class relations. From this point of view, what is required is a *combination* of cultural and economic analyses in order to grasp the totality of 'social class'. It is a matter of both/and, not of either/or (see Bradley 1996; Fenton and Bradley 2002).

The alternative 'unitary' approach depicts culture and economy as constituting an indivisible *totality*. As Du Gay and Pryke have argued:

> Instead of viewing a market or firm as existing prior to and hence independently of descriptions of it, the turn to culture instigates a reversal of this perception, by indicating the ways in which objects are *constituted* through the discourses used to describe them and act upon them. (Du Gay and Pryke 2002: 2, our emphasis)

From this point of view, no distinctions can be drawn between economic and cultural practices, for they are one and the same thing. For example, commercial success or failure in retailing (and in many other industries as well) depends on the quality of their interactive service delivery. Employees in these organisations are trained, through a variety of interpersonal and communication management techniques, to exhibit the capacities and conduct that produce certain meanings for customers and thus sales for the company. In such jobs, it is argued, cultural and economic practices are fused. For Du Gay and Pryke, therefore, 'cultural economic analysis' is '...an emergent form of enquiry concerned with the practical material-cultural ways in which "economic" objects and persons are put together from disparate parts' (ibid.: 8).

The unitary or 'cultural economy' approach, as described by Du Gay and Pryke, has parallels with Bourdieu's approach to stratification. As Devine and Savage have noted in their summary of Bourdieu in Chapter 1: 'There is no question of there being a relationship between "base" and "superstructure" or between "economic" class and "social" class; these terms are simply meaningless within a Bourdieuvian perspective' (p. 14).

Whether culture and economy are viewed as dual (albeit closely related) systems or as forming a totality has major implications for empirical research. A dual systems approach to culture/economy, furthermore, is perfectly compatible with quantitative, variable-oriented approaches to stratification, which may be extended to incorporate cultural as well as economic variables. It is also compatible with the relatively orthodox sociological and anthropological approaches characteristic of previous community and occupational case study work.

A unitary approach to culture and economy is, arguably, not only more restricted in its methods but is also an area where intensive methodological developments are required. It is clear that 'variable oriented' methods would be far less appropriate (but see Stewart *et al*. 1980). The methods employed are likely to be fine-grained, ethnographic, and historical. As Du Gay and Pryke (2002: 8) note, what is required for cultural economic analysis are the 'grey, meticulous and patiently documentary' genealogical methods recommended by Foucault).

Another issue of some importance in relation to recent theoretical debates is the relative significance of the 'cultural' *per se*. Put simply, the discussion focuses on whether, under the conditions of contemporary capitalism, the distinctions between economy and culture have blurred, and indeed 'cultural' considerations, broadly conceived, are driving economic activities. That is, 'cultural' rather than 'economic' issues may have become more significant for our understanding of contemporary society. Indeed, many advocates of the unitary position have suggested that the shift from 'economics' to 'culture' involves a larger societal shift, an epochal change towards post-modern social conditions (Crook *et al*. 1992; Lash and Urry 1994; Pakulski and Waters 1996). In relation to class, this argument has taken a variety of guises. There has been, for example, a discussion of whether consumption is more significant than production in shaping class identities. It has been argued that more and more areas of the economy are, effectively, devoted to cultural production and reproduction with all the myriad repercussions for employment and class that this involves. There has also been a debate as to whether the 'aesthetisation of production' has meant that sign value has become more important than exchange value in the structuring of commodities (Baudrillard 1972).

In terms of strict logic, if economy and culture are seen to be fused, then the unitary approach cannot even raise the question of whether economic or cultural factors are more significant in social explanation. The economic and the cultural are one and the same thing, and they cannot even be analytically separated. Indeed, it may be suggested that one limitation of a strict application of this totalising 'cultural economy' approach is precisely that the possibilities for causal explanation are significantly restricted. 'Grey, meticulous and patiently documentary' research may produce insightful historical and ethnographic descriptions, but its advocates tend to ignore the fact that the purpose of social research, particularly in the area of class and stratification, is not merely to describe but also to explain social and economic inequalities.

In practice, however, many of those who are ostensibly committed to a unitary approach are nevertheless prepared to make assertions relating to the changing importance or significance of 'culture'. In common with the 'cultural turn' more generally, these assertions are usually to the effect that culture has become somehow more significant in determining social positions. Advocates of the dual systems approach, however, are less convinced that such a change has occurred. This may be because, having evaluated the 'cultural primacy' arguments empirically and theoretically, they consider them to be mistaken (Sayer and Walker 1992). They recognise the embeddedness of the economic in the cultural, and they note that this recognition is long overdue in class and stratification research, but this does not necessarily imply that the claim that culture has become more important. Yet others are relatively agnostic or uncommitted on this issue, simply emphasising the need to explicitly recognise and study what has previously been neglected.

In this section we have drawn out two themes emanating from the turn to culture. First, whether culture and economy should properly be viewed as a unitary system or as a dual system; and second, whether cultural, as opposed to economic, factors have become generally more significant in the determining of economic and social position (class) in contemporary societies. We have suggested that an answer to the second question requires some element of 'dual systems' thinking, even if it does not go all the way back to the older 'structure and consciousness' approach.

The contributions to this book

The theoretical and methodological issues discussed above are all reflected in the various chapters included in this book.

The most 'orthodox' position is, perhaps, that of Devine, who directly approaches the question of the use of the language of 'class'. Reviewing the conventional approaches to this question, she traces the changing use of class labels by the middle classes in America and Britain. Using her own data, she shows how ideas of 'class' are often equated, in fact, with the Weberian idea of 'status' in a larger conception of 'social class'. She shows, however and rather surprisingly, that the language of class was used by a higher proportion of people in America than in Britain. This she explains in terms of the differing cultural resonances of the term 'middle class'.

This approach is broadened by Anthias, whose concern is to look at the non-class factors in social differentiation and inequality and, in particular, divisions of gender and race/ethnicity. She identifies three models of stratification, which relate closely to the distinctions that we have made. She rejects both the 'reductionist' model, which is associated with attempts to reduce gender and ethnicity to class relations, and the 'identity' model, which is associated with trends in post-modernist theory. In place of these, she allies herself with a modified variant of what she calls the 'intersectionality' model. According to this model, people must be seen as occupying multiple and overlapping social positions which may be either reinforcing or contradictory in their effects on both inequality and collective identity. Anthias argues that a recognition of this 'translocational positionality' of social inequality must not focus on the purely descriptive, but must highlight the processes through which such multiple positions are reproduced. In arguing this point, she develops an unacknowledged reformulation of Lenski's (1954) argument on 'status inconsistency' in multidimensional systems of social stratification.

Blokland's chapter turns from class labels to class communities. She makes the obvious, but nevertheless important, point that a felt sense of community is not the automatic result of the ways in which people categorise themselves, though she glosses rather the even more important question of whether people's own categorisations are an authentic result of their objective structural location. As we have argued above, the latter linkage is far from automatic, and we suspect that Blokland would not disagree. She concentrates on the social construction of community among residents of a locality in the Netherlands that is seen by policy makers as a working-class 'problem' area. She places particular emphasis on collective memory and the narrative accounts that people produce to explain their lives to themselves and to each other. She shows how the demise of a distinctive working-class identification was associated with an increase in the ethnic diversity of the area.

Savage and his colleagues break new ground through the use of Bourdieu to explore similar issues. They develop his approach through the use of a local case study of Cheadle, which they believe will allow them to develop a richer descriptive account of class processes. They reject conventional arguments about the decline or fragmentation of the working class and argue that a distinctive class habitus can still be found among workers living in Cheadle. Rooted in manual skills, this involves shared cultural values and a sense of belonging. They suggest that the apparent disappearance of the working class as a focus of academic concern is as much a consequence of pressures on academics that have made it more problematic for them to take an oppositional stance as structural changes in class relations themselves. Although Savage and his colleagues engage with newer theoretical frameworks, their work may be seen as, in part, a return to the 'community studies' tradition of the 1960s and 1970s. It lacks, however, the central premise on which some of these early studies foundered – that is, their work does not seek to define 'community' in precise, spatial, terms but rather emphasises the inter-weaving of employment and place in the generation of identity.

The unitary view of culture and economy is most clearly developed by Skeggs, who argues that there has not been a shift *from* economy *to* culture (understood dualistically), but rather a deployment of culture as an economic resource. Economics, she argues, has been reduced to culture, and the economy becomes a 'symbolic economy'. Skeggs focuses on the symbolic production of class: the ways in which individuals and groups attain value through symbolic exchange, and how this constrains their movement through social space. She argues that cultural practices have become central to class formation because of their role in this symbolic exchange. This enhanced importance of culture is seen as a consequence of a 'de-materialisation' of commodity production: an orientation of production towards more mobile commodities that are desired for their symbolic meaning as much as – if not more than – their physical properties. This de-materialisation, she argues, is manifested most clearly in such things as branding and the use of image in advertising. Here she looks, in particular, at the middle-class cultural appropriation of the working class and its experiences as symbolic objects of cultural consumption. Despite pointing to the persistence of capitalist structures, these are not incorporated as autonomous structuring principles. They appear, at best, as residual factors that are untheorisable except as cultural forms.

The chapter by Phillips and Western takes up general issues of identity formation, arguing that, in the contemporary world, the links between stable (typically 'class') identities and stable social structures have broken down and each side of the relationship has become highly fragmented. Contemporary identities, they claim, are fluid and are specific to particular concrete contexts. They do not, however, follow post-modernist ideas on this. They remain closer to the views of Giddens, who sees a continuing importance for social structures as shaping and conditioning factors in social life. From this point of view, the construction of identity is a 'reflexive project' through which people attempt to construct a sense of stability. Phillips and Western use these ideas to identify the socio-historical formation of identity in Australia. They find that territorial and structural identities remain as important factors in identity formation and that class is especially salient for the youngest cohort in their study. Overall, they conclude, Australia is firmly 'modern' rather than 'post-modern', so far as the fluidity of individual and collective identities is concerned.

Like Phillips and Western, Vester uses Durkheim's concept of the social milieu. Where the former link this to the territoriality of action, however, Vester allies it with Bourdieu's approach to social fields and sees the social milieu in cultural terms rather than in the material 'morphological' terms stressed by Durkheim himself. The central part of his chapter is an analysis and mapping of class positions and an exploration of the 'hegemonic' relations among these positions. For each position, Vester examines the characteristic background and orientation of its members. He looks at the dissolution of class and class culture in Germany, and the emergence of 'new' milieux for identity formation. These new milieux – those of the 'vanguard' – are rooted in the expansion of knowledge and information, especially since the 1960s, and the consequent enhanced importance of cultural capital. The relations among these positions and their relative sizes reflect

		Importance of culture	
		'Agnostic' on culture	*Culture more important*
Culture–economy relationship	*Unitary*	Vester	Skeggs
	Dual	Devine, Phillips and Western, Anthias, and Savage *et al.*	Blokland

Figure 9.1 The culture–economy relationship and the relative significance of culture and economy in sociological explanation

generational relations: the traditional working class milieu, Vester argues, is now characteristic of the 'grandparent generation', while the 'modern employee' position comprises the 'grandchildren' generation of the 1960s. Within the latter, however, generational effects are also at work, as – by contrast with the findings of Phillips and Western – it is the newest recruits who show the strongest development of the new habitus.

The different approaches to the incorporation of culture (broadly defined) into 'class analysis' (defined equally broadly) suggest there is no 'one best way' to approach the topic. Thus (and in some contrast with the first chapter in this book), in developing new approaches to class analysis, we would not lay a major emphasis on the widespread adoption of Bourdieu's approach, but rather advocate the development of a range of culturally sensitive approaches to class and stratification. In relation to the distinctions we have identified in this chapter, we would suggest that the chapters in this book may be usefully mapped as in Figure 9.1.

The strange problem of the baby and the bathwater

Our conclusion from reviewing the contributions to this book is that there is no one 'best way' as is often implied by those who have taken up Bourdieu. There are, rather, a range of culturally sensitive approaches to class and stratification. What, then, have been the benefits to our understanding of issues in class and stratification of the cultural turn? It is difficult to give a straightforward answer to this question. The main positive effects of the cultural turn might, with hindsight, be seen to be indirect rather than direct. The theoretical debates associated with the turn to culture did serve to challenge the tendency to subsume other social differentiations – such as gender and ethnicity – within the 'class' problematic. As has been argued in the Introduction, the *impasse* reached in the debate on class consciousness, together with the dominance of an economistic, variable-oriented approach to class analysis, merely served to divert attention away from the role of culture in social and economic structuring. To the extent that the cultural turn has re-inserted cultural issues into stratification debates, this is to be warmly welcomed. It remains the case, however, that this re-balancing of research in class and stratification that was brought about by the turn to culture also had a negative impact. In particular, it tended to write class itself out of the agenda of social theory and research, virtually replacing it with discussions of culture, consumption, and identity alone.

This has had unfortunate consequences for sociological thinking in relation to issues of inequality. Inequality was always central to the class enterprise, and indeed the capacity to measure (and to some extent to account for) inequality has been central to the major justifications offered for the enterprise itself (Goldthorpe and Marshall 1992). Central to the old mainstream of class analysis had been the measurement of inequality and the distribution of advantages and disadvantages by class situation. Employment-based classes were found to be located in relatively clear and sharp gradients according to their life chances, and these were recognised as the major determinants of differences in style of life, collective consciousness, and political action. Research into social mobility showed the high degree of closure that existed in recruitment patterns to class situations and, therefore, the ways in which opportunities for advancement were constrained by class position. It is not possible to summarise such research here, but we might highlight, for Britain, the joint and separate works of Goldthorpe and Lockwood on the working class and the middle class (Lockwood 1959; Goldthorpe *et al.* 1968a,b, 1969), Savage and Devine on the working class (Savage 1987; Devine 1992a), Goldthorpe (1980, 1987); the work of Payne (1987) on social mobility; of Crompton on the intermediate or 'white-collar' classes (Crompton and Jones 1984); of Townsend (1976) on poverty; of Scott (1991) on the upper class, and the evidence compiled by Reid (1998).

Such a research focus was all-but-lost with the turn to culture, and this has major implications for social policy debates. As an increasing number of authors have noted (O'Neill 1999; Frank 2000), an emphasis on the reflexive individual and a focus on individual identities rather than collective actions and outcomes have many resonances with neoliberalism. The promotion of individual rights and recognition meshes well with the arguments of those who have criticised the way in which collective provision has disempowered individuals. Thus, as O'Neill (1999: 85) argues, there has been something of a '...convergence of a postmodern leftism with neoliberal defences of the market'.

Thus 'identity politics' associated with the cultural turn have serious consequences for the politics of equality. If individual recognition is to be the primary political objective, then issues of redistribution fall by the way-side. It is paradoxical (to put it mildly) that this theoretical shift took place at precisely the same time that the intensification of capitalist economic activity was actually generating increasing levels of inequality. As O'Neill (2001) puts it: 'the fragmentation of social citizenship is now accelerated by the New Right's curious adoption of left cultural relativism'. There is a very real danger of 'winning cultural battles but losing the class war'.

A further tension in identity politics is that the pressure for individual recognition can over-simplify group identities, thus promoting separatism and indeed perpetuating negative within-group inequalities deriving from, for example, patriarchalism and authoritarianism. Fraser (2000) has described this as a problem of 'reification'. She has recently suggested a rethinking of these theoretical tensions between redistribution and recognition politics through an analysis that draws upon Weberian class concepts (she cites the extracts from Weber in Gerth and Mills 1948; see also Scott 1996, 2002).

Fraser's argument rests on the analytic separation of culture and economy, following what we have described as the dual systems approach. She suggests that the 'culturalist' theories of contemporary society that fuse economic inequality seamlessly into the cultural hierarchy result in an all-too-present danger of 'displacement'. That is, economic inequalities are effectively subsumed within, or displaced onto, cultural concerns. In such a model,

> to revalue unjustly devalued identities is simultaneously to attack the deep sources of economic inequality; (and) no explicit politics of redistribution is needed. (2000: 111)

Such 'vulgar culturalism' is nothing more than the mirror image of the 'vulgar economism' that characterised cultural or status differences as deriving directly from economic inequalities (a position criticised, for example, in Lockwood 1988). However, in contrast to vulgar culturalism and as we have argued above, the current reality in capitalist societies is that the economic mechanisms of distribution are at least partially decoupled from cultural patterns.

Fraser argues that the theoretical problems of 'reification' and 'displacement' can be resolved by returning to the Weberian distinction between 'class' and 'status' that we have highlighted above. 'Class' involves relationships that are constituted in economic terms as specific market situations, most typically defining specific employment and property relations. The 'status' order, on the other hand, involves 'socially entrenched patterns of cultural value... culturally defined categories of social actors' (Fraser 2000; see also Scott 1996 for a systematic elaboration of this distinction). This distinction allows Fraser to highlight two analytically distinct dimensions of social justice, one involving the distribution of disposable resources and one involving the allocation of recognition. The latter – central for advocates of the cultural turn – concerns the effects of institutionalised meanings and norms on the relative standing of social actors. Where Weber saw this as relating to collective identities and styles of life, Fraser recognises that, under contemporary conditions, this relates far more to individual variations in lifestyle:

> what requires recognition is not group-specific identity but the status of individual group members as full partners in social interaction. Misrecognition, accordingly, does not mean the depreciation and deformation of group identity, but social subordination... to redress this injustice still requires a politics of recognition, but in the 'status model' this is no longer reduced to a question of identity. (Fraser 2000: 113; see also Scott 2002)

Claims for both economic redistribution and cultural recognition, Fraser argues, can be appraised against the same evaluative standard of 'participatory parity' (Fraser 2000). Such evaluative standards concern the question of what social arrangements will permit all adult members of society to interact with one another as peers. This argument implicitly resurrects Marshall's (1948) idea of citizenship. The idea of citizenship concerns the civil, political, and social rights that make possible the effective participation of a person in the society of which they are a member. It comprises the conditions that make it possible to enjoy the styles of life and range of individual choices that members of a society have come to regard as normal.[5]

Fraser's particular concern is with the ways in which the citizenship idea can generate valid claims to cultural recognition (see also Pakulski 1997). Thus, she argues that not all recognition claims can be met. Elements of (collective) identity claims that discriminate against certain categories of group members, such as women, for example, would not be valid on this basis.

Fraser's resolution of the 'equality versus difference' conundrum, as we have noted, rests upon a 'dual systems' approach to economy and culture. We suggest that this further strengthens our general argument that to view culture and economy as unitary places unnecessary limitations on research and analysis in class and stratification. We would suggest that Bourdieu's approach, which has been extensively drawn upon by a number of contributors to this volume, may be interpreted in either a 'unitary' or a 'dual' fashion. Particularly in his earlier writings, Bourdieu can be 'read' as taking a dual systems approach, although some of his contemporary followers (see Chapter 4) take a 'unitary' perspective. There is, therefore, some ambiguity as far as Bourdieu's position is concerned.[6] However, we do not think that it would be particularly fruitful to enter into a debate on 'what Bourdieu really meant'. Rather, we have simply suggested that some of his contemporary followers have adopted a *de facto* 'unitary' approach, and have sought to explore the implications of this position.

In conclusion, therefore, we have suggested that the move beyond the cultural turn has resulted in a diversity of responses. Culture and economy are inter-twined, but as long as they are seen, for the purposes of analysis, as dual systems then this inter-twining may be explored using both variable-oriented as well as case-study research methods. Similarly, the question of whether cultural factors (or status) have become more important in the determination of class position (social and economic positioning) may be systematically investigated through the study of a variety of locales, occupations, institutions, and social groups. In short, in our conclusions to this volume we would re-affirm our pluralistic stance in relation to research on class and stratification, and would not advocate recourse to current interpretations of Bourdieu alone.

Notes

1. Here an exception must be made in the case of Marx, who argued that pre-capitalist societies are 'class' stratified. However, Marx's conceptualisation of pre-capitalist 'classes' has many parallels with Weber and Tonnies status/ gemeinschaft groupings.
2. For this reason, we do not here seek to identify one 'best' definition of class, or one best way of undertaking class analysis. In our introduction to the first volume for this seminar series (Crompton *et al.* 2000) we concluded that the multidimensional character of stratification means that a genuine pluralism is

required in analysis and research. Genuine pluralism, however, is not the same thing as relativism or agnosticism. If there is no single over-arching concept of 'class' it follows that some approaches to the concept will have strengths that others do not, and vice versa. See the general account of this epistemological position in Scott (in May and Williams 1998).

3. See, for example, the debates relating to Durkheim's *Suicide* (Cicourel 1964; Douglas 1967).

4. The issue has been extensively debated in a special issue of *Comparative Social Research*, Volume 16, 1997.

5. This argument was used by Townsend (1976) in his construction of analyses and redistributive claims concerning the level of poverty and deprivation, and similar arguments have been made by Scott (1994) for the existence and assessment of wealth and privilege.

6. For example, Bourdieu (1977a: 507) writes of '... the relative autonomy enjoyed by the academic market on account of the fact that the structure of distribution of cultural capital is not exactly the same as the structure of economic capital and of power'.

Bibliography

Abbott, A. (2001) *Chaos of Disciplines*, Chicago: University of Chicago Press.

Abrams, M., Rose, R. and M. Hindon (1960) *Must Labour Lose?*, Harmondsworth: Penguin.

Adkins, L. (2002) *Revisions: Gender in Late Modernity*, Milton Keynes: Open University Press.

Adkins, L. and C. Lury (1999) 'The labour of identity: performing identities, performing economies', *Economy and Society*, 28: 598–614.

Aitkin, D. (1982) *Stability and Change in Australian Politics*, Canberra: Australian National University Press.

Alexander, J. (1994) *Contemporary Social Theory*, London: Verso.

Allan, G. and G. Crow (1994) *Community Life: An Introduction to Local Social Relations*, London: Harvester.

Anderson, B. (1983) *Imagined Communities*, London: Verso.

Anthias, F. (1998a) 'Rethinking social divisions: some notes towards a theoretical framework', *Sociological Review*, 46: 506–535.

—— (1998b) 'Evaluating diaspora: beyond ethnicity?', *Sociology*, 32: 557–580.

—— (2001) 'New hybridities, old concepts: the limits of culture', *Ethnic and Racial Studies*, 24: 617–641.

—— (2002) 'Where do I belong? Narrating collective identity and translocational positionality', *Ethnicities*, 2: 491–515.

Anthias, F. and N. Yuval Davis (1983) 'Contextualising feminism: ethnic gender and class divisions', *Feminist Review*, 15: 62–75.

—— (1992) *Racialised Boundaries: Race, Nation, Gender, Colour and Class and the Anti-Racist Struggle*, London: Routledge.

Archer, M. (1988) *Culture and Agency*, Cambridge: Cambridge University Press.

Archer, M.S. (1995) *Realist Social Theory*, Cambridge: Cambridge University Press.

Back, L. and V. Quaade (1993) 'Dream utopias, nightmare realities: imagining race and culture within the world of Benatton advertising', *Third Text*, 22: 65–80.

Baethge, M. (1991) 'Arbeit, Vergesellschaftung, Identität: Zur zunehmenden Subjektivierung der Arbeit in Wolfgang Zapf (ed.), *Die Modernisierung moderner Gesellschaften*, Frankfurt/Main, New York: Campus, pp. 260–278.

Baudrillard, J. (1972) *For a Critique of the Political Economy of the Sign*, St Louis, MO: Telos Press.

—— (1981) *For a Critique of the Political Economy of the Sign*, St Louis, MO: Telos Press.

Bauman, Z. (1982) *Memories of Class*, London: Routledge.

—— (1988) *Freedom*, Milton Keynes: Open University Press.

—— (1992) *Intimations of Postmodernity*, London: Routledge.

Bean, C. (1999) 'The forgotten cleavage? Religion and politics in Australia', *Canadian Journal of Political Science*, 32: 551–569.

Beck, U. (1992) *Risk Society*, London: Sage.

Becker, U., Becker, H. and W. Ruhland (1992) *Zwischen Angst und Aufbruch. Das Lebensgefuehl der Deutschen in Ost und West nach der Wiedervereinigung*, Duesseldorf: Econ.

Behagg, C. (1986) 'Myths of cohesion: capital and compromise in the historiography of nineteenth-century Britain', *Social History*, 11: 375–384.

Bell, C. and H. Newby (1975) 'The sources of variation in agricultural workers images of society' in M. Bulmer (ed.), *Working-Class Images of Society*, London: Routledge & Kegan Paul.

Bell, D. (1973) *The Coming of Post-Industrial Society: A Venture in Social Forecasting*, New York: Basis Books.

Bellah, R.N., Madsen, R., Sullivan, W.M., Swidler, A. and S. Tipton (1996) *Habits of the Heart*, second edition, Berkeley: University of California Press.

Bennett, T. (1998) *Culture: A Reformers Science*, London: Sage.

Bennett, T., Emmison, M. and J. Frow (1999) *Accounting for Tastes, Everyday Australian Cultures*, Cambridge: Cambridge University Press.

Berlant, L. (2000) 'The subject of true feeling: pain, privacy, politics' in S. Ahmed, J. Kilby, C. Lury, M. McNeil and B. Skeggs (eds), *Transformations: Thinking Through Feminism*, London: Routledge.

Beynon, H. (1975) *Working for Ford*, London: Penguin.

Beynon, H. and T. Austin (1994) *Masters and Servants: Class and Patronage in the Making of a Labour Organization*, London: Rivers Oram Press.

Bianchi, S. (1995) 'Changing Economic Roles of Women and Men' in R. Farley (ed.), *State of the Union: America in the 1980s*, Volume 1: *Economic Trends*, New York: Russell Sage Foundation.

Blackburn, R. (1967) 'The unequal society' in R. Blackburn and A. Cockburn (eds), *The Incompatables*, Harmondsworth: Penguin.

Blauner, R. (1964) *Alienation and Freedom*, Chicago: University of Chicago Press.

Bledstein, B.J. (2001) 'Introduction: storytellers to the middle class' in B.J. Bledstein and R.J. Johnston (eds), *The Middling Sorts*, New York: Routledge.

Blokland, T.V. (2001) 'Bricks, mortar, memories: neighbourhood and networks in collective acts of remembering', *International Journal of Urban and Regional Research*, 25: 268–283.

Blokland-Potters, T.V. (1998) *Wat stadsbewoners bindt: Sociale relaties in een achterstandswijk*, Kampen: Kok Agora.

Bonnett, A. (1998) 'How the British working class become white: the symbolic (re)formation of racialised capitalism', *Journal of Historical Sociology*, 11: 316–340.

Bosmans, J. (1988) 'Het maatschappelijk-politiek leven in Nederland 1918–1940' in J.C. Boogman (ed.), *Geschiedenis van het moderne Nederland: politieke, economische en sociale ontwikkelingen*, Houten: De Haan.

Bourdieu, P. (1977a) 'Cultural reproduction and social reproduction' in J. Karabel and A.H. Halsey (eds), *Power and Ideology in Education*, Oxford: Oxford University Press.

—— (1977b) *Outline of a Theory of Practice*, Cambridge: Cambridge University Press.

—— (1984) *Distinction: A Social Critique of the Judgement of Taste*, London: Routledge.

—— (1986) 'The forms of capital' in J.E. Richardson (ed.), *Handbook of Theory of Research for the Sociology of Education*, New York: Greenwood Press.

—— (1987) 'What makes a social class? On the theoretical and practical existence of groups', *Berkeley Journal of Sociology*, 32: 1–8.

—— (1989) 'Social space and symbolic power', *Sociological Theory*, 7: 14–25.
—— (1990a) 'L'economie de la maison', *Actes de la Recherche en Sciences Sociales*, 52: 81–82.
—— (1990b) *The Logic of Practice*, Oxford: Polity.
—— (1993) *Sociology in Question*, London: Sage.
—— (1997) 'The forms of capital' in A.H. Halsey, H. Lauder, P. Brown and A.S. Wells (eds), *Education, Culture, Society, Economy*, Oxford: Oxford University Press.
—— (1999a) *Pascalian Mediations*, Oxford: Polity.
—— (1999b) *The Weight of the World*, Cambridge: Polity.
Bourdieu, P. and J.-C. Passeron (1977) *Reproduction in Education, Society and Culture*, London: Sage.
Boyne, R. (2002) 'Bourdieu: from class to culture', *Theory, Culture and Society*, 19: 117–128.
Bradley, H. (1996) *Fractured Identities: Changing Patterns of Inequality*, Cambridge: Polity.
—— (1999) *Gender and Power in the Workplace*, London: Macmillan.
Brah, A. (1991) 'Difference, diversity, differentiation' in S. Allen, F. Anthias and N. Yuval Davis (eds), *Commonalities and Differences, International Review of Sociology*, Series 2: 53–73.
—— (1996) *Cartographies of the Diaspora*, London: Routledge.
Breen, R. and C. Rotman (1995) *Class Stratification: A Comparative Perspective*, London: Harvester.
Bremer, H. (1999) *Soziale Milieus und Bildungsurlaub*, Hannover: agis texte.
Bromley, R. (2000) 'The theme that dare not speak its name: class and recent British film' in S. Munt (ed.), *Cultural Studies and the Working Class: Subject to Change*, London: Cassells.
Brown, R. and P. Brannen (1970) 'Social relations and social perspectives among shipbuilding workers', *Sociology*, 4: 1.
Brown, W. (1995) 'Wounded attachments: late modern oppositional political formations' in J. Rajchman (ed.), *The Identity in Question*, New York and London: Routledge.
—— (2001) *Politics out of History*, Princeton, NJ: Princeton University Press.
Brubaker, R. and F. Cooper (2000) 'Beyond "identity"', *Theory and Society*, 29: 1–47.
Brunsdon, C. (1997) *Screen Tastes: Soap Opera to Satellite Dishes*, London: Routledge.
Buckingham, A. (1999) 'Is there an underclass in Britain', *Sociology*, 3: 49–75.
Bulmer, M. (1975a) 'Introduction' in M. Bulmer (ed.), *Working-Class Images of Society*, London: Routledge & Kegan Paul.
—— (1975b) 'Some problems of research on class imagery' in M. Bulmer (ed.), *Working-Class Images of Society*, London: Routledge & Kegan Paul.
—— (1978) 'Social structure and social change in the twentieth century' in M. Bulmer (ed.), *Mining and Social Change: Durham County in the Twentieth Century*, London: Croam Helm.
—— (1986) *Neighbours: The Work of Phillip Abrams*, Cambridge: Cambridge University Press.
Burgers, J. (2000) 'Rotterdam, wereldhaven' in G. Engbersen and J. Burgers (eds), *Illegale vreemdelingen in Rotterdam*, Amsterdam: Boom.
Butler, J. (1993) *Bodies that Matter*, London: Routledge.
—— (1998) 'Merely cultural', *New Left Review*, 227: 33–44.

Cannadine, D. (1999) *The Rise and Fall of Class in Britain*, New York: Columbia University Press.

Carchedi, G. (1977) *On the Economic Identification of Social Classes*, London: Routledge.

Castles, S. and G. Kosack (1973) *Immigrant Workers in the Class Structure in Western Europe*, Oxford: Oxford University Press.

Centres, R. (1949) *The Psychology of Social Class*, Princeton, NJ: Princeton University Press.

Cerulo, K.A. (1997) 'Identity constructions: new issues, new directions', *Annual Review of Sociology*, 23: 385–409.

Chaney, D. (1994) *The Cultural Turn*, London: Routledge.

Charlesworth, S. (2000) *A Phenomenology of Working-Class Experience*, Cambridge: Cambridge University Press.

Charnock, D. (2001) 'National identity, partisanship and populist protest as factors in the 1999 Australian republic referendum', *Australian Journal of Political Science*, 36: 271–291.

Cicourel, A.V. (1964) *Method and Measurement in Sociology*, New York: Free Press.

Cockburn, C. (1991) *In the Way of Women: Men's Resistance to Sex Equality in Organisations*, London: Macmillan.

Cohen, A.P. (1986) 'Of symbols and boundaries, or, does Ertie's greatcoat hold the key?' in A.P. Cohen (ed.), *Symbolising Boundaries: Identity and Diversity in British Cultures*, Manchester: Manchester University Press.

Cohen, P. (1988) 'The perversions of inheritance' in P. Cohen and H. Bains (eds), *Multi Racist Britain*, Basingstoke: Macmillan.

—— (1992) '"It's racism what dunnit": Hidden narratives in theories of racism' in J. Donald and A. Rattansi (eds), *'Race', Culture and Difference*, London: Sage.

Coleman, J. and L. Rainwater (1978) *Social Standing in America*, London: Routledge & Kegan Paul.

Collins, Hill P. (1990) *Black Feminist Thought*, London: Harper Collins.

—— (1993) 'Toward a new vision: race, class and gender as categories of analysis and connection', *Race, Sex and Class*, 1(1): 25–45.

Coward, R. and J. Ellis (1977) *Language and Materialism*, London: Routledge & Kegan Paul.

Craib, I. (1998) *Experiencing Identity*, London: Sage.

Crenshaw, K. (1994) 'Mapping the margins: intersectionality, identity politics and vilence against women of color' in, M.A. Fineman and R. Mykitiuk. *The Public Nature of Private Violence*.

Crewe, I. and B. Sarvlik (1981) *Decade of Dealignment*, Cambridge: Cambridge University Press.

Crompton, R. (1998) *Class and Stratification*, second edition, Cambridge: Polity.

Crompton, R. and G. Jones (1984) *White-Collar Proletariat*, London: Macmillan.

Crompton, R. and M. Mann (eds) (1986) *Gender and Stratification*, Cambridge: Polity.

Crompton, R., Devine, F., Savage, M. and J. Scott (eds) (2000) *Renewing Class Analysis*, Cambridge: Blackwell.

Crook, S., Pakulski, J. and M. Waters (1992) *Postmodernization*, London: Sage.

Crossley, N. (2002) *Making Sense of Social Movements*, Milton Keynes: Open University Press.

Crow, G. and G. Allan (1990) 'Constructing the domestic sphere: the emergence of the modern home in post-war Britain' in H. Corr and L. Jamieson (eds), *Politics of Everyday Life: Continuity and Change in Work and the Family*, London: Macmillan.

Dahrendorf, R. (1957) *Soziale Klassen und Klassenkonflikt in der industriellen Ge-sellschaft*, Stuttgart: Enke [*Class and Class Conflict in an Industrial Society*], London: Routledge (1959).

Davies, A. (1992) *Leisure, Gender and Poverty: Working-Class Culture in Salford and Manchester, 1900–1939*, Manchester: Manchester University Press.

Davies, A., S. Fielding and T. Wyke (1992) 'Introduction' in A. Davies and S. Fielding (eds), *Workers' Worlds: Cultures and Communities in Manchester and Salford 1880–1939*, Manchester: Manchester University Press.

Davies, M. (1994) 'Feminist appropriations: law, property and personality', *Social and Legal Studies*, 3: 365–391.

Davis, M. (1990) *City of Quartz*, London: Verso.

—— (1997) *Gangland: Cultural Elites and the New Generationalism*, St Leonards: Allen and Unwin.

Day, G. (2001) *Class*, London: Routledge.

de Regt, A. (1984) *Arbeidersgezinnen en Beschavingsarbeid*, Meppel: Boom.

De Swaan, A. (1995) 'Widening circles of identification: emotional concerns in sociogenetic perspective', *Theory, Culture and Society*, 12: 25–39.

Deleuze, G. and F. Guattari (1977) *Anti-Oedipus: Capitalism and Schizophrenia*, New York: Viking Press.

Dennis, N., Henriques, F. and C. Slaughter (1956) *Coal is Our Life: An Analysis of a Yorkshire Mining Community*, London: Eyre and Spottiswoode.

Der Stern (2000) *MarktProfile*, Hamburg: Stern.

Derrida, J. (1981) *Dissemination*, Chicago: Chicago University Press.

Devine, F. (1992a) *Affluent Workers Revisited*, Edinburgh: Edinburgh University Press.

—— (1992b) 'Social identities, class identity and political perspectives', *Sociological Review*, 40: 229–252.

—— (1997) *Social Class in America and Britain*, Edinburgh University Press.

—— (1998) 'Class analysis and the stability of class relations', *Sociology*, 32: 23–42.

—— (2004a) *Class Practices: How Parents Help Their Children Get Good Jobs*.

——(2004b) 'Talking about class in Britain' in F. Devine and M. Waters (eds), Social Inequalities in Comparative Perspective, Malden, MA: Blackwell.

Diawara, M. (1998) 'Homeboy cosmopolitan: Manthia Diawara interviewed by Silvia Kolbowski', *October*, 83: 51–70.

Donald, J. and A. Rattansi (eds) (1992) 'Introduction', *Race, Culture and Difference*, London: Sage.

Douglas, J. (1967) *The Social Meanings of Suicide*, Princeton: Princeton University Press.

Du Gay, P. and M. Pryke (2002) *Cultural Economy*, London: Sage.

Durkheim, E. (1893/1984) *The Division of Labour in Society*, Houndsmills: Macmillan (also 1902), Ueber soziale Arbeitsteilung, Frankfurt a.M.

Durkheim, Émile (1961) [1894] *Die Regeln der soziologischen Methode*, Neuwied.

Eaton, S.E. (2001) *The Other Boston Busing Story*, New Haven: Yale University Press.

Edgell, S., Hetherington, K. and A. Warde (eds) (1997) *Consumption Matters*, Oxford: Blackwells.

Elias, N. and J.L. Scotson (1985) *The Established and the Oustiders: A Sociological Inquiry into Community Problems*, Den Haag: Ruward (Dutch Translation).

Emmison, M. and M. Western (1990) 'Social class and social identity: a comment on Marshall *et al.*', *Sociology*, 24: 241–253.

Engels, F. (1844/1958) *The Condition of the Working-Class in England*, St Albans, Herts.: Panther.

Erickson, B. (1991) 'What is good taste for?', *Canadian Review of Sociology and Anthropology*, 28: 255–278.

Erickson, B. (1996) 'Culture, class and connections', *American Journal of Sociology*, 102: 217–251.

Erikson, R. and J.H. Goldthorpe (1992) *The Constant Flux*, Oxford: Clarendon Press.

Evans, G. (1992) 'Is Britain a class-divided society? A re-analysis and extension of Marshall *et al.*'s study of class consciousness', *Sociology*, 26: 233–258.

—— (1996) 'Putting men and women into classes', *Sociology*, 30: 209–234.

—— (2001) *The End of Class Politics?*, Oxford: Clarendon.

Fanon, F. (1986) *Black Skin, White Masks*, London: Pluto.

Farley, R. (ed.) (1995) *State of the Union*, Volume Two: *Social Trends*, New York: Russell Sage Foundation.

Featherstone, M. (1991) *Consumer Culture and Postmodernism*, London: Sage.

Fenton, S. and H. Bradley (2002) *Ethnicity and Economy: Race and Class Revisited*, Basingstoke: Palgrave.

Fentress, J. and C. Wickham (1992) *Social Memory: New Perspectives on the Past*, Oxford: Basil Blackwell.

Fine, B. (2001) *Social Capital versus Social Theory: Political Economy and Social Science at the Turn of the Millenium*, London: Routledge.

Flaig, Berthold B., Meyer, T. and J. Ueltzhoeffer (1993) *Alltagsaesthetik und politische Kultur*, Bonn.

Forde-Jones, C. (1998) 'Mapping social boundaries: gender, race and poor relief in Barbadian plantation society', *Journal of Women's History*, 10: 9–31.

Foucault, M. (1972) *The Archaelogy of Knowledge*, London: Tavistock.

—— (1979) *The History of Sexuality*, Volume One: *An Introduction*, London: Penguin.

Frable, D. (1997) 'Gender, racial, ethnic, sexual, and class identities', *Annual Review of Psychology*, 48.

Frank, T. (2000) *One Market under God*, New York: Doubleday.

Frankenberg, R. (1966) *Communities in Britain: Social Life in Town and Country*, London, Penguin.

Franklin, S., Lury, C. and J. Stacey (2000) *Global Nature, Global Culture*, London: Sage.

Fraser, N. (1995) 'From redistribution to recognition? Dilemmas of justice in "post-socialist" age', *New Left Review*, 212: 68–94.

—— (2000) 'Rethinking recognition', *New Left Review*, May/June.

Freud, S. (1949) *Group Psychology and the Analysis of the Ego*, New York: Liverlight.

Gallie, D. (1983) *Social Inequality and Class Radicalism in France and Britain*, Cambridge: Cambridge University Press.

Gamson, W. (1992) *Talking Politics*, New York: Cambridge University Press.

Gans, H.J. (1962) *The Urban Villages: Group and Class in the Life of Italian-Americans*, New York: Free Press.

—— (1988) *Middle American Individualism*, New York: Free Press.

Garfinkel, H. (1956) 'Conditions of successful degradation ceremonies', *American Journal of Sociology*, 61: 420–424.

Geiger, T. (1932) *Die soziale Schichtung des deutschen Volkes*, Stuttgart: Enke.

—— (1949) *Die Klassengesellschaft im Schmelztiegel*, Koeln und Hagen: Kiepenheuer.

Gerteis, J. and M. Savage (1998) 'The salience of class in Britain and America: a comparative analysis', *British Journal of Sociology*, 49: 252–274.

Gerth, H.H. and C.W. Mills (eds) (1948) *From Max Weber: Essays in Sociology*, London: Routledge & Kegan Paul.

Gibson-Graham, J.K. (1996) *The End of Capitalism (as we knew it)*, Oxford: Blackwell.

Giddens, A. (ed.) (1974) *Positivism and Sociology*, London: Heinemann.

Giddens, A. (1984) *The Constitution of Society*, Cambridge: Polity Press.

—— (1990) *The Consequences of Modernity*, Stanford: Stanford University Press.

—— (1991a) *Modernity and Self-Identity: Self and Society in the Late Modern Age*, Cambridge, UK: Polity Press.

—— (1991b) *The Condition of Modernity*, Cambridge: Polity Press.

—— (1997) *Jenseits von Links und Rechts*, Die Zukunft radikaler Demokratie, Frankfurt a.M.

—— (1999) *Der dritte Weg: Die Erneuerung der sozialen Demokratie*, Frankfurt a.M.

Gilman, S.L. (1992) 'Black bodies, white bodies: towards an iconography of female sexuality in late nineteenth century art, medicine and literature' in J. Donald and A. Rattansi (eds), *'Race', Culture and Difference*, London: Sage.

Gilroy, P. (1987) *There Ain't no Black in the Union Jack*, London: Hutchinson.

—— (1993) *The Black Atlantic*, London: Verso.

Gimenez, M. (2001) 'Marxism and class, gender and race: rethinking the trilogy', *Race, Gender and Class*, 8: 23–33.

Gittins, I. (2002) 'Crimwatch', *The Guardian*, Manchester.

Glaser, B. and A. Strauss (1968) *The Discovery of Grounded Theory*, Chicago: Aldine.

Goldthorpe, J.H. (1980) (in association with C. Llewellyn and C. Payne) *Social Mobility and Class Structure in Modern Britain*, first edition, Oxford: Clarendon Press.

—— (1987) (in association with C. Llewellyn and C. Payne) *Social Mobility and Class Structure in Modern Britain*, second edition, Oxford: Clarendon Press.

—— (1988) 'Intellectuals and the working class' in D. Rose (ed.), *Social Stratification and Economic Change*, London: Hutchinson.

—— (1996) 'Class analysis and the reorientation of class theory: the case of persisting differentials in educational attainment', *Sociology*, 47: 481–506.

—— (2000) *On Sociology: Numbers, Narratives and the Integration of Research and Theory*, Oxford: Oxford University Press.

Goldthorpe, J.H. and G. Marshall (1992) 'The promising future of class analysis', *Sociology*, 26: 381–400.

Goldthorpe, J.H., Lockwood, D., Bechhofer, F. and J. Platt (1968a) *The Affluent Worker: Industrial Attitudes and Behaviour*, Cambridge: Cambridge University Press.

—— (1968b) *The Affluent Worker: Political Attitudes and Behaviour*, Cambridge: Cambridge University Press.

—— (1969) *The Affluent Worker in the Class Structure*, Cambridge: Cambridge University Press.

Granovetter, M. and R. Swedberg (eds) (1992) *The Sociology of Economic Life*, Boulder: Westview Press.

Grusky, D.B. and R.M. Hauser (1984) 'Comparative social mobility revisited: models of convergence and divergence in 16 countries', *American Sociological Review*, 49: 19–38.

Grusky, D.B. and J.B. Sorensen (1998) 'Can class analysis be salvaged?', *American Journal of Sociology*, 103: 1187–1234.

Habermas, J. (1981a) *Theory of Communicative Action*, Volume 1: *Reason and the Rationalisation of Society*, London: Heinemann.

—— (1981b) *Theory of Communicative Action*, Volume 2: *The Critique of Functionalist Reason*, London: Heinemann.

Hage, G. (1998) *White Nation*, Melbourne and London: Pluto Press.

Hall, S. (1978) 'The political and the economic in Marx's theory of class' in A. Hunt (ed.), *Class and Class Structure*, London: Lawrence & Wishart.

—— (1990) 'Cultural identity and diaspora' in J. Rutherford (ed.), *Identity: Community, Culture, Difference*, London: Lawrence & Wishart.

Hall, S. and S. Jefferson (eds) (1975) *Resistance through Rituals*, London: Hutchinson.

Hall, S. and T. Jefferson (1977) *Resistance through Rituals: Youth Subcultures in Post-War Britain*, London: Hutchinson.

Hall, S., Critcher, C., Jefferson, T., Clarke, J. and B. Roberts (1978) *Policing the Crisis: Mugging, the State and Law and Order*, London: Hutchinson.

Hall, S., Held, D. and T. Mcgrew (eds) (1992) *Modernity and its Futures*, Cambridge: Open University Press.

Halle, D. (1984) *America's Working Man*, Chicago: University of Chicago Press.

Halle, D. and F. Romo (1991) 'The blue-collar working class' in A. Wolfe (ed.), *America at Century's End*, Berkeley: University of California Press.

Halman, L. (1995) 'Is there a moral decline? A cross-national inquiry into morality in contemporary society', *International Social Science Journal*, 145: 419–439.

Halsey, A.H. *et al.* (1980) *Origins and Destinations*, Oxford: Clarendon Press.

Hardt, M. and A. Negri (2000) *Empire*, Cambridge, MA: Harvard University Press.

Harre, R. (1983) 'Identity projects' in G. Breakwell (ed.), *Threatened Identities*, Chichester: John Wiley & Sons.

Hartmann, M. (1998) 'Homogenitaet und Stabilitaet. Die soziale Rekrutierung der deutschen Wirtschaftselite im europaeischen Vergleich' in Peter A. Berger and V. Michael (eds), *Alte Ungleichheiten: neue Spaltungen*, Opladen: Leske + Budrich, pp. 171–187.

Haylett, C. (2000) 'This is about us, this is our film! "personal and popular discourses of underclass"' in S. Munt (ed.), *Cultural Studies and the Working Class: Subject to Change*, London: Routledge.

—— (2001) 'Illegitimate subjects? Abject whites, neoliberal modernisation and middle-class multiculturalism', *Environment and Planning D: Society and Space*, 19: 351–370.

Heath, A., Jowell, R. and J. Curtice (1985) *How Britain Votes*, Oxford: Pergamon.

Hechter, M. (1987) 'Nationalism as group solidarity', *Ethnic and Racial Studies*, 10: 415–426.

Herz, Thomas A. (1990) 'Die Dienstklasse: Eine empirische Analyse ihrer demographischen, kulturellen und politischen Identitaet' in Peter A. Berger and S. Hradil (Hg.), *Lebenslagen, Lebensstile, Goettingen*: Otto Schwartz (Soziale Welt, Sonderband 7), S. 231–252.

Hill, J. (1986) *Sex, Class and Realism, British Cinema 1956–1963*, London: British Film Institute.

Hobsbawm, E. (1984) *Worlds of Labour: Further Studies in the History of Labour*, London: Weidenfeld & Nicholson.

Hodge, R.W. and D.W. Treiman (1968) 'Class identification in the United States', *American Journal of Sociology*, 73: 535–547.

Hoggart, R. (1957) *The Uses of Literacy*, London: Chatto.

Holmwood, J. and A. Stewart (1983) 'The role of contradictions in modern theories of social stratification', *Sociology*, 17.

Honneth, A. (1995) *The Struggle for Recognition*, Cambridge, MA: MIT Press.

Hout, M. (1988) 'More universalism, less structural mobility: the American occupational structure in the 1980s', *American Journal of Sociology*, 93: 358–400.

Hueting, E. (1989) *De permanente herstructuring van het welzijnswerk*, Zutphen: De walburg Press.

Hunt, P. (1980) *Gender and Class Consciousness*, London: Macmillan.

Inglehart, R. (1997) *Modernization and Postmodernization*, Princeton, NJ: Princeton University Press.

Inglehart, R. and W. Baker (2000) 'Modernization, cultural change and the persistence of traditional values', *American Sociological Review*, 65: 19–51.

Jackman, M. and R. Jackman (1983) *Class Awareness in the United States*, Berkeley: University of California Press.

Jackson, B. and D. Marsden (1962) *Education and the Working Class*, London: Routledge.

Jameson, F. (1991) *Postmodernisation, or the Cultural Logic of Late Capitalism*, London: Verso.

Jencks, C. *et al.* (1979) *Who Gets Ahead?* New York: Basic Books.

Jenkins, R. (1992) *Pierre Bourdieu*, London: Routledge.

—— (1996) *Social Identity*, London: Routledge.

Johnson, R. (1979) '"Introduction" in Centre for Contemporary Cultural Studies', *Unpopular Education: Schooling and Social Democracy in England Since 1944*, London: Hutchinson.

Johnson, R.D. (2001) 'Conclusion: Historians and the American middle class' in B.J. Bledstein and R.J. Johnston (eds), *The Middling Sorts*, New York: Routledge.

Jones, F.L. and J. McMillan (2001) 'Scoring occupational categories for social research', *Work, Employment and Society*, 15: 539–563.

Kahl, J.A. and J.A. Davis (1955) 'A comparison of indexes of socio-economic status', *American Sociological Review*, 20: 317–325.

Kahn, J.S. (2001) *Modernity and Exclusion*, London: Sage.

Katznelson, I. (1981) *City Trenches*, New York: Pantheon Books.

—— (1985) *Marxism and the Metropolis*, Oxford: Oxford University Press.

Kellner, D. (1992) 'Popular culture and the construction of postmodern identities' in S. Lash and J. Friedman (eds), *Modernity and Identity*, Oxford, UK: Blackwell.

Kemp, D. (1978) *Class and Party in Australia*, St Lucia: University of Queensland Press.

Kidd, A.J. and K.W. Roberts (eds) (1985) *City, Class and Culture: Studies of Cultural Production and Social policy in Victorian Manchester*, Manchester: Manchester University Press.

Kingston, P.W. (2000) *The Classless Society*, Stanford, CA: Stanford University Press.

Kirk, N. (1991) '"Traditional" working-class culture and "the rise of labour": some preliminary questions and observations', *Social History*, 16: 203–216.

Kuper, A. (1973) *Anthropologists and Anthropology: The British School, 1922–72,* Harmondsworth: Penguin.

Lacan, J. (1977) *Ecrits,* London: Tavistock.

Lamont, M. (1992) *Money, Morals and Manners: The Culture of French and American Upper Class,* Chicago: University of Chicago Press.

—— (2000) *The Dignity of Working Men,* New York: Russell Sage Foundation.

Landry, B. (1988) *The New Black Middle Class,* Chicago: University of Chicago Press.

—— (1991) 'The enduring dilemma of race in America' in A. Wolfe (ed.), *America at Century's End,* Berkeley University of California Press.

Lash, C. (1991) *The True and Only Heaven: Progress and its Critics,* New York: W.W. Norton.

Lash, S. and J. Urry (1994) *Economies of Sign and Space,* London: Sage.

Lawler, S. (2000a) *Mothering the Self,* London: Routledge.

—— (2000b) 'Escape and escapism: representing working-class women' in S. Munt (ed.), *Cultural Studies and the Working Class: Subject to Change,* London: Cassell.

Leijdesdorff, S. (1987) *Wij Hebben als Mensen Geleefd: het Joods Proletariaat van Amsterdam, 1900–1940,* Amsterdam: Meulenhoff.

Lemert, C. (1995) *Sociology after the Crisis,* Boulder: Westview Press.

Lenski, G. (1954) 'Status crystallization: a non-vertical dimension of social status' in reprinted in J. Scott (ed.) (1996), *Class,* Volume 1, London: Routledge & Kegan Paul.

Levitas, R. (1998) *The Inclusive Society? Social Exclusion and New Labour,* London: Macmillan.

Lijpahrt, A. (1968) *Verzuiling, Pacificatie en Kentering in de Nederlandse Politiek,* Haarlem: Becht.

Lipovetsky, G. (1994) *The Empire of Fashion: Dressing Modern Democracy,* Princeton, NJ: Princeton University Press.

Lis, C. and H. Soly (1993) 'Neighborhood social change in Western European cities', *International Review of Social History,* 38: 1–30.

Littlejohn, J. (1963) *Westrigg: The Sociology of a Cheviot Parish,* London: Routledge & Kegan Paul.

Lloyd, Warner W. *et al.* (1949) *Democracy in Jonesville: A Study in Equality and Inequality,* New York: Harper & Row.

Lockwood, D. (1956) 'Some remarks on "the social system"', *British Journal of Sociology,* 7: 2.

—— (1959) *The Black Coated Worker,* London: Allen & Unwin.

—— (1966) 'Sources of variation in working-class images of society', *Sociological Review,* 14: 244–267.

—— (1975) 'Sources of variation in working-class images of society' in M. Bulmer (ed.), *Working-Class Images of Society,* London: Routledge & Kegan Paul.

—— (1988) 'The weakest link in the chain' in D. Rose (ed.), *Social Stratification and Economic Change,* London: Unwin Hyman.

—— (1992) *Solidarity and Schism: The Problem of Disorder in Durkheimian and Marxist Sociology,* Oxford: Clarendon.

—— (1996) 'Civic integration and class formation', *British Journal of Sociology,* 43: 531–550.

Longhurst, B. and M. Savage (1996) 'Social class, consumption and the influence of Bourdieu: some critical issues' in S. Edgell, K. Hetherington and A. Warde (eds), *Consumption Matters,* Oxford: Blackwell.

Lukas, J.A. (1985) *Common Ground*, New York: Alfred A. Knopf, Inc.

Lury, C. (1996) Consumer Culture, second edition, Oxford: Blackwell.

—— (1998) *Prosthetic Culture: Photography, Memory and Identity*, London: Routledge.

—— (2000) 'The united colours of diversity: essential and inessential culture' in S. Franklin, C. Lury and J. Stacey (eds), *Global Nature, Global Culture*, London: Sage.

Lyman, P. (1986) 'Domestic life in Coventry 1920–1939' in B. Lancaster and T. Mason (eds), *Life and Labour in a Twentieth Century City: The Experience of Coventry*, Coventry: Cryfield.

Lyon, D. (2000) 'Post-modernity' in G. Browning, A. Halcli and F. Webster (eds), *Understanding Contemporary Society*, London: Sage.

Lyotard, J.-F. (1979) *The Postmodern Condition: A Report on Knowledge*, Minneapolis: University of Minnesota Press.

—— (1988) *The Different: Phases in Dispute*, Manchester: Manchester University Press.

Mann, M. (1970) 'The social cohesion of liberal democracy', *American Sociological Review*, 35: 423–431.

—— (1973) *Consciousness and Action among the Western Working Class*, London: Macmillan.

Mannheim, K. (1996) 'The problem of generations' in W. Sollors (ed.), *Theories of Ethnicity: A Classical Reader*, London: Macmillan.

Mare, R.D. (1995) 'Changes in educational attainment and school enrollment' in R. Farley (ed.), *State of the Union: America in the 1990s*, Volume 1: *Economic Trends*, New York: Russell Sage Foundation.

Marshall, G. (1988) 'Some remarks on the study of working-class consciousness' in D. Rose (ed.), *Social Stratification and Economic Change*, London: Hutchinson.

Marshall, G. and D. Rose (1990) 'Out-classed by our critics', *Sociology*, 24: 2.

Marshall, G., Rose, D., Newby, H. and C. Vogler (1988) *Social Class in Modern Britain*, London: Unwin Hyman.

Marshall, T.H. (1948) 'Citizenship and social class', in *Sociology at the Crossroads*, London: Heinemann.

Marx, K. (1972) 'Wage labour and capital' in R.C. Turner (ed.), *The Marx-Engels Reader*, New York: W.W. Norton.

Massey, D. and N. Denton (1993) *American Apartheid*, Cambridge, MA: Harvard University Press.

May, T. (2001) 'A future for critique: positioning, belonging and reflexivity', *European Journal of Social Theory*, 3: 157–173.

May, T. and M. Williams (eds) (1998) *Knowing the Social World*, Buckingham: Open University Press.

McAllister, I. (1994) *Political Behaviour*, Melbourne: Longman Cheshire.

McCarthy, C. (2000) 'Reading the American popular: suburban resentment and the representation of the inner city in contemporary film and TV' in D. Fleming (ed.), *Formations: A 21st-Century Media Studies Textbook*, Manchester: Manchester University Press.

McClintock, A. (1995) *Imperial Leather: Race, Gender and Sexuality in the Colonial Context*, London: Routledge.

McCrone, D., Stewart, R., Keily, R. and F. Bechhofer (1998) 'Who are we? problematising national identity', *Sociological Review*, 46: 629–652.

McDonald, K. (1999) *Struggles for Subjectivity*, Melbourne: Melbourne University Press.

McKenna, M. (1991) 'The suburbanization of the working-class population of Liverpool between the wars', *Social History*, 16: 173–189.

McLennan, G. (2000) 'The new positivity' in A. Witz, J. Eldridge, S. Scott and C. Warhurst (eds), *For Sociology*, York: Sociology Press.

McNay, L. (1999) 'Gender, habitus and the field: Pierre Bourdieu and the limits of reflexivity', *Theory, Culture and Society*, 16: 95–117.

Melucci, A. (1996) *Challenging Codes: Collective Action in the Information Age*, Cambridge: Cambridge University Press.

Merleau-Ponty, M. 1965 [1945] *Phaenomenologie der Wahrnehmung*, Berlin.

Merton, R.K. (1949) *Social Theory and Social Structure*, New York: Harper and Row.

—— (1968) *Social Theory and Social Structure*, New York: The Free Press (revised and enlarged edition).

Miles, R. (1993) *Racism after Race Relations*, London: Routledge.

Modood, T. (1988) 'Black, race equality and Asian identity', *New Community*, 14: 397–404.

Mollenkopf, J. and M. Castells (eds) (1991) *The Dual City*, New York: Russell Sage.

Moore, R.S. (1975) 'Religion as a source of variation in working-class images of society' in M. Bulmer (ed.), *Working-Class Images of Society*, London: Routledge & Kegan Paul.

Moran, L. and B. Skeggs (2001a) 'Property and propriety: fear and safety in gay space', *Social and Cultural Geography*, 2: 407–420.

—— (2001b) 'The property of safety', *Journal of Social Welfare and Family Law*, 23: 1–15.

Morris, L. (1994) *Dangerous Classes: The Underclass and Social Citizenship*, London: Routledge.

Mueller, D. (1990) *'Zum Typus der "neuen ArbeiterInnen", Forschungsprojekt Sozialstrukturwandel und neue soziale Milieus'*, working paper, Hannover.

Murray, C. (1990) *The Emerging Underclass*, London: Institute of Economic Affairs.

Myrdal, G. (1969) *An American Dilemma*, New York: Harper & Row.

Nead, L. (1988) *Myths of Sexuality: Representations of Women in Victorian Britain*, Oxford: Blackwell.

Neij, R. (1989) *De Organisatie van het Maatschappelijk werk*, Zutphen: De Walburg Pers.

Newby, H. (1977) *The Deferential Worker*, Harmondsworth: Allen Lane.

—— (1982) *The State of Research into Social Stratification in Britain*, London: ESRC.

Norris, C. (2000) 'Post-modernism: a guide for the perplexed' in G. Browning, A. Halcli and F. Webster (eds), *Understanding Contemporary Society*, London: Sage.

O'Byrne, D. (1997) 'Working class culture: local community and global conditions' in J. Eade (ed.), *Living the Global City*, London: Routledge.

Offe, C. (1985) *Disorganized Capitalism*, Cambridge: Polity Press.

Oliver, M.L. and T.M. Shapiro (1995) *Black Wealth/White Wealth*, New York: Routledge.

O'Neill, J. (ed.) (1973) *Modes of Individualism and Collectivism*, London: Heinemann.

—— (1999) 'Economy, equality and recognition' in L. Ray and A. Sayer (eds), *Culture and Economy after the Cultural Turn*, London: Sage.

—— (2001) 'Oh! my others, there is no other: capital culture, class and otherwiseness', *Theory, Culture and Society*, 18: 2.

Ortner, S. (1991) 'Reading America: preliminary notes on class and culture' in G.R. Fox (ed.), *Recapturing Anthropology: Working in the Present*, Santa Fe, NM: School of American Research Press.

Oudenaarden, J. (1995) *Met Brede Vleugelslagen: De Geschiedenis van 75 Jaar Instituut voor de Rijpere Jeugd*, Rotterdam: Phoenix and Den Oudsten.

Pahl, R.E. (1985) *Divisions of Labour*, Oxford: Blackwell.

—— (1989) 'Is the emperor naked?', *International Journal of Urban and Regional Research*, 13: 711–720.

—— (1993) 'Does class analysis with class theory have a future?', *Sociology*, 27: 253–258.

Pakulski, J. (1997) 'Cultural Citizenship', *Citizenship Studies*, 1.

Pakulski, J. and M. Waters (1996) *The Death of Class*, London: Sage.

Parkin, F. (1972) *Class Inequality and Political Order*, London: Paladin.

Parsons, T. (1937) *The Structure of Social Action*, New York: Free Press.

Payne, G. (1987) *Mobility and Change in Modern Society*, Basingstoke: Macmillan.

Payne, G. (ed.) (2000) *Social Divisions*, Basingstoke: Macmillan.

Penn, R. (1981) 'The nuffield class categorisation', *Sociology*, 15.

Phillips, A. and B. Taylor (1980) 'Sex and skill: moves towards a feminist economics', *Feminist Review*, 6: 79–88.

Phillips, T. (1996) 'Symbolic boundaries and national identity in Australia', *British Journal of Sociology*, 47: 113–134.

—— (1998) 'Popular views about Australian identity: research and analysis', *Journal of Sociology*, 34: 281–302.

Phizacklea, A. and R. Miles (eds) (1980) *Labour and Racism*, London: Routledge & Kegan Paul.

Poovey, M. (1995) *Making a Social Body: British Cultural Formation, 1830–1864*, Chicago: University of Chicago Press.

Poulantzas, N. (1973) *Political Power and Social Classes*, London: New Left Books.

Ragin, C. (1992) 'Introduction' in C. Ragin. and H.S. Becker (eds), *What is a Case?*, Cambridge: Cambridge University Press.

Ragin, C. (ed.) (1991) 'Introduction' to *Issues and Alternatives in Comparative Social Research*, Leiden: E.J. Brill.

Ray, L. and A. Sayer (ed.) (1999) *Culture and Economy after the Cultural Turn*, London: Sage.

Reay, D. (1998) *Class Work: Mothers' Involvement in their Children's Primary Schooling*, London: UCL Press.

Reid, I. (1998) *Class Differences in Britain*, Cambridge: Polity Press.

Roberts, E. (1995) *Women and Families: An Oral History 1940–1970*, Oxford: Basil Blackwell.

Roberts, I. (1993) *Craft, Class and Control*, Edinburgh: Edinburgh University Press.

Roberts, K. (2001) *Class in Modern Britain*, Basingstoke: Palgrave.

Roberts, R. (1974) *The Classic Slum*, Harmondsworth: Penguin.

Roderick, M. and R.H. Fryer (1975) 'The deferential worker?' in M. Bulmer (ed.), *Working-Class Images of Society*, London: Routledge & Kegan Paul.

Rose, D. (1997) *Constructing Classes: Towards a New Social Classification for the UK*, Swindon: ESRC.

—— (1999) *Powers of Freedom*, Cambridge: Cambridge University Press.

Rouse, R. (1995) 'Thinking through transnationalism: notes on the cultural politics of class relations in the contemporary united states', *Public Culture*, 7(2): 353–402.

Rowbotham, S. and H. Beynon (eds) (2001) *Looking at Class*, London: Rivers Oram.
Rowe, K. (1995) *The Unruly Woman: Gender and the Genres of Laughter*, Austin: University of Texas Press.
Rupp, Jan C.C. (1995) 'Les classes populaires dans un espace social à deux dimensions', *Actes de Recherche en Sciences Sociales*, no. 109, October, pp. 93–98.
—— (1997) 'Rethinking Cultural and Economic Capital' in John R. Hall (ed.), *Reworking Class*, Ithaca (NY): Cornell University Press, pp. 221–241.
Sassen, S. (1991) *The Global City: New York, London, Tokyo*, Princeton, NJ: Princeton University Press.
Saunders, P. (1989) 'Left-write in sociology', *Network*, 44: 3–4.
—— (1990a) *A Nation of Homeowners*, London: Unwin Hyman.
—— (1990b) *Social Class and Stratification*, London: Tavistock.
Saussure, de F. (1959) *Course in General Linguistics*, New York: McGraw.
Savage, M. (1987) *The Dynamics of Working-Class Politics*, Cambridge: Cambridge University Press.
—— (1996) 'Space, networks and class formation' in N. Kirk (ed.), *Social Class and Marxism: Defences and Challenges*, Aldershot: Scolar Press.
—— (2000) *Class Analysis and Social Transformation*, Buckingham: Open University Press.
Savage, M., Barlow, J., Dickens, P. and A.J. Fielding (1992) *Property, Bureaucracy and Culture: Middle-Class Formation in Contemporary Britain*, London: Routledge.
Savage, M., Bagnall, G. and B. Longhurst (2001) 'Ordinary, ambivalent and defensive: class identities in the Northwest of England', *Sociology*, 35: 875–892.
—— (2002) 'The comforts of place: belonging and identity in the Northwest of England' in T. Bennett and E. Silva (eds), *Everyday Life Cultures*, Brighton: Sociology Press.
Sayer, A. (2001) 'What are you worth? recognition, valuation and moral economy', *British Sociological Association Annual Conference*, Manchester.
Sayer, A. and R. Walker (1992) *The New Social Economy*, Oxford: Blackwell.
Scase, R. (1977) *Social Democracy in a Capitalist Society*, London: Croom Helm.
—— (1992) *Class*, Buckingham: Open University Press.
Scherzer, K.A. (1992) *The Unbounded Community: Neighborhood and Social Structure in New York City 1830–1875*, Durham: Duke University Press.
Schreurs, C.J. (1962) *De Afrikaanderwijk: Een Proeve van Verkenning*, Rotterdam: Stichting Byzonder Gezinswerk.
Scott, J. (1991) *Who Rules Britain*, Cambridge: Polity Press.
—— (1994) *Poverty and Wealth: Citizenship, Deprivation and Privilege*, London: Longman.
—— (1996) *Stratification and Power*, Cambridge: Polity Press.
—— (1998) 'Relationism, cubism, and reality: beyond relativism' in T. May and M. Williams (eds), *Knowing the Social World*, Buckingham: Open University Press.
—— (2002) 'Class and stratification', *Acta Sociologica*, 32.
—— (forthcoming) *Central Questions in Sociology*, London: Sage.
Scott, J. and L. Morris (1996) 'The attenuation of class analysis', *British Journal of Sociology*, 56: 10–20.
Sennett, R. and J. Cobb (1977) *The Hidden Injuries of Class*, Cambridge: Cambridge University Press.
Shotter, J. and K.J. Gergen (1989) *Texts of Identity*, London: Sage.
Skeggs, B. (1994) 'Refusing to be civilized: "race", sexuality and power' in M. Maynard (ed.), *The Dynamics of Race and Gender*, London: Taylor & Francis.

—— (1997) *Formations of Class and Gender*, London: Sage.

—— (2003) *Class, Self, Culture*, London: Routledge.

Smelser, N. and R. Swedberg (eds) (1994) *The Handbook of Economic Sociology*, Princeton: Princeton University Press.

Sorensen, A. (2000) 'Employment relations and class structure' in R. Crompton, F. Devine, M. Savage and J. Scott (eds), *Renewing Class Analysis*, Oxford: Blackwell/ Sociological Review.

SPD (1984) Planungsdaten fuer die Mehrheitsfaehigkeit der SPD. Ein Forschungsprojekt des Vorstandes der SPD, Bonn: Parteivorstand der SPD.

'Spiegel' Verlag/manager magazin (Hrsg.) (1996) 'Spiegel'-Dokumentation Soll und Haben 4, Hamburg: Spiegel Verlag.

Stacey, M. (1960) *Tradition and Change: A Study of Banbury*, Oxford: Oxford University Press.

Stanley, L. (1993) 'On auto/biography in sociology', *Sociology*, 27: 41–52.

Stewart, A., Prandy, K. and R.M. Blackburn (1980) *Social Stratification and Occupations*, London: Macmillan.

Stolcke, V. (1995) 'Talking culture: new boundaries, new rhetorics of exclusion in Europe', *Current Anthropology*, 36: 1–24.

Strathern, M. (1992) *After Nature: English Kinship in the Late Twentieth Century*, Cambridge: Cambridge University Press.

Studlar, D. and S. Welch (1981) 'Mass attitudes on political issues in Britain', *Comparative Political Studies*, 14: 327–355.

Swartz, S. (1997) *Culture and Power: The Sociology of Pierre Bourdieu*, Chicago: University of Chicago Press.

Szreter, S. (1996) *Fertility, Class and Gender in Britain*, 1860–1940, Cambridge: Cambridge University Press.

Tasker, Y. (1998) *Working Girls: Gender and Sexuality in Popular Culture*, London: Routledge.

Taylor, C. (1994) 'The politics of recognition' in D.T. Goldberg (ed.), *Multiculturalism: A Critical Reader*, Oxford: Blackwell.

Taylor, S.J.L. (1998) *Segregation in Boston and Buffalo*, Albany: SUNY.

Thoburn, N. (2001) 'Autonomous production? On Negri's "new synythesis"', *Theory, Culture and Society*, 18: 75–96.

Thompson, E.P. (1963) *The Making of the English Working Class*, London: Gollancz.

Thompson, P. (1988) *The Voice of the Past*, Oxford: Oxford University Press.

Tilly, C. (1984) *Big Structures, Large Processes, Hugh Comparisons*, New York: Russell Sage.

—— (1999) *Durable Inequalities*, Berkeley: University of California Press.

Townsend, P. (1976) *Poverty in the UK*, Harmondsworth: Penguin.

Turner, B.S. (1999) 'The sociology of generations' in B.S. Turner (ed.), *Classical Sociology*, London: Sage.

Turner, B.S. and C. Rojek (2001) *Society and Culture*, London: Sage.

Turner, J.C. (1984) 'Social identification and psychological group formation' in H. Tajfel (ed.), *The Social Dimension*, Volume 2, Cambridge: Cambridge University Press.

Urry, J. (2000) *Sociology Beyond Societies*, London: Routledge.

Valten, D. (1988) *Tuindorp Vreewijk: Een Geschiedschrijving over de Vennootschap, haar Woningen en haar Huurders, 1913–1988*, Rotterdam: De Waterstad/Centrum voor Bedrijfsgeschiedenis: Erasmus Universiteit Rotterdam.

Van der Ree, D. (1995) *A Suitcase in Berlin: Researching Collective Memories in Berlin and Amsterdam*, Paper presented on the 2nd *Theory, Culture & Society* Conference, Berlin.

Van Dijk, H. (1976) *Rotterdam 1810–1880: Aspecten van een Stedelijke Samenleving*, Rotterdam: Erasmus Universiteit Rotterdam.

Van Zuylen, W.H. (ed.) (1966) *Het werk Uwer handen: Geschiedenis van een Gereformeerde kerk Rotterdam-Zuid (Katendrecht)*, Rotterdam: Van Haspel.

Vanneman, R. and L.W. Cannon (1987) *The American Perception of Class*, Philadephia: Temple University Press.

Vicinus, M. (1974) *The Industrial Muse: A Study of Nineteenth Century British Working Class Literature*, London: Croom Helm.

Vester, M. (1970) 'Die Entstehung des Proletariats als Lernprozess, Frankfurt: Europaeische Verlagsanstalt.

—— (1992) 'Die Modernisierung der Sozialstruktur und der Wandel von Mentalitaeten' in S. Hradil (ed.), *Zischen Bewusstsein und Sein*, Opladen: Leske + Budrich, pp. 223–249.

—— (1998) 'Was wurde aus dem Proletariat?' in J. Friedrichs Lepsius, M. Rainer and Mayer, K. Ulrich (eds), *Die Diagnosefaehigkeit der Soziologie*, Opladen: Westdeutschger Verlag, pp. 164–206.

—— (2001) 'Milieus und soziale Gerechtigkeit' in Karl-Rudolf Korte and Werner Weidenfeld (Hg.), *Deutschland-TrendBuch*, Opladen 2001, S. 136–183.

Vester, M., Hofmann, M. and I. Zierke (1994) *Soziale Milieus in Ostdeutschland*, Koeln: Bund.

Vester, M., von Oertzen, P., Geiling, H., Hermann, T. and D. Mueller (2001) [1993] *Soziale Milieus im gesellschaftlichen Strukturwandel. Zwischen Integration und Ausgrenzung*, 2. Aufl., Frankfurt/Main.

Voegele, W., Bremer, H. and M. Vester (Hg.) (2002) *Soziale Milieus und Kirche*, Wuerzburg.

von Bismarck, Klaus (1957) *Kirche und Gemeinde in soziologischer Sicht, Zeitschrift fuer evangelische Ethik*, H. 1, 1957, S. 17–31.

von Saldern, A. (1990) 'The workers' movement and cultural patterns on urban housing estates and in rural settlements in Germany and Austria during the 1920s', *Social History*, 15: 333–354.

Walkowitz, D.J. (1999) *Working with Class*, Chapel Hill: University of North Carolina.

Walton, J.K. (1987) *Lancashire: A Social History, 1558–1939*, Manchester: Manchester University Press.

Ward, I., Leach, M. and G. Stokes (2000) 'The rise and fall of one nation' in M. Leach, G. Stokes and I. Ward (eds), *The Rise and Fall of One Nation*, St Lucia: University of Queensland Press.

Warde, A. (1997) *Consumption, Food and Taste*, London: Sage.

Warner, W.L. *et al.* (1949) *Social Class in America*, New york: Harper & Row.

Walkerdine, V. and H. Lucey (1989) *Democracy in the Kitchen: Regulating Mothers and Socialising Daughters*, London: Virago.

Waters, M. (1995) *Globalisation*, London: Routledge.

Weakliem, D. and M. Western (1999) 'Class voting, social change and the Left in Australia, 1943–1996', *British Journal of Sociology*, 50: 609–630.

Weber, M. (1964) [1921] *Wirtschaft und Gesellschaft: Grundriss der verstehenden Soziologie*, Koeln/Berlin: Kiepenheuer & Witsch.

Weigert, A.J., Teitge, J.S. and D.W. Teitge (1986) *Society and Identity: Toward a Sociological Social Psychology*, Cambridge: Cambridge University Press.

Western, M.C. (1999) 'Who thinks what about capitalism: class consciousness and attitudes to economic institutions', *Journal of Sociology*, 35: 351–370.

Whittier, N. (1997) 'Political generations, micro-cohorts, and the transformation of social movements', *American Sociological Review*, 62: 760–778.

Wiebke, G. (2002) 'Traditionslinie von Macht und Besitz: Das Konservativ-gehobene Milieu' in W. Voegele, H. Bremer and M. Vester (Hg.), *Soziale Milieus und Kirche*, Wuerzburg: Ergon, pp. 297–309.

Wievorka, M. (1998) 'Is multiculturalism the solution?', *Ethnic and Racial Studies*, 21: 881–910.

Wiggers, A.J., Lissens, R.F., Devreker, A., Kooy, G.A. and H.A. Lauwerier (eds) (1975) *Grote Winkler Prins Encyclopedie in Twintig Delen*, Amsterdam: Elsevier.

Williams, R. (1961) *The Long Revolution*, New York: Columbia University Press.

—— (1963) *Culture and Society 1780–1950*, Harmondsworth: Penguin.

—— (1976) *Keywords*, London: Fontana.

—— (1977) *Marxism and Literature*, Oxford: Oxford University Press.

Willis, P. (1977) *Learning to Labour*, Saxon House: Farnborough.

Wolfe, A. (1998) *One Nation, After All*, New York: Viking Penguin.

Wright, E.O. (1985) *Classes*, London: Verso.

—— (1996) *Class Counts*, Cambridge: Cambridge University Press.

Wright, P. (1985) *On Living in an Old Country: The National Past in Contemporary Britain*, London: Verso.

Yeo, E. (1996) *The Contest for Social Science: Relations and Representations of Gender and Class*, London: Rivers Oram.

Young, M. and P. Willmott (1957) *Family and Kinship in East London*, London: Routledge.

Zizek, S. (1997) 'Multiculturalism, or, the cultural logic of multinational capitalism', *New Left Review*, 225: 28–52.

Zussman, R. (1985) *Mechanics of the Middle Class*, Berkeley, California: University of California.

Zwieg, F. (1961) *The Worker in an Affluent Society*, London: Heinemann.

Index